NUCLEAR ENERGY NOW

NUCLEAR ENERGY NOW

WHY THE TIME HAS COME FOR THE WORLD'S MOST MISUNDERSTOOD ENERGY SOURCE

ALAN M. HERBST
GEORGE W. HOPLEY

John Wiley & Sons, Inc.

Published by John Wiley & Sons, Inc., Hoboken, New Jersey.
Published simultaneously in Canada.

Wiley Bicentennial Logo: Richard J. Pacifico

For general information on our other products and services or for technical support, please contact our Customer Care Department within the United States at (800) 762-2974, outside the United States at (317) 572-3993 or fax (317) 572-4002.

Wiley also publishes its books in a variety of electronic formats. Some content that appears in print may not be available in electronic books. For more information about Wiley products, visit our Web site at www.wiley.com.

Library of Congress Cataloging-in-Publication Data:

Herbst, Alan M., 1964–
 Nuclear energy now : why the time has come for the world's most misunderstood energy source / Alan M. Herbst, George W. Hopley.
  p. cm.
 Includes bibliographical references and index.
 978-0-470-05136-8 (cloth)
  1. Nuclear industry—United States. 2. Energy policy—United States.
I. Hopley, George W., 1963–. II. Title.
HD9698.U52H46 2007
333.792'40973—dc22

2006036781

Printed in the United States of America.

10 9 8 7 6 5 4 3 2 1

To my wife, Adina, for her love,
understanding, and unyielding support.

Contents

Illustrations

Figures

Tables

Preface

The U.S. nuclear industry, while a major producer of electric power for the nation, has not had a new reactor licensed or built for decades. This clean source of electricity generation has been greatly underutilized during the last quarter-century as a result of misinformation, negative press accounts, and a prior history of cost overruns and financing difficulties.

Since the last new U.S. nuclear reactors were built, significant changes have taken place within the nuclear industry, but many of these changes have gone virtually unnoticed by the public. Enhanced regulatory oversight, improved management, and industry consolidation now make the U.S. nuclear industry a model of cost-efficient, safe, and reliable electricity generation.

Our growing dependence on imported energy and concerns over greenhouse gas emissions and global warming created from the combustion of fossil fuels require that we limit to the fullest extent possible our further reliance on oil, coal, and natural gas, and recommit ourselves to nuclear energy to help meet our future energy demands.

The U.S. nuclear industry is now poised for a rebirth. Utility executives realize they must bring significant amounts of cost-effective generation on line over the next decade, and they have taken the initial steps to obtain the required permits and licenses from receptive federal authorities to construct such facilities.

Nuclear Energy Now provides an unbiased and informed description of the historic development, enhanced safety, considerable operating and environmental benefits, and limited drawbacks of nuclear energy relative to other fuels, both conventional and renewable. One of the goals of this book is to clear up many of the pervasive misconceptions regarding this proven technology. Once the public as well as local and state government officials become better informed of the benefits of this technology, it is hoped they will become supporters and advocates for the continued growth of this industry.

This book highlights the key developments in nuclear power, along with the continued operating and safety improvements in nuclear reactors. It also examines nuclear energy's global growth, which in recent years has significantly outpaced that in the United States, the onetime industry leader. It also identifies the strategic steps the U.S. government has taken to jump-start this critical industry.

Acknowledgments

Writing a book is never an easy task. While we have both written numerous energy-related studies, reports, and articles throughout our professional careers, producing a book for a considerably broader, general audience proved to be a unique and challenging endeavor.

We would like to take this opportunity to thank our editors at John Wiley & Sons for their support and guidance in every stage of this effort. Special thanks go to Bill Falloon, who recognized the potential for a timely title on the merits of nuclear power, for his assistance in helping us craft our message and ultimately bring this book to market. We would also like to thank Emilie Herman, our Senior Development Editor, for her advice, patience, and critical eye. She kept us on message and away from descending into a world of technical jargon. We are also grateful to the other talented individuals at Wiley for their interest and professionalism in producing and marketing this title.

We would be negligent if we did not recognize the considerable efforts put forth by the Energy Information Administration, the statistical arm of the U.S. Department of Energy, and other U.S. government agencies, such as the Nuclear Regulatory Commission, who work tirelessly producing accurate and dependable energy sector data and analytics. This material proved to be invaluable in researching and writing this work.

Last, and most important, writing this book diverted our time and attention from our loved ones. We would like to publicly thank them for their patience, understanding, support, and sacrifice, without which writing this book would not have been possible.

Alan M. Herbst
George W. Hopley

About the Authors

Alan M. Herbst has two decades' experience with global energy markets and professional consulting services. He specializes in the analysis of commodity fundamentals, pricing, commercial trading, and risk management opportunities and has performed work in the oil, natural gas, and electric power sectors. In recent years, he has focused his efforts on emerging energy technologies and markets, specifically nuclear power, the Alberta oil sands, coal gasification technologies, and the growing global liquefied natural gas (LNG) market.

Mr. Herbst is the General Partner of Utilis Energy, LLC, a consulting and market research firm with offices in New York and London. Prior to his tenure with Utilis Energy, he held the position of U.S. Energy Practice Area Manager for Datamonitor Inc., where he focused on strategic planning and developing the group's research, analysis, and marketing efforts. Mr. Herbst has also held energy analysis and consulting positions with the PIRA Energy Group and Standard & Poor's.

Mr. Herbst has also been an energy industry expert to various media outlets, making numerous television and radio appearances. He has been interviewed extensively and widely quoted on energy issues by both the trade and general press, has spoken at international energy conferences, and has been widely published as a contributor in numerous trade journals.

Mr. Herbst has an MBA in Finance and International Business from New York University's Stern School of Business. He has a BA in History and Biology from Washington University in St. Louis, Missouri. In addition, he possesses a Series 3 Certification (Futures and Commodities) from the National Association of Securities Dealers (NASD) and has been a registered Power Marketer.

He resides in Manhattan with his wife Adina, is an avid exercise enthusiast and world adventure traveler, and has been known to hammer a finger or two while volunteering at various Habitat for Humanity build sites.

George Hopley has been involved in energy markets since 1990, principally analyzing supply and demand fundamentals of U.S. and international power and gas markets. In addition to studying the individual market sector components, he focuses on dynamics of price formation as well as forecasting forward price curves for power and underlying fuels.

Mr. Hopley is Associate Director at Barclays Capital, the investment banking division of Barclays Bank, PLC, the UK-based financial services group. He is the lead commodities analyst for North American natural gas, electric power, and plastics markets. Prior to this, he was senior director of energy market analysis for Duke Energy North America in Houston, focusing on short-term market dynamics. Prior to that, he held similar positions with the New Power Company and Enron North America. He also worked in the electric power practice of PIRA Energy Group in New York.

At Barclays Capital, Mr. Hopley writes extensively on market and price dynamics, and he has been widely published by financial and energy market publications.

Mr. Hopley has an MBA in Finance from New York University's Stern School of Business. He has a BA in Economics from Trinity College in Hartford, Connecticut.

He lives in Manhattan with his wife Elizabeth and daughter Alexandra, and is an active sailor.

Introduction

Top Misconceptions Concerning Nuclear Power

Informed, rational debate requires that the participants thoroughly understand the benefits of nuclear power first, but opinions have and continue to be easily skewed by emotional rhetoric put forth by groups with an antinuclear agenda. This rhetoric has created numerous misconceptions about nuclear power and its ability to safely generate large quantities of low-cost electricity. The following introduction outlines the main arguments against nuclear power and responds with a brief rebuttal. These issues are explored in greater length in the chapters that follow.

Nuclear Power Is Harmful to the Environment

To some individuals, anything relating to nuclear fission and radiation *must* be bad for the environment. Screaming supermarket tabloid headlines and images of the effects of radiation have led many to think that nuclear power is inherently dangerous both to people and to the environment.

This quite simply is not the case. Chapter 2 explains the safety features of nuclear power and identifies just how vastly superior it is to most other energy-producing fuels, due to the fact that it can create electricity without the production of greenhouse gases and other emissions that contribute to global warming. This fact has won over prominent environmentalists who, after educating themselves on the issue, now support the further development nuclear energy in the United States.

Nuclear Power Is Too Expensive

Headlines of dramatic cost overruns many decades ago have prompted many to view nuclear power cost projections with much cynicism. But those who believe that nuclear power just isn't a cost-effective way to produce electricity don't properly understand utility sector economics. Chapter 2 shows that while the cost of constructing nuclear units is at a premium to the construction of fossil fuel–based power plants, decades of operating data show that once these nuclear plants are operating, the cost of the power produced is below that of fossil fuels.

Additionally, the industry's notoriety for high construction costs and cost overruns has also begun to change due to greater standardization, which has led to efficiencies in the planning, permitting, construction, and operation of these nuclear units.

Nuclear Power Is Not Safe

It's not wrong to put a premium on safety. In fact, it would be irrational *not* to do so. Chapter 5 highlights the fact that over approximately 60 years of development, the operating safety of nuclear power facilities has continuously been enhanced. While the industry has accumulated hundreds of thousands of hours of safe operation, many continue to focus on a single event or two that dramatically shapes their perception of this industry. However, when the facts are examined, one can state that no one has ever been in killed in the United States from a civilian nuclear plant. The same cannot be said about other U.S. electricity-generating facilities.

This safety record is the result of stringent government and regulatory oversight of nuclear generation operations.

Nuclear Power Is Vulnerable to Attack

Critics against the expansion of U.S. nuclear power believe that both existing and potential new facilities will be vulnerable to terrorist attack. Unfortunately, in the post-9/11 world in which we live, the security of all critical infrastructure assets is of significant importance. Since 2001, there have been considerable security upgrades to the nation's 103 commercially operating nuclear units. Additional measures have been enacted to protect these assets from air attack, and while there have been differing opinions regarding the structural integrity of such facilities if hit with a commercial airliner, those familiar with aviation note that the likelihood of hitting such a relatively small target while traveling at high speed is extremely remote.

Nuclear Power Has a Waste Problem

Nuclear facilities do produce waste, but the amount of waste is substantially less than the waste produced from coal- and oil-fired generation facilities. The tons of coal and millions of barrels of oil used for conventional electricity generation produce particulate waste products that remain on site while other waste is released into the environment. Chapter 4 explains how, with nuclear power, a small amount of fissionable material produces a great amount of energy and even smaller amounts of waste. This waste has varying levels of radioactivity and must be kept in a secure environment. A centralized facility is currently being developed to house this waste in one secure location.

Public Opinion Is Firmly Against Nuclear Power

Vocal opposition to U.S. nuclear power operations and their further development gives the impression that the vast majority of the public is against nuclear power. While at times during the past two or three decades nuclear opposition forces have rallied, various public opinion polls cited in Chapter 1 show that the majority of the U.S. public is in favor of nuclear power and that its favorability rating has actually increased in recent years due to rising energy prices and concerns over our dependence on imported oil.

Nuclear Power Hasn't Evolved

The general public tends to view nuclear power as a technology that has not evolved since reactors first commercialized the atom for peaceful purposes; they assume that the hundreds of nuclear units currently in operation are identical to or little changed from 1950s technology. This, however, is not the case, as shown in Chapter 1, which chronicles reactor improvements. Reactors currently operating are safer and more efficient that those used in preceding decades, and new reactor designs, described in Chapter 5, have been developed that possess even greater safety and operating efficiencies than units currently operating.

Nuclear Power, the Right Technology for the Right Time

Once people gain a better understanding of nuclear power and the role that it has played and will continue to play in providing the U.S. economy with huge quantities of environmentally friendly power, a greater reliance on this energy technology in the years to come will be recognized as a prudent course of action.

NUCLEAR ENERGY NOW

1

From Warheads to Washing Machines: Post-World War II Nuclear Development

Post-World War II development of nuclear power in the United States can be classified as a long endurance march. While reactors in the 1950s produced electricity just like their more modern counterparts operating today, it's a misconception that nuclear power technology and the industry haven't changed very much over the years. Actually, six decades of advances in reactor performance and economics have aided in the commercial development of nuclear power in the United States. These advances have not occurred in a vacuum; economic ups and downs, politics, and public opinion have both hindered and aided the commercial development of nuclear power.

The rest of the world has accepted nuclear power as a significant contributor to helping the world's population meet its ever-increasing demand for energy. The Vienna-based International Atomic Energy Agency (IAEA) puts the number of nuclear reactors currently under construction at 29. Broader-based estimates put the number of nuclear reactors either under construction, in the planning stage, or under consideration around the globe at 130. While there are plans for a number of new reactors in the United States, construction has not yet begun. The United States will continue to fall behind the rest of the world in building and operating nuclear power facilities, which is ironic considering it was the initial developer of this technology.

To understand the current and future prospects for nuclear generation in the United States, one must understand how the industry developed and the obstacles it continues to face.

A Developmental Time Line—
From Isotopes to Megawatts

Following is a general time line for this postwar development of nuclear power in the United States:

1946   The first nuclear reactor-produced radioisotopes for peacetime civilian use are made available by the U.S. Army's Oak Ridge facility in Tennessee. Radioisotopes are shipped to the Brainard Cancer Hospital in St. Louis.

1946   The U.S. Congress passes the Atomic Energy Act to establish the Atomic Energy Commission, the successor to the Manhattan Project. The commission is charged with overseeing the use and development of nuclear technology.

1948   The U.S. government's Argonne National Laboratory and the Westinghouse Corporation's Bettis Atomic Power Laboratory announce plans to commercialize nuclear power to produce electricity for consumer use.

1954   The U.S. Congress passes the Atomic Energy Act of 1954— grants the Atomic Energy Commission the power to license private companies to use nuclear materials and also to build and operate nuclear power plants.

1955   BORAX-III reactor provides Arco, Idaho, with all of its electricity for more than an hour.

1955   The USS Nautilus becomes the world's first nuclear-powered submarine.

1957   The International Atomic Energy Agency is formed with 18 member countries to promote peaceful uses of nuclear energy.

1957	The first U.S. commercial nuclear power plant begins operation in Shippingport, Pennsylvania.
1962–1969	Several new reactor types are in development.
1974	The Energy Reorganization Act splits the Atomic Energy Commission into the Energy Research and Development Administration (ERDA) and the Nuclear Regulatory Commission (NRC). ERDA oversees the development and refinement of nuclear power, while the NRC focuses on the safe handling of nuclear materials.
1979	The nuclear facility at Three Mile Island near Harrisburg, Pennsylvania, experiences a major failure when a secondary cooling system water pump in the facility's Unit 2 reactor malfunctions.
1986	The Chernobyl nuclear accident occurs during unauthorized experiments when four pressurized-water reactors overheat, releasing their water coolant as steam. The hydrogen formed by the steam results in two major explosions and a fire, releasing radioactive particles into the atmosphere.
1990s	The U.S. Naval Nuclear Propulsion Program pioneers new material fabrication techniques, radiological control, and quality control standards.
2000	The fleet of 103 nuclear power plants in the United States achieves world record reliability benchmarks, operating annually at more than 90 percent capacity for the past decade.
2002	The Nuclear Power 2010 program is established to aid in the renewed development of U.S. nuclear power via a cost-sharing initiative with the industry.
2002	Nevada's Yucca Mountain is named as a permanent repository for nuclear waste.
2005	The U.S. Energy Policy Act was signed into law in August 2005. The Act provides several key financial incentives for the renewed development of nuclear power in the United States.

(SOURCE: National Academy of Engineering. Reprinted with permission from *A Century of Innovation*, © by the National Academy of Sciences, Courtesy of the National Academies Press, Washington, D.C.)

In the past 60 years we have seen the successful transformation of the atom from a military weapon to a vast source of electricity that benefits the public's lives, powering everyday activities from using washing machines to surfing the Internet. This relatively seamless transformation has been accomplished through effective government regulation and the development of new technology. The following sections examine recent regulatory changes and their impact on U.S. commercial nuclear development, and how these and the resulting industry changes have been perceived by the general public.

U.S. Energy Policy Act

The passage of the U.S. Energy Policy Act in 2005 is one of the cornerstones to the renaissance of nuclear power in the United States.

The passage of the U.S. Energy Policy Act in 2005 is one of the cornerstones to the renaissance of nuclear power in the United States since it provides several key financial incentives in the form of loan guarantees and tax credits. For "new-build" advanced nuclear plants—defined as those including a reactor design approved after December 31, 1993, by the Nuclear Regulatory Commission (NRC)—the Act provides:

- Substantial loan guarantees.
- Risk insurance for nuclear developers.
- Production tax credits.

Loan Guarantees

The Energy Policy Act gives the U.S. Secretary of Energy broadly defined authority to approve loan guarantees for up to 80 percent of the cost of "innovative technologies" that "avoid, reduce or sequester air pollutants for anthropogenic emissions of greenhouse gases." The provisions, although aimed primarily at new nuclear plant construction, could also be used for renewable energy projects and even some clean coal efforts. The Department of Energy (DOE) may enter into contracts with sponsors of a new facility including up to six reactors, consisting of not more than three different designs.

Risk Insurance

The Act creates a new category of risk insurance for the first new-build nuclear plants in the United States. This insurance covers financial risks caused by licensing delays in the new combined construction and operating license (COL) process, or by litigation that delays licensing or plant operation. This type of risk insurance will be particularly attractive to nuclear power plant developers due to their past experiences with licensing difficulties. Two utilities that could have benefited from this risk insurance were the Tennessee Valley Authority (TVA) and the now defunct Long Island Lighting Company (LILCO).

The TVA has the distinction of activating the last new nuclear reactor in the United States at Watts Bar near Spring City, Tennessee, in 1996. The reactor took more than two decades to build and ended up with a price tag of more than $6 billion for construction and financing; it was originally predicted to cost one-tenth that amount. The excessive cost of the nuclear reactor forced the TVA and other utilities to scrap future nuclear reactor construction in the 1980s and 1990s.

The Long Island Lighting Company planned to build a nuclear power plant on New York's Long Island. The project, initiated in 1965 to help the utility meet its rapidly growing customer electricity demand, was sited on the Island's north shore near the small town of Shoreham. After LILCO applied to the NRC and received a license to construct the nuclear facility, excessive cost overruns ultimately pushed the project's price tag to around $6 billion.

But the Shoreham project's greatest challenge, and ultimate downfall, centered on LILCO's failure to receive an operating license from the NRC due to the fact that, because of geographic constraints, they were unable to produce a satisfactory emergency evacuation plan should there be a problem at the reactor. Besides limited ferry service and personal watercraft, the only way to leave Long Island is via automobile or train through New York City, which is adjacent to the extreme western end of Long Island. Several proposed evacuation plans submitted to the NRC were rejected and LILCO, in the face of massive cost overruns and the inability to receive an operating license, simply discontinued the project.

In the end, the utility's ratepayers were left responsible for the utility's poor planning and had to pay off the billions, leaving them with some of the highest electric rates in the country. This was ultimately the downfall of the utility and resulted in its takeover by the state of New York in the late 1990s and the creation of the Long Island Power Authority (LIPA).

Other utilities took note of LILCO's difficulties in obtaining an operating license. This potential license uncertainty added considerable economic risk and created another hurdle for developers of U.S. nuclear power plants. The NRC's new licensing procedure, known as Part 52, alleviates this situation and streamlines the process by allowing applicants to file for the aforementioned combined COL.

Following the passage of the Energy Policy Act, the first two reactors that receive COLs and are under construction will receive insurance coverage for 100 percent of any potential cost of delay, up to $500 million per contract. This would also cover delays in full-power operation caused by the "failure of the NRC to comply with schedules for review and approval of inspections, tests, analyses, and acceptance criteria established under the combined license," as well as delays caused by litigation. The next four units will be covered for 50 percent of the costs of the covered delays, up to $250 million per contract, after an initial 180-day period.

Production Tax Credit

The Energy Policy Act allows a 1.8 cent per kilowatt-hour (c/kWh) production tax credit for energy generated from new nuclear power plants. The tax credit is limited to the first 6,000 electrical megawatts (MWe) of generation capacity, equivalent to from five to seven conventionally sized nuclear units, for eight years of operation, capped at $125 million.

Limitations of the Energy Policy Act

The tax credits that form the bulk of the incentive program are not guaranteed to all market participants. They are limited to the first 6,000 megawatts of nuclear power produced—as few as four reactors and possibly no more than six, depending on reactor size. Since the insurance payout is restricted to six reactors, this clearly benefits firms willing to exercise "first mover advantage." It is presumed that after the initial reactors are built, incentives won't be necessary to sustain a nuclear revival.

Since building a reactor is seen as a huge financial undertaking with potential costly delays, the incentives could amount to half the cost of financing and constructing the unit. The value of these tax credits could therefore potentially be $2 billion (divided among six utilities).

The new Energy Policy Act also extends the Price-Anderson Act's liability coverage for a period of 20 years. This Act is the framework of nuclear industry self-funded liability insurance against catastrophic accidents, and requires all utilities to meet federal reliability standards for transmission grids.

Some critics of this plan describe the incentive package signed into law, which exceeds $8 billion in value, as "corporate welfare" for various Fortune 500 corporations and assert that the industry would never consider building new nuclear units without the U.S. taxpayer taking on the associated risk. Still others in the nuclear sector wonder whether the incentives are enough to stimulate a nuclear revival. The tax credits don't start until the reactor is built, which could take up to 10 years, but likely less, and the insurance provisions are conditioned on unpredictable economic factors.

Squeezing Out Every Last Megawatt: Enhanced Operational Performance

Over the past 15 years, the improved management of U.S. nuclear facilities has achieved noticeable advances in their operational efficiency, safety, and overall profitability. Data from the Energy Information Agency show that in the early 1990s, U.S. nuclear plants had operating efficiencies of only 70 percent on average (see Table 1.1). However, by 2004 these operational efficiencies were in excess of 90 percent. The associated gains in reactor utilization have been equivalent to incremental output increases equal to approximately 25 new nuclear units on the U.S. power grid since 1990, without building any new nuclear facilities.

Such improvements can be attributed largely to the consolidation of nuclear plant ownership. Indeed, over the past 10 years, the number of nuclear operators in the United States has declined from 46 to 23. This has resulted in safer, more cost-effective, and more reliable plant operations. As a result of this success, most U.S. nuclear plants are expected to apply for renewed licenses that will extend their operations into the middle of this century.

In addition, the NRC has approved 2,300 megawatts (MW) of "uprates," which increase the maximum power level at which a nuclear power

Table 1.1   **U.S. Nuclear Generation and Utilization, 1990–2004**

	Billion kWh	% Utilization
1990	576,974	66.0
1991	612,642	70.2
1992	618,841	70.9
1993	610,367	70.5
1994	640,492	73.8
1995	673,402	77.4
1996	674,729	76.2
1997	628,644	71.1
1998	673,702	78.2
1999	728,254	85.3
2000	753,893	88.1
2001	767,299	89.3
2002	780,220	90.9
2003	763,744	88.4
2004	788,556	90.5

SOURCE: Utilis Energy/Energy Information Agency.

plant can operate. Another 1,100 megawatts of uprates are currently under review by the NRC, which has also approved 20-year extensions of the operating licenses of 30 reactors. Another 16 applications are under review, and 22 more are yet to be submitted, which means that, all told, owners of two-thirds of the nuclear power plants in the United States have committed to apply for license renewals by 2010, and others are expected to follow. This is expected to increase the amount of nuclear power available to the market without necessitating the construction of new reactors. This efficiency and uprate strategy was a successful plan to pursue in the wake of the events at Three Mile Island and Chernobyl, which occurred in 1979 and 1986, respectively, and considerably hindered the development of new nuclear assets on a global basis.

Nuclear Power 2010 Program

Gains from greater reactor utilization will only go so far in helping the United States keep pace with growing electricity demand. To reawaken the industry and ultimately to construct a new generation of nuclear reactors will require direct involvement from the federal government.

The government's Nuclear Power 2010 program, established in 2002 and now part of the Energy Policy Act of 2005, creates a partnership between the government and industry to share costs in order to:

> *The government's Nuclear Power 2010 program creates a partnership between the government and industry to share costs.*

- Demonstrate new, untested NRC licensing processes.
- Find sites on which to build new plants.
- Certify state-of-the-art (or Generation III+) designs for new nuclear power plants.

The program also conducts economic studies and analyses that focus on the barriers to the construction of new plants.

Thus far, utilities such as Dominion Resources, Exelon Nuclear, and Entergy are cooperating with the NRC to obtain early site permits for sites located in Virginia, Illinois, and Mississippi. At the time of this writing, the NRC is reviewing the utilities' applications and is expected to issue permits during 2006 and 2007. Once this is complete, the utilities will have sites that are preapproved by regulators to host new plants. This process will avoid the siting problems that vastly escalated the costs of some plants in the 1980s and led to the abandonment of others.

In November 2004, the Nuclear Power 2010 program took a major step forward by approving two projects of utility-led consortia to implement plans that could lead to the construction and operation of new U.S. nuclear plants. Central to this effort, these projects demonstrate the NRC's combined construction and operating license (or "one-step" license) process. These projects could result in a new nuclear power plant order by 2009 and a new nuclear power plant constructed by the private sector and in operation by 2014.

In response to this increase in activity, the program's budget rose significantly in 2005 to just below $50 million. Recent appropriations for the Nuclear Power 2010 program are shown in Figure 1.1.

President Bush's budget supports the continuation of the Nuclear Power 2010 initiative in 2006 with a request of $56 million (an increase of

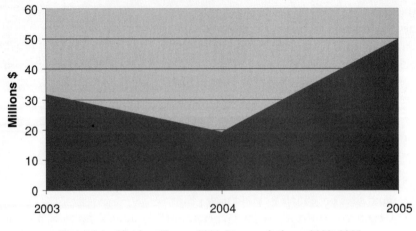

Figure 1.1   **Nuclear Power 2010 Appropriations, 2003–2005**
SOURCE: Utilis Energy/OMB.

$6.4 million compared to 2005). In addition, the Offices of Nuclear Energy, Science, and Technology within the Department of Energy requested $511 million (an increase of $25 million compared to 2005) for investment in nuclear research, education, and infrastructure to support the development of new nuclear generation technologies and advanced energy products. This will provide significant improvements to the economics, sustainability, safety, and reliability of nuclear-based energy, as well as its resistance to pro-liferation and terrorism.

Changing Public Opinion

While the U.S. nuclear industry has marched forward with new designs, enhanced performance, and a recent increase in support from the federal government, its acceptance by the general public has tended to wax and wane over the decades. After years of disinterest, especially in the United States, the nuclear power industry is now positioned for a comeback. The drivers behind this comeback are:

• Growing concerns over the adequacy of fossil-based energy supply.
• Increased interest in environmental issues.
• Rising energy prices.

Adequacy of Energy Supply

According to the Energy Information Agency, the U.S. Department of Energy's statistical arm, total U.S. electricity sales are expected to increase by 50 percent, from 3,567 billion kilowatt-hours in 2004 to 5,341 billion kilowatt-hours in 2030. To meet this anticipated increase in demand, additional energy infrastructure assets–especially power plants–must be built. However, until recently, this has been easier said than done.

For many years the public gave little thought to energy issues and continued to take electricity for granted. Simply stated, electricity was always there. All a person had to do to receive it was flick a switch and remember to pay the monthly bill. This attitude worked well in an environment of low prices and plenty of spare generation capacity, but when market fundamentals change it was an entirely different story.

U.S. economic growth in the last decades of the twentieth century, coupled with the public's general unwillingness to permit new electric generation and transmission projects, slowly eroded the nation's electricity supply surplus. As a result, as demand crept upward, certain markets were left vulnerable to supply outages. This was the case with the rolling blackouts experienced in California during 2001. With reserves of fossil fuels dwindling, the U.S. government now views nuclear energy as a partial solution to this growing energy supply problem.

Besides being a virtually unlimited source of supply, nuclear power also offers considerable enhancements in energy reliability. For example, when Hurricane Katrina was bearing down on the U.S. Gulf Coast in late August 2005, Entergy Corporation declared a precautionary "unusual event" and shut down its Waterford nuclear reactor in St. Charles Parish, 30 miles east of New Orleans. Just two weeks later, Entergy was given permission by the NRC to reactivate the unit since it had suffered no significant damage, due to its robust construction. Other energy infrastructure and assets in the region were not so fortunate, and it took weeks and months after the hurricane to restore operations to various refineries and pipelines in the affected region.

The ultimate impact of Katrina on the nuclear power industry is likely to be considerably

Even before Katrina's market impact, the rising cost of natural gas and imported oil prompted various firms to reexamine the potential for constructing new nuclear assets.

greater than a brief shutdown of a single reactor. Damage to natural gas facilities on the Gulf Coast sent already-high natural gas prices even higher, and in the wake of Hurricane Rita these prices reached $14 per thousand BTUs (MMBtu). Even before Katrina's market impact, the rising cost of natural gas and imported oil prompted various firms to reexamine the potential for constructing new nuclear assets. The two 2005 U.S. Gulf Coast hurricanes have also reinforced concerns of overdependence on any one source of energy and concentrating too much infrastructure in one region of the United States.

Concerns over Climate Change

James Lovelock, a founder of Greenpeace, said, "Only nuclear power can halt global warming."

There is increasing agreement within the climate change lobby that greater utilization of nuclear power must be considered in order to reduce the threat of global warming. Unlike fossil fuels, nuclear power generation does not emit carbon dioxide, the main catalyst of climate change. This has created an unlikely alliance between the nuclear industry and many environmentalists, who are looking for ways to reduce carbon dioxide emissions. A statement made by James Lovelock, a founder of Greenpeace, that "Only nuclear power can halt global warming" offers an example of this alliance.

Rising Costs of Fossil Fuels

In many markets today, electricity generated from nuclear power is some of the cheapest power available. The cost of nuclear power produced by existing plants is likely to be lower than from newly built plants because of the high capital start-up costs of new nuclear plants. However, the nuclear industry has promised that new reactor designs will cost only $1,500 per kilowatt (kW) of installed capacity (assuming ideal conditions and no construction delays). Others believe a more realistic assessment would be to estimate the cost of new plants at closer to $2,000 per kilowatt. In any event, the anticipated rebirth of the U.S. nuclear power market will be greatly influenced by its associated costs.

The Evolution of Public Opinion

According to a March 2006 survey conducted by Bisconti Research and GfK NOP for the Nuclear Energy Institute, 73 percent of the 1,000 U.S. adult respondents polled would accept a new nuclear reactor at an existing plant site and 68 percent would favor the use of nuclear energy as one of the ways to provide electricity to the United States, while only 29 percent of those polled oppose nuclear power. The data are consistent with public opinion results obtained by Bisconti Research in May 2005 which showed that 70 percent of Americans favored nuclear power.

Bisconti's research has shown over the past decade a widening gap between those who favor nuclear energy and those in opposition to the technology. Public opinions on the issue since 1983 are shown in Figure 1.2.

In recent years Bisconti's research has also shown a widening gap between those *strongly* in favor and strongly against nuclear power. (See Figure 1.3.) These recent polling results are the latest figures of a decade-long attempt to mold U.S. public opinion. The following sections illustrate the change in the public's attitude toward nuclear power over the past 40 years.

Much of the public's perception of nuclear energy tends not to be based on facts but rather on past images, such as mushroom clouds and ill-

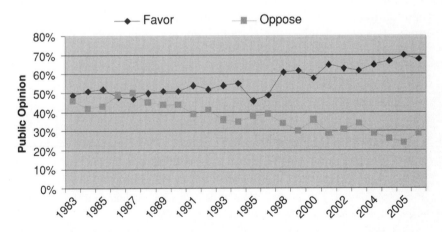

Figure 1.2 **Bisconti Research: Increasingly Favorable Public Opinion**
SOURCE: Utilis Energy/Bisconti Research.

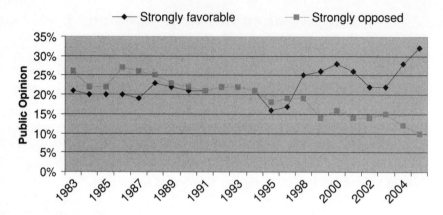

Figure 1.3   **Bisconti Research: Strongly Favorable versus Strongly Opposed**
SOURCE: Utilis Energy/Bisconti Research.

ness caused by radiation and radioactive fallout. These perceptions have changed over the decades. By understanding what has influenced the public's perception, one can form a more objective opinion regarding the merits of nuclear energy.

Prior to the 1970s

There has always been some sort of bias against nuclear energy. Public opinion has basically been shaped by the only concrete example of unrestrained nuclear power the world has known: the atomic bombs used against Japan in the closing days of World War II. This public anxiety toward the atom was further exacerbated by the efforts of Albert Einstein immediately following the war. In 1946, Albert Einstein and eight other scientists formed an organization to educate the American people about the nature of nuclear weapons and nuclear war. This organization, the Emergency Committee of Atomic Scientists, more commonly known as the "Einstein Committee," carried out an educational campaign over a five-year period that featured a documentary film about nuclear weapons and explained to the public the implications of nuclear warfare. Atomic energy, however, has little to do with nuclear weapons.

In the early decades of U.S. commercial nuclear development, the government and nascent nuclear industry relied on public relations campaigns to counteract any antinuclear bias generated by groups such as the

Einstein Committee. These PR campaigns featured slogans such as President Eisenhower's "Atoms for peace" and such headline-catching statements as electricity "too cheap to meter," coined in 1954 by Lewis Strauss, then head of the Atomic Energy Commission. During this era, attempts were made to link nuclear technology to social progress, economic growth, and a better standard of living. With U.S. demand for electricity doubling approximately each decade during this time, nuclear power was positioned as one of the keys to the country's continued success, a source of energy that would give us a competitive advantage over other nations, such as the Soviet Union, and provide a very attractive carrot to U.S. allies who could potentially share in the utilization of this closely held technology.

If Americans thought little about energy supply and related costs in the 1980s and 1990s, this general indifference pales in comparison to the public's attitude toward energy consumption and prices in the 1960s and early 1970s, when oil prices were generally stagnant, conservation was basically unheard of, and supplies were always abundant.

A global event halfway around the world changed these perceptions virtually overnight and prompted many Americans to rethink their nation's reliance on imported oil. This event, the Arab oil embargo of 1973, was the result of the October Arab/Israeli Yom Kippur War. As part of their political strategy in reacting to the Yom Kippur War, the Organization of Arab Petroleum Exporting Countries (OAPEC)—consisting of Saudi Arabia, Iran, Iraq, the United Arab Emirates, and Qatar, a subset of nations belonging to OPEC—unilaterally cut oil production 25 percent; placed an embargo on shipments of crude oil to the West, in particular the United States and the Netherlands; and raised posted prices by 17 percent to $3.65 a barrel (still a bargain when compared to $70 crude today).

Overnight, U.S. oil imports from Arab nations dropped from 1.2 million barrels per day to roughly 20,000 barrels per day. The price of oil increased to nearly $12.00 per barrel in January 1974. At the pump, prices rose from about 35 cents to $1.20 a gallon at the apex of the crisis. While the embargo was lifted on March 18, 1974, the incident was a wake-up call to public officials and private citizens, demonstrating the negative consequences of the United States' growing dependence on foreign oil.

In response to the embargo, the United States introduced a few half-hearted conservation measures, such as implementing a national maximum speed limit of 55 miles per hour and extending daylight savings time. The largest legislative initiative in response to the crisis was the approval by the U.S. Congress on November 13, 1973, of a trans-Alaskan oil pipeline, designed to supply the U.S. with 2 million barrels of oil a day. The massive pipeline project was completed in 1977. For the past 30 years the pipeline has been effectively transporting crude to the Port of Valdez, whence it is then shipped over water to the U.S. West Coast, then refined and sold to U.S. consumers. It should be noted, however, that Alaska's North Slope oil production has declined over the decades as those oil fields mature. Today the Alaskan pipeline delivers less than 1 million barrels a day to U.S. consumers.

The artificial supply shortage created by OAPEC resulted in a significant upward price event, effectively ending years of energy price lethargy. It also prompted many in the United States to increase their efforts to further develop nuclear power as a potential solution that would provide the country with energy independence.

Mid-1970s Nuclear Backlash

The renewed interest in the further development of nuclear power was dampened in the mid-1970s, when consumer advocates such as Ralph Nader argued that the industry had become a powerful special interest group in need of reform. These advocates demanded greater amounts of public accountability within the nuclear industry. During this same time, environmentalists began to advocate other alternative sources of energy such as solar, hydroelectric, and wind generation, and other interest groups questioned the cost-effectiveness of nuclear energy production. These developments took some public support away from the nuclear camp, but this loss of support was relatively minor compared to developments at the end of the decade.

Nuclear power almost received its knockout blow during the Three Mile Island accident in 1979. This incident (discussed in greater detail later in this book) occurred only 12 days after the commercial release of the motion picture *The China Syndrome*. In the film's fictional disaster scenario, a nuclear accident created a superheated mass of molten reactor fuel, which burned though a steel reactor vessel and the plant's reinforced concrete foundation into the earth below. The film portrayed the nuclear industry as being cloaked in secrecy and incompetently run and gave the impression that the technology required to safely operate nuclear units had a great potential to run out of control.

The movie became a Hollywood hit and its title became the new catch phrase for the antinuclear movement in the U.S. Less than two weeks later, when the Three Mile Island incident occurred, the issues raised in the movie—public accountability and the risk of runaway technology—became the major talking points in the media, which greatly influenced public opinion. An example of the media reaction to this event is illustrated by the April 9, 1979, cover of *Time* magazine, which declared Three Mile Island to be a "Nuclear Nightmare."

The Three Mile Island accident set in motion public scrutiny of all U.S. commercial nuclear facilities. Investigators aggressively sought to unearth industry examples of:

- Construction flaws
- Incompetent management
- Potential operating risks

The accident at Three Mile Island also galvanized opposition to nuclear power. There were demonstrations in the streets and musicians took to the stage. A group called Musicians United for Safe Energy (MUSE) gathered for five nights at benefit concerts in New York City in September 1979. The proceeds from these events went to fund pro-solar energy organizations.

These media messages were so intense that since 1979 there have been no new nuclear power plants built in the United States. In 1986, the Chernobyl disaster further reinforced hostile media messages against the nuclear industry. While coverage of both events created an opportunity for media outlets to attract an audience, most of them failed to provide any context for this event and did not identify the safety track record of the U.S. nuclear industry.

> *The accident at Three Mile Island galvanized opposition to nuclear power.*

Reintroducing the Public to Nuclear Energy

The U.S. nuclear power industry most certainly had a bloody nose at the hands of the media as it entered the twenty-first century. As a result of Three Mile Island and Chernobyl news coverage and associated special interest group campaigns, few people or organizations not directly associated with the sector had anything positive to say about nuclear power, and the idea of constructing new nuclear facilities was not thought to be realistic.

In 2001, against the backdrop of rising energy costs, which were just beginning to accelerate, the Bush administration launched an energy independence campaign that prominently featured nuclear energy. At this point, whispers from utility executives were heard, mentioning the possibility of building new nuclear power plants. It seemed that nuclear energy, already producing roughly 20 percent of America's electricity with little fanfare, was about to arise from the dead.

The terrorist attacks of September 11, 2001, temporarily delayed the renaissance of nuclear power in the United States. Media reports focusing on the potential vulnerability of U.S. nuclear facilities not only put industry expansion plans into a state of hibernation, but there was also considerable talk of closing nuclear power plants located near population centers, such as New York's Indian Point facility. While some individuals and groups may never believe these facilities are secure from attack, the passage of time and increasing pressures to rely less on foreign sources of energy have again sparked interest in building new nuclear units in the United States.

In 2006, the Bush administration attempted to solidify public support for nuclear energy by clearly identifying nuclear power as a means to significantly reduce greenhouse gas emissions. On the talk show circuit, former New Jersey governor Christie Whitman and EPA administrator and Greenpeace co-founder Patrick Moore aggressively promoted nuclear energy as "cleaner, cheaper, and safer" than many other fuel alternatives currently available in the market and in the United States. Both called for the public and private sectors to renew their investment in nuclear power to achieve the goal of reducing greenhouse gas emissions. President Bush continued to champion this message; on May 24, 2006, while visiting Pennsylvania's Limerick Nuclear Generation Station, he said:

> Let's quit the debate about whether greenhouse gases are caused by mankind or by natural causes; let's just focus on technologies that deal with the issue. Nuclear power will help us deal with the issue of greenhouse gases.

In addition to appealing to the public's environmental concerns, President Bush also linked nuclear power development with independence, greater national security, and economic development by saying:

For the sake of economic security and national security, the United States of America must aggressively move forward with the construction of nuclear power plants. Other nations are. Interestingly enough, France has built 58 plants since the 1970s, and now gets 78 percent of its electricity from nuclear power. . . . China has nine nuclear plants in operation and they got-plan to build 40 more over the next two decades. They understand that in order to be an aggressive nation, an economic nation that is flourishing so that people can benefit, they better do something about their sources of electricity.

Negative Media Messages

The media wield a tremendous power to send messages that can easily sway public opinion. A declining number of the U.S. public reads newspapers on a regular basis, but opinions can be molded through visual media such as movies and television. Many opponents of nuclear energy have effectively utilized these forms of entertainment to lobby against the continued use and growth of nuclear power. Just days before the Three Mile Island accident and in the five years that followed, there were a number of high-profile films and television programs that helped to galvanize antinuclear sentiment in the United States.

The China Syndrome

The first of these was the film *The China Syndrome*. The movie and its message, considered by many to be a product of California's vocal antinuclear community of the 1970s, was heavily influenced by three technical consultants, Dale Bridenbaugh, Richard Hubbard, and Gregory Minor. These three engineers left General Electric's nuclear power division in February 1976 and became heavily involved in the campaign for Proposition 15, a state initiative opposing the use of nuclear power. The three engineers eventually formed MHB Technical Associates, and the firm was retained to consult on set design, technical sequences, and nuclear terminology for the film.

The China Syndrome quickly became the cult classic for antinuclear activists, but most energy industry experts believe the film gave a heavily skewed interpretation of electric utility and nuclear power operations in the United States and featured many misleading statements relating to utility economics and NRC oversight, along with technical inaccuracies.

The Day After *and* Threads

The Day After, an ABC TV movie dramatization of the effects of a hypothetical nuclear attack on the United States and the town of Lawrence, Kansas, in particular, was one of the biggest media events of the 1980s. Aired on Sunday, November 20, 1983, *The Day After* was watched by an estimated half of the adult population, approximately 100 million people, the largest audience for a made-for-TV movie up to that time.

Prior to the movie being aired, it was screened by the U.S. Joint Chiefs of Staff, who were shocked by its content. When aired, the majority of Americans responded with equal shock. ABC set up toll-free phone lines and distributed a half million viewer guides to help the audience psychologically deal with the material. Discussions among experts, the media, and the general public first introduced the term *nuclear winter*, an event depicted in the film.

The Day After went on to be nominated for 12 Emmy Awards and won 2. The film was released theatrically to 40 countries, an idea proposed by Brandon Stoddard, then president of ABC Motion Picture Division, who had been impressed by the film *The China Syndrome*. Three weeks after its U.S. broadcast, an edited version of the film was shown in Britain on the ITV commercial network, accompanied by a Campaign for Nuclear Disarmament recruitment drive.

Threads, a British antinuclear film broadcast in 1984, offered an even more extreme picture of a nuclear exchange than the one presented in *The Day After*. The film depicted the results of a full nuclear exchange in the United Kingdom, the ensuing nuclear winter, and its effects 13 years into the future.

Threads was first broadcast on BBC television in 1984 and then again in 1985 as part of a week of programs marking the fortieth anniversary of the atomic bombings of Hiroshima and Nagasaki. In 1985, it was shown on PBS stations as part of fund-raising drives. *Threads* was also syndicated in the United States to commercial television stations, as well as Superstation TBS; the latter followed the film with a panel discussion on nuclear war.

Late-Night Laughs

Discussion about nuclear power in popular media isn't limited to movies with frightening images or doomsday scenarios. Public opinion can also be influenced by comments made by comedians and established comedy shows. NBC's long-running late-night comedy show *Saturday Night Live* spoofed the 1979 Three Mile Island accident shortly after its occurrence when, in a skit, a soft drink spilled on a control room panel triggered a meltdown scare at the "Two Mile Island" nuclear plant. The skit included then President Jimmy Carter visiting the crippled facility and getting a little too close to the melting core. The spoof also featured a utility-sponsored mime troop, in a hopelessly amateurish attempt to show the benefits of nuclear energy.

While popular culture references about nuclear safety have waned in the years following Three Mile Island, they haven't totally disappeared. In fact, America's favorite animated family, *The Simpsons*, lives in the shadow of the fictitious Springfield nuclear reactor, and its patriarch, the bumbling Homer Simpson, is employed at the facility. This setting doesn't create a high degree of public trust in the capabilities of the nuclear industry.

Putting Nuclear Power in a Positive Light

The U.S. nuclear industry has made plans to roll out a multiyear advertising campaign to build public support for new nuclear generation plants. In early 2006, the Nuclear Energy Institute (NEI) finalized plans for an ad campaign with the PR firm Hill & Knowlton to promote a "nuclear renaissance." The goal of the campaign is to build greater bipartisan support inside and outside the D.C. beltway for greater use of nuclear power in the United States. The print ad campaign (Figure 1.4) features a young girl with a blue-sky background and declares, "Clean air is so twenty-first century" and "Our generation is demanding lots of electricity . . . and clean air."

As a proindustry advocacy group, the NEI has an interest in closely monitoring the changing sea of U.S. public opinion. It commissioned Bisconti to quantify the U.S. public's opinions on nuclear power. While it can be said that opinion polls paid for by advocacy groups generally yield more industry-friendly results than polls conducted by potentially more

NUCLEAR.
Electricity & Clean Air
Today & Tomorrow.

Kids today are part of the most energy-intensive generation in history. They demand lots of electricity. And they deserve clean air.

That's why nuclear energy is so important to America's energy future. Nuclear energy already produces electricity for 1 of every 5 homes and businesses. And our 103 nuclear power plants don't produce any greenhouse gases or emissions that harm our air quality.

We need secure, domestic sources of electricity for the 21st Century—and we also need clean air. With nuclear energy, we can have both.

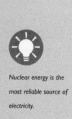

Nuclear energy is the most reliable source of electricity.

NUCLEAR.
CLEAN AIR ENERGY.

NEI
WWW.NEI.ORG

Figure 1.4   **An NEI Ad from Its "Clean Air" Campaign**
SOURCE: Nuclear Energy Institute.

objective organizations or independent polling firms, recent nuclear energy opinion polls tend to show a strong correlation with Bisconti's results.

Gallup Polling Results

On four occasions since 1994, the Gallup organization asked respondents: "Overall, do you strongly favor, somewhat favor, somewhat oppose, or strongly oppose the use of nuclear energy as one of the ways to provide electricity for the U.S.?" On three occasions—in 1994, 2005 and 2006—responses were generally around 55 percent, but never reached 60 percent approval. Only in 2001, the same year as the 9/11 terror attacks, did the public's favorable response dip to 46 percent. (See Figure 1.5.)

ABC News Polling Results

At various times since Three Mile Island, ABC News has asked respondents: "In general, would you favor or oppose building more nuclear power plants at this time?" While prior to the Three Mile Island accident these replies were just above 50 percent positive, for the ensuing 25 years public approval for new reactor construction has been generally below 40

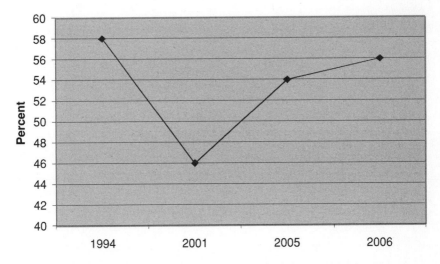

Figure 1.5   **Gallup Poll Tracking Public's Attitude toward Nuclear Power**
SOURCE: Data courtesy of Gallup.

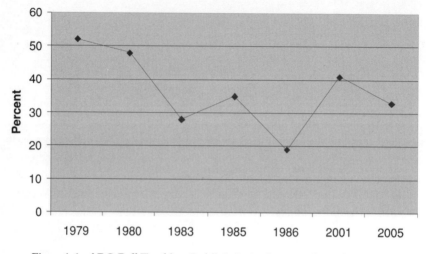

Figure 1.6   **ABC Poll Tracking Public's Attitude toward Nuclear Power**
SOURCE: Utilis Energy/ABC.

percent; the nadir occurred in 1986 when less than one person in five, or 20 percent, approved of new reactor construction. ABC's most recent poll, in 2005, put support of new nuclear power plant construction below 40 percent, but in the wake of recent energy price increases and the administration's efforts to create support for nuclear power, the poll's measurement of a favorability rating greater than 50 percent should occur in the near future. (See Figure 1.6.)

CBS News Polling Results

CBS News asked respondents: "Would you approve or disapprove of building more nuclear power plants to generate electricity?" Prior to the Three Mile Island accident, responses to CBS's poll were extremely favorable, with almost 70 percent of respondents approving the construction of new nuclear power facilities. Similar to the results of other polls, the post–Three Mile Island favorability drop was significant. However, by 1990 opinions reversed again, and by 2001 just over half of the respondents approved of building more nuclear power plants to generate electricity. (See Figure 1.7.)

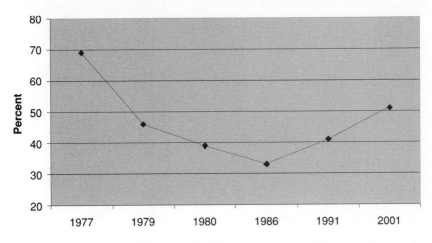

Figure 1.7 **CBS Poll Tracking Public's Attitude toward Nuclear Power**
SOURCE: Utilis Energy/CBS.

While the general public may favor investment in nuclear energy, when asked about the location of such a power plant the "not in my backyard" (NIMBY) syndrome has a tendency to kick in, but poll results have begun to show that this, too, is slowing changing with regard to nuclear power.

In its own poll, the NEI asked respondents: "If a new power plant were needed to supply electricity, would it be acceptable to you or not acceptable to you to add a new reactor at the site of the nearest nuclear power plant that already is operating?" Along the same lines, the Gallup organization asked respondents: "Overall, would you strongly favor, somewhat favor, somewhat oppose, or strongly oppose the construction of a nuclear energy plant in your area as one of the ways to provide electricity for the U.S.?" The results of these two polls are shown in Figure 1.8 and show a growing public tolerance for the citing of nuclear reactors.

Some groups will always be opposed to nuclear power and the construction of new plants in the United States. However, as the passage of time separates us from negatively perceived events, such as Three Mile Island and Chernobyl, and should there be no other negative events, the public's approval of and openness to further nuclear energy expansion in the United States should continue to increase.

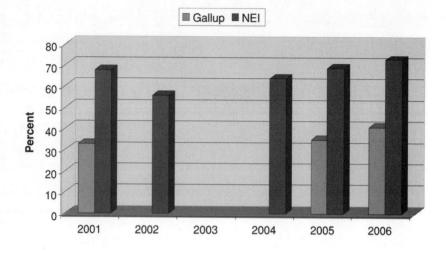

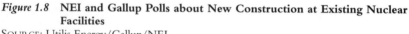

Figure 1.8   **NEI and Gallup Polls about New Construction at Existing Nuclear Facilities**
SOURCE: Utilis Energy/Gallup/NEI.

Challenges to Overcome

Several years ago most electricity market analysts believed the majority of new U.S. power generation capacity would be natural gas-fired. Changing economics, tightening natural gas availabilities, and environmental pressures now have utilities reconsidering the nuclear power option, but significant hurdles remain.

Financial Hurdles

It is still difficult to find utility executives willing to publicly commit to building a new reactor, due to the $3 to $4 billion investment required. Following Enron's demise in 2001 and the retrenchment of the deregulated wholesale merchant sector of the electricity industry, public utilities have been attempting to restructure their debt-laden balance sheets and increase stock performance, not to take on huge new projects and their related liabilities. Wall Street is also worried about the potential backlash resulting from any company's announcement to build a new reactor, fearing that environmental groups will quickly launch an aggressive campaign against it.

Waste Disposal

Besides financial concerns, there is in the United States an ongoing nuclear waste disposal problem to tackle. At the center of the waste dispute is the federal government's plan to transport spent nuclear fuel and high-level radioactive waste across the country and permanently store it at Yucca Mountain in Nevada.

Changing economics, tightening natural gas availabilities, and environmental pressures now have utilities reconsidering the nuclear power option, but significant hurdles remain.

Opponents to the further development of U.S. nuclear power frequently bring up the nuclear waste question. Nuclear reactors, through their normal operation, create relatively small quantities of radioactive waste, compared to other power sources. This nuclear waste can either be stored in a secure area or reprocessed into additional nuclear fuel.

Currently nuclear waste is kept on site at the operating reactors found throughout the United States. These distributed sites must be secure, must have accurate records, and are inspected at regular intervals to ensure proper compliance with NRC regulations. Table 1.2 shows that between 1968 and 2002, approximately 47,000 metric tonnes of nuclear waste had been produced by commercial U.S. reactors.

The Yucca Mountain facility has several obstacles to overcome before it becomes the nation's repository for nuclear waste. While political and legal battles have entangled the proposal for years, the Bush administration and U.S. Congress have endorsed the development of nuclear energy and vowed that the nation will have a permanent nuclear waste site. The DOE supports the Yucca Mountain project and believes that "sound science" is on its side. However, the project continues to have strong opponents, including key congressional leaders.

In September 2005, the NRC approved a temporary radioactive material waste site on the Skull Valley Goshute Reservation, located approximately 45 miles from Salt Lake City. This move is a major step on the road to developing Yucca Mountain, a site that would store 77,000 tons of nuclear waste in an area about 90 miles away from Las Vegas. Skull Valley, which could house 44,000 tons of waste in steel containers, would warehouse spent fuel until it is ready to be sent to Yucca Mountain. In the meantime, the U.S. House of Representatives has voted to allocate $10 million to move nuclear waste out of the hands of utilities and toward a more permanent location.

Table 1.2   **U.S. Commercial Reactor Waste Production, 1968–2002**

Reactor Type	Number of Assemblies		
	Stored at Reactor Sites	Stored at Away-from-Reactor Facilities	Total
Boiling-water reactor	90,398	2,957	93,355
Pressurized-water reactor	69,800	491	70,291
High-temperature gas-cooled reactor	1,464	744	2,208
Total	**161,662**	**4,192**	**165,854**
	Metric Tonnes of Uranium (MTU)		
Boiling-water reactor	16,153.6	554	16,707.6
Pressurized-water reactor	30,099.0	192.6	30,291.6
High-temperature gas-cooled reactor	15.4	8.8	24.2
Total	**46,268.0**	**755.4**	**47,023.4**

MTU = Metric tonnes of uranium.

Notes: A number of assemblies discharged prior to 1972, which were reprocessed, are not included in this table (no data available for assemblies reprocessed before 1972).

Totals may not equal sum of components because of independent rounding.

SOURCE: Energy Information Administration, Form RW-859, "Nuclear Fuel Data" (2002).

The DOE must meet certain NRC standards if it is to win approval to develop the Yucca Mountain site. Department officials hope to begin delivering waste to the proposed national repository by 2012. To get to that point, however, the Yucca developers must complete an application for the NRC, which is substantially behind schedule.

The Yucca Mountain site has received approval from the U.S. government's General Accounting Office (GAO) with regards to safety and possible terrorist vulnerability. The GAO stated that the likelihood of any attacks being successful are "very low" and "extremely unlikely" because the material is hard to disperse and would be stored in protective containers.

Waste Reprocessing

The other approach to the nuclear waste issue is not to store it but to reprocess it into nuclear fuel. This is done in other countries—France, for example. On February 6, 2006, the U.S. Department of Energy announced the Global Nuclear Energy Partnership (GNEP). This "supplier nation" partnership potentially between Russia, Japan, China, the United Kingdom, and France, with a $250 million budget for fiscal year 2007, plans to leverage technology to recycle spent nuclear fuel without producing plutonium as a by-product of the reaction. Reprocessing allows for the greater extraction of energy from nuclear fuel, reduces the amount of waste requiring permanent disposal, and greatly reduces the risk of nuclear proliferation, which can lead to the development of nuclear weapons. By utilizing reprocessing technology, the United States will not need any additional storage facilities besides Yucca Mountain.

> *This "supplier nation" partnership potentially between Russia, Japan, China, the United Kingdom, and France, with a $250 million budget for fiscal year 2007, plans to leverage technology to recycle spent nuclear fuel without producing plutonium.*

The United States stopped reprocessing in 1970 because the technology of that day separated plutonium, which presented a significant terrorist and proliferation concern. The United States now proposes to develop, in partnership with these other nations, technologies that will allow for the recycling of spent fuel but not separate plutonium, and to couple them with fast reactors that can burn down the spent fuel. One proposal under the GNEP plan is to have Australia become the world's nuclear bank, leasing enriched uranium to other countries to generate power and then storing depleted fuel rods in its vast, empty outback. Under this scenario, technologically advanced nuclear nations will provide nuclear fuel and recycling services for energy generation to other countries, who would in turn forgo their own development of nuclear technologies.

Economics of Nuclear Power

When all costs are considered, including rising natural gas and coal prices and costs associated with global warming, nuclear units are becoming increasingly inexpensive. New regulatory restrictions on emissions of carbon dioxide increase the costs of fossil fuel-generated electricity; at the same time, fears of climate change have softened opposition among some environmentalists.

While the government must still solve the problems associated with nuclear waste, security, and the challenge of climate change, the United States is proposing expanding its nuclear generation as an affordable low-carbon energy alternative.

The billion dollar-plus cost of building a nuclear power plant is large compared with that of gas-fired plants, but once a nuclear plant is built, it can steadily generate enormous amounts of power without being subject to the volatile fuel prices that have plagued utility customers in recent years. Thus, it offers greater relative price stability.

The Nuclear Energy Cost Debate

A new 1,000-megawatt nuclear plant costs $1.5 to $2.0 billion and takes at least five years to construct. This compares to $1.2 billion and three to four years for a coal-fired facility, and $500 million for a combined-cycle gas plant.

A 2004 report from the University of Chicago funded by the DOE compared the levelized power costs of prospective nuclear, coal, and gas-fired power generation in the United States. Various nuclear options were included, and for advanced boiling-water reactors (ABWR) or AP1000 type reactors (discussed in subsequent chapters) the initial costs ranged from 4.3 to 5.0 cents per kilowatt-hour on the basis of:

- Overnight capital costs of $1,200 to $1,500/kW.
- A 60-year plant life.
- Five-year construction.
- Operation at 90 percent capacity.

Table 1.3 Nuclear Plant(s) Projected Electricity Costs (Cents/kWh)

Overnight Capital Cost $/kW		1,200	1,500	1,800
First unit	7-year build, 40-year life	5.3	6.2	7.1
	5-year build, 60-year life	4.3	5.0	5.8
Fourth unit	7-year build, 40-year life	4.5	4.5	5.3
	5-year build, 60-year life	3.7	3.7	4.3
Eighth unit	7-year build, 40-year life	4.2	4.2	4.9
	5-year build, 60-year life	3.4	3.4	4.0

SOURCE: Utilis Energy/University of Chicago.

This compares with coal at 3.5 to 4.1 cents per kilowatt-hour and natural gas (combined-cycle gas turbine, or CCGT) at 3.5 to 4.5 cents per kilowatt-hour.

While coal and natural gas appear to have the initial cost advantage, if a series of eight nuclear units of the same kind are considered, and assuming increased efficiency due to experience, the levelized power costs drop 20 percent from those just quoted. When the nuclear engineering costs are also amortized, they drop 32 percent, bringing the cost to about 3.4 cents per kilowatt-hour. Multiple-unit estimated cost reductions in the University of Chicago study are shown in Table 1.3.

Waste Contrasts and Comparisons

For coal-burning power plants, solid waste is a problem. Approximately 10 percent of the content of coal is ash. Ash often includes metal oxides and alkalis. These residues must be disposed of as solid wastes. Natural gas does not produce significant volumes of combustion-based solid wastes.

The waste from nuclear power plants consists primarily of solid spent fuel, along with some process chemicals, steam, and heated cooling water. Such nuclear waste differs from a coal plant's waste in that its volume and mass are small relative to the electricity produced.

Nuclear waste also differs from fossil fuels in that the spent fuel is radioactive, while only a minute share of the waste from a fossil plant is radioactive. Solid waste from a nuclear plant or from a fossil fuel plant can be toxic or damaging to the environment, often in ways unique to the particular category of plant and fuel. Waste from the nuclear power plant is managed to the point of disposal, while a substantial part of fossil fuel waste is unmanaged after release from the facility.

The issue of whether nuclear plants actually present a net positive environmental gain compared to fossil fuels also depends on the values that are placed on the wastes that each type of plant produces. However, in general, it can be said that:

- Nuclear power provides an environmental benefit by almost entirely eliminating airborne wastes and particulates generated during power generation.
- Nuclear power creates a cost in the form of relatively small volumes of radioactive wastes that are produced that must be managed prior to ultimate disposal.

Fossil fuels also produce unwanted solid wastes, though the problems associated with these wastes differ from spent nuclear fuel. Neither waste stream is desirable, but on a pound-per-pound basis, the potential environmental cost of waste produced by a nuclear plant is usually viewed as higher than the environmental cost of most wastes from fossil fuel plants. Nevertheless, the volume of waste from the nuclear plant is substantially lower and better controlled.

Regulatory Nuclear Waste Restrictions

There are legislative and regulatory restrictions on the disposal of nuclear waste, which usually vary with the type of waste. Because wastes produced from power plants vary with the fuel, potential environmental controls consequently vary with the type of power plant.

By far the greatest environmental waste concern at an operating nuclear power plant is spent-fuel disposal. The spent fuel has different radiation and chemical characteristics from the initial nuclear fuel, necessitating special handling of the waste above and beyond the handling of the initial fuel. The expenses of such handling need to be included in the costs of nuclear power production.

In the United States, for both policy and economic reasons, final disposal of spent nuclear fuel is accomplished through burial. Reprocessing and transmutation of the fuel remain options that are under periodic policy consideration, though such processes also involve the ultimate burial of spent-fuel components. Reprocessing and transmutation would alter the timing, volume, duration, and conditions of such burials. They would also increase the costs of nuclear power plant operation, probably significantly.

Spent Fuel

The DOE has statutory responsibility for the disposal of spent nuclear fuels, which is funded by a surcharge on the cost of nuclear fuels. Presently this charge is 0.1 cent per kilowatt-hour of power generated. This charge is intended to cover the costs of disposal of nuclear wastes, though they are levied against power generated and not the amount of waste produced.

There are questions over whether the funds provided by nuclear power generators adequately cover the costs relating to the disposal of nuclear waste. The targeted ultimate burial site for spent fuels, Yucca Mountain in Nevada, has not yet been opened and has been challenged in the courts. Ultimate disposal has thus not occurred for most spent fuels, which are now in temporary storage at the reactors where they were produced or at alternative sites.

Nuclear power generation produces around 2,000 metric tonnes of spent fuel per annum. This amounts to 0.006 pounds per megawatt-hour. A typical nuclear power plant of 1,000 MWe capacity operating 91 percent of the time produces around 45,758 pounds, or slightly less than 23 tons of waste per year. The issue with waste from a nuclear power plant is not its volume, which is comparatively small, but the special handling required for satisfactory disposal. A similar amount of electricity from coal would yield over 300,000 tons of ash, assuming 10 percent ash content in the coal.

Opponents of the Yucca Mountain plan, which include Nevada state officials, are seeking government funding to store the spent waste on sites where it is generated. They also favor investing in waste "reprocessing" techniques that are used by other nations. Such technology recycles nuclear waste, extracting usable plutonium and uranium from spent fuel. Many believe it doesn't make sense, from a practical point of view, to move nuclear waste across the country and store it at Yucca Mountain. Other groups believe the plan to use Yucca Mountain as a permanent nuclear waste site is inadequate.

The issue of whether to proceed with Yucca Mountain appears to be trapped in a never-ending quagmire of debate. Nevada was considered an ideal location for such storage, given the aridity of the land. At the same time, more than 100 nuclear bomb tests have already been detonated underground in the state. However, opponents counter that volcanic activity is ever-present in the region, which could enable radioactive materials to escape in the event of seismic activity.

Currently, the United States' 103 commercial nuclear reactors store 70,000 tons of waste at 72 commercial and military sites in 39 states. The DOE says it will take 24 years to fill the Yucca site. Thus far, more than 20 years and $4 billion have been spent studying the Yucca Mountain concept, but it has yet to be approved.

Summary

The past 60 years have brought considerable change to the nuclear power industry. At first, this exotic technology was relatively unproven and was viewed with significant levels of concern. While opposition to this form of electricity generation increased following two highly publicized accidents, public opinion in favor of nuclear power has remained strong. Now, after many years of quietly operating and producing approximately 20 percent of the United States' electricity, the nuclear industry appears to have weathered the storm of negative events and the backlash of public opinion.

Decades of proven operations have even most of its critics acknowledging the technology's ability to create vast amounts of commercial electric power—power badly needed by the general public to run the everyday life conveniences that we now take for granted, such as throwing a load of laundry in the washing machine or going online to surf the Internet. Current market fundamentals and economics now favor the expansion of the U.S. nuclear industry, and numerous utilities have begun the process to build and operate additional nuclear generation plants. During the summer of 2006, plans were in the works to build 18 new facilities, most of which would be sited next to existing nuclear units.

In today's environment of increasing energy demand and geopolitical instability, nuclear power remains a technology that has not been utilized to its fullest potential. The chapters that follow show how and why the U.S. nuclear sector is poised for renewed growth and identify the drivers behind this anticipated growth.

2

The Nuclear Paradigm Shift

*Thirty years on, my views have changed, and the rest of the
environmental movement needs to update its views, too, because nuclear
energy may just be the energy source that can save our planet from
another possible disaster: catastrophic climate change.*

*Look at it this way: More than 600 coal-fired electric plants in the
United States produce 36 percent of U.S. emissions—or nearly 10
percent of global emissions—of CO_2, the primary greenhouse gas
responsible for climate change. Nuclear energy is the only large-scale, cost-
effective energy source that can reduce these emissions while continuing to
satisfy a growing demand for power. And these days it can do so safely.*

—Patrick Moore, co-founder of Greenpeace, in the *Washington
Post*, April 16, 2006. (Patrick Moore is also chairman and
chief scientist of Greenspirit Strategies Ltd. He and Christine
Todd Whitman are co-chairs of a new industry-funded
initiative, the Clean and Safe Energy Coalition, which
supports increased use of nuclear energy.)

The United States is approaching a critical juncture at which it
must resolve how to meet future electricity demands with a co-
herent and actionable strategy. Simply stated, the issues that have
brought us to this point are the fact that demand for power continues to

increase; energy costs are already high and rising, and remain exposed to unsettled geopolitical situations; and environmental issues have moved to the fore, dictating the cost and availability of future supply options. Power planners worldwide, not just domestically, are being forced to make decisions incorporating these disparate concerns, fully cognizant that actions taken currently will have long-lasting consequences that stretch far beyond current economic and political cycles. Within this context, nuclear power emerges as a vital component of the energy supply portfolio. Yet legacy issues have weighed down the growth of nuclear energy over the past decade.

The Current Situation

The last new nuclear power reactor in the United States went into commercial operation in 1996, after receiving its construction permit in 1973. The larger share of nuclear-generating units came online in the 1970s and 1980s, essentially capping an era of rapid power plant growth throughout the country. Since then there has been a noticeable trend toward development of other power generation resources, notably natural gas–fired power plants. There are numerous reasons for this shift, including negative public sentiment (discussed in Chapter 1) and the perception that construction of nuclear power plants would be both expensive and time-consuming.

In response, the domestic nuclear energy industry has spent this period proving its economic worth and demonstrating its safety record. During this time, the Nuclear Regulatory Commission (NRC) has also evolved, creating an environment wherein the nuclear plant operators are more proactive in achieving high safety and maintenance standards, and providing good operators the opportunity to improve effective utilization of their existing assets.

U.S. Fuel Mix

In today's domestic electric power market, traditional fossil fuel technologies dominate the supply function. Coal-fired generation typically provides almost 50 percent of total U.S. electricity supply, with natural gas– and oil-based technology providing a combined 20 percent. Thus, over two-thirds of

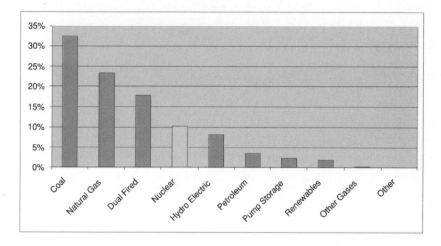

Figure 2.1 **U.S. Electric Power Industry Net Capacity, Summer 2004**
SOURCE: Energy Information Administration, Form EIA-860, "Annual Electric Generator Report."

the total energy consumed in the electricity sector comes from burning fossil fuels. The balance of U.S. electricity production consists mainly of nuclear energy, at 20 percent, and hydroelectric power, at 6.5 percent. These in turn overshadow the contributions of renewable energy (principally solar, wind, and biomass), which, combined, only amount to 2.5 percent of the total market. Figure 2.1 shows summer 2004 net capacity of U.S. generation assets with nuclear power providing 10 percent of the nation's available electricity generation capacity.

The lengthy process of planning, permitting, financing, and constructing any of these types of power-generating facilities dictates that the nation's current supply profile will change very little over the next few years. In fact, the biggest change to the generating mix has just gone through its mature stages—that of the rapid additions of natural gas plants from the middle 1990s to the early 2000s. Figure 2.2 shows that from 1993 to 2004, natural gas generating capacity grew by 342 percent, from 65,523 megawatts to 224,257 megawatts, while every other supply source either stayed the same, shrank, or logged just marginal growth. *Dual-fired* resources, in this figure, represent units that are capable of burning either oil or gas; the changes therein reflect the overall growth in addition to the improvement of technology, from older steam type units

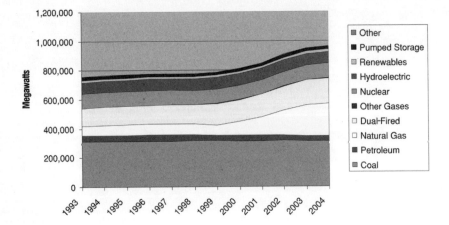

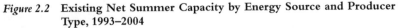

Figure 2.2   **Existing Net Summer Capacity by Energy Source and Producer
        Type, 1993–2004**
SOURCE: Energy Information Administration.

to newer combined-cycle ones. Note that the *renewables* category rose 28
percent, but only increased its share of the total market by 0.2 percent, as
it is still a small amount in absolute figures.

In a little over 10 years' time, the total U.S. energy-generation market
has grown by more than 25 percent, from approximately 750,000
megawatts to just under 1,000,000 megawatts. Table 2.1 shows the considerable gains made by natural gas over this decade, increasing from approximately 65,000 to just under 225,000 megawatts, while nuclear power has
not shown any appreciable growth. The immediate questions that arise
are: How will capacity growth be addressed in the U.S. market, and what
role will nuclear power play in this growth?

U.S. Nuclear Capacity Growth

The majority of nuclear capacity growth took place during the 1970s and
1980s with plants that had been issued construction licenses in the 1960s.
As the federal government was fostering the growth of the nuclear power
industry in the 1940s, creating the Atomic Energy Commission (AEC) in
the process, a true and desirable separation of the regulatory function from

Table 2.1 Existing Net Summer Capacity by Energy Source and Producer Type, 1993–2004 (Megawatts)

Period	Coal	Petroleum	Natural Gas	Dual-Fired	Other Gases	Nuclear	Hydroelectric	Renewable	Pumped Storage	Other	Total
1993	310,148	44,019	65,523	120,157	1,931	99,041	77,410	14,656	21,146	550	754,582
1994	311,415	42,695	70,685	123,110	2,093	99,148	78,041	15,021	21,208	550	763,967
1995	311,386	43,708	75,438	121,958	1,661	99,515	78,562	15,300	21,387	550	769,463
1996	313,382	43,585	74,498	128,570	1,664	100,784	76,437	15,309	21,110	550	775,890
1997	313,624	43,202	76,348	129,384	1,525	99,716	79,415	15,351	19,310	774	778,649
1998	315,786	40,399	75,772	130,399	1,520	97,070	79,151	15,444	19,518	810	775,868
1999	315,496	35,587	73,562	146,039	1,909	97,411	79,393	15,942	19,565	1,023	785,927
2000	315,114	35,890	95,705	149,833	2,342	97,860	79,359	15,572	19,522	523	811,719
2001	314,230	39,714	125,798	153,482	1,670	98,159	79,484	16,180	19,096	440	848,254
2002	315,350	38,213	171,661	162,289	2,008	98,657	79,354	16,755	20,373	641	905,301
2003	313,019	36,429	208,447	171,295	1,994	99,209	78,694	18,199	20,522	638	948,446
2004	313,020	33,702	224,257	172,170	2,296	99,628	77,641	18,763	20,764	700	962,942

SOURCE: Energy Information Administration.

39

sponsorship never really existed. The rush to bring nuclear plants, then still a new technology, onto the market created a spurt of growth domestically in which more plants were under consideration than were in operation. Combine that acceleration phase of development with the keen interest of nuclear technology providers (i.e., General Electric and Westinghouse) to gain market share, and the immediate result was the proliferation of plants and plant types with an oversight function that was ill-prepared to handle proper regulation of this new and safety-intense technology.

In 1962 the AEC predicted that by the year 2000, 50 percent of total U.S. electricity supply would originate from nuclear plants. This turned out to be exceedingly overoptimistic.

Initial enthusiasm for nuclear power persisted through the 1950s, which represented the beginning of a surging interest in adopting nuclear technology, yet by the early 1960s only 6 commercial facilities had been brought on line that were not built by the U.S. government, compared with the 85 units that had been sold by reactor vendors through 1968. According to the NRC's "A Short History of Nuclear Regulation, 1946–1999" (www.nrc.gov/who-we-are/short-history.html), this era was referred to as the Great Bandwagon Market. In fact, in 1962 the AEC predicted that by the year 2000, 50 percent of total U.S. electricity supply would originate from nuclear plants. This turned out to be exceedingly overoptimistic.

Safety considerations (described in Chapter 5) also affected nuclear generation growth and evolved at the same that the boom in nuclear planning took place. To mitigate the risks of accidents at nuclear plants, plant sites far from metropolitan areas were preferred, and plans to have some nuclear facilities within major metropolitan cities (e.g., Con Edison's Ravenswood nuclear plant intended for New York City) were shelved. In addition, reliance on accumulated experience with nuclear power increased and conservative engineering standards—multiple back-ups and safety design redundancies—were mandated. Clifford K. Beck, then the AEC's deputy director of regulation, told the Joint Committee in 1967 that "no one is in a position to demonstrate that a reactor accident with consequent escape of fission products to the environment will never happen. . . . No one really expects such an accident, but no one is in a position to say with full certainty that it will not occur." (www .nrc.gov/who-we-are/short-history.html#Bandwagon)

Public opinion was integral to the pattern of growth of nuclear generating capacity from the outset. The changes in sentiment that eventually reduced the public's interest in the technology sprang from issues with nuclear power itself,—which gained more public exposure from the development of weapons technology—and the fallout implications of the buildup during the Cold War. Debate about adequacy of nuclear plant design, absent of any experience with a major disaster, meant that once questions arose and gained currency, there was little beyond theory and controlled laboratory results that could counter speculation surrounding potential occurrences like the aforementioned "China syndrome." These reactor meltdowns, resulting from potential cooling system failure, occupied AEC staff during the mid-1960s.

With each new application filed with the AEC during this time, wider consideration of the prospect of the fleet of nuclear plants fueling everyone's power needs brought more questions to the surface. These issues included:

- Emergency core cooling
- Thermal pollution
- Radiation exposure
- Environmental impact
- Radioactive waste

In the late 1970s, after the Three Mile Island accident, the reluctance to embrace the technology was palpable. In fact, the immediate impact on nuclear plant development after the Three Mile Island accident in March 1979 was that the AEC stopped granting operating licenses for plants already under construction. (The AEC lifted the sanction one year later in February 1980, and granted the next operating license in August of that year.) The impact of the groundswell of public opinion moving against nuclear power was financially draining on the utilities that still had plans to develop plants.

Nuclear Power Plant Financing

The capital costs of financing nuclear power development suddenly increased as the timeline for development was extended. The hold on granting operating licenses for plants already under construction, if not at completion, also caused plants early in execution or still on the drawing board to be delayed for an even longer period of time. Forcing this delay to persist even beyond the reaction to the high-profile incident was the fact that many plants had design differences and, in some cases, significant design flaws. The due diligence required to review all nuclear power plant designs, both online and still under planning, lengthened the time period that was already materially longer than originally anticipated.

Compounding the time delay was the financial environment that characterized the mid- and late 1970s. The oil embargo of 1973–1974 sensitized the general public to energy costs (those related primarily to transportation) and the consequences of relying on foreign oil, but given the relatively lesser share of electricity from oil-fired plants (except along the East Coast) the impact on electricity was to halt the growth of oil-based generation (its peak was in 1978, 365 billion kilowatt-hours versus 115 billion kilowatt-hours in 2005). In addition, the coincident rise in inflation as measured by the consumer price index (CPI), shown in Figure 2.3, and in interest rates (both long and short term), meant that large-scale projects, such as nuclear power facilities, which took long periods of time and utilized large quantities of raw materials, all financed in public markets, were especially hard hit.

U.S. interest rates soared to 10 percent and beyond by 1980, from under 6 percent at the start of the 1970s. Inflation popped during the oil embargo to 11 percent, retreated briefly to 6 percent in 1977, but then ratcheted back over 13 percent in 1980, the worst combination of increased finance cost and rising material charges in the post–World War II era.

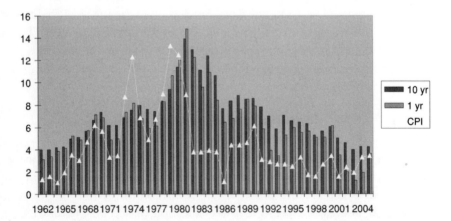

Figure 2.3 **Average Annual Interest Rates and Consumer Price Index**
SOURCE: Federal Reserve/Bureau of Labor Statistics.

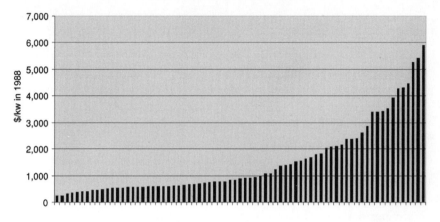

Figure 2.4 **Capital Costs for Nuclear Plant Construction since 1988**
SOURCE: Platts.

The impact of this inflation on reactor capital costs was substantial. Original estimates for the overnight cost of construction were less than $2,000/kilowatt, ideally under $1,000/kilowatt, which would allow these assets to operate competitively with coal-based and other base-load technologies. Figure 2.4 shows the construction costs for 75 nuclear plants (operating, retired, or cancelled). In effect two-thirds of the capacity that made it into the construction cycle actually came in below $1,500/kilowatt. These lower cost units typically were designed and built earlier, making it through the licensing process before the early 1980s. The newer and safer units dominate the one-third of plants whose costs soared above $1,500/kilowatt, even reaching above $5,000, or more than four times the average cost of all the others.

As previously stated, the rising costs and cost overruns associated with U.S. nuclear reactor construction severely hurt its economic viability. During the 1980s these costs soared. Examples of these delay-associated cost overruns, according to the NRC, include:

- Shoreham Power Station. The Long Island–based nuclear reactor received its NRC operating license in April 1989. The plant was permanently shut down in June of that same year without commercially generating electricity because a working area evacuation plan could not be produced. Ratepayers were left to foot the $5.5 billion bill.

- Nine Mile Point Reactor. Located in Oswego, New York, the Niagara Mohawk facility began construction in 1974 and after 14 years received its operating license. The total cost of the project was well over budget at $6.3 billion.
- Seabrook Nuclear Station. The two New Hampshire-based reactors had an initial price tag of $900 million. In 1989, Unit 2 was cancelled after $900 million had been spent. When reactor Unit 1 began operations in 1990, the unit's price tag was $6.5 billion.
- Washington Nuclear. The Washington State utility initiated efforts to construct four nuclear reactors in the early to mid-1970s. These were later cancelled or mothballed from 1982 to 1995 due to mismanagement, delays, and cost overruns. The utility eventually defaulted on $2.25 billion in bonds financing these units and the costs were passed along to ratepayers.
- Watts Bar Power Station. The two-unit nuclear facility in Tennessee received its construction license in 1973, but only one unit was eventually built. Construction lasted 23 years and the project had a final price tag of $6.9 billion.
- Comanche Peak. The two-unit Texas nuclear facility was issued construction permits in December 1974, but its reactors did not begin operations until 1990 and 1993 at a total cost of $9.1 billion.

Costs Favor Coal

If cost issues alone did not serve to force consideration of cheaper and more quickly constructed sources of electric power, then the combination of safety concerns and cost considerations together pushed nuclear energy out of favor. Electric utilities had no choice but to concentrate their generation building efforts on conventional fossil fuels, and coal became king. Figure 2.5 shows the impact of inflation on the price of electricity, and the overall price rise due to rising fuel costs during the 1970s.

Interest in burning greater amounts of coal for electricity production shows up in Figure 2.6, the chart depicting fuel consumption during the post-WWII era, as the amount of coal consumed during the 1970s accelerated rapidly, from 320 million short tons in 1970 to 569 in 1980 and 781 in 1990. Throughout this time, however, coal's share of total U.S. electric output stayed in a steady range between 49 and 50 percent.

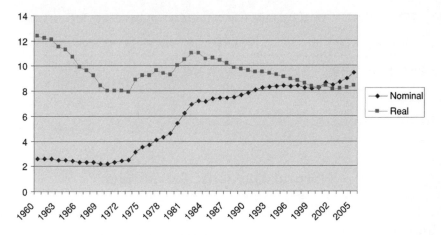

Figure 2.5 **Average Residential Retail Price of Electricity, Nominal versus Real**
SOURCE: Energy Information Administration.

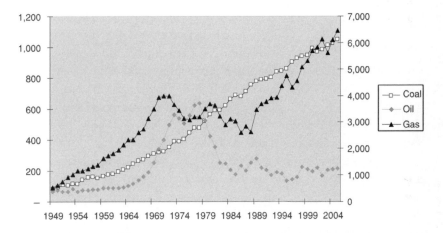

Figure 2.6 **Annual Fossil Fuel Consumption for Electricity Production**
Note: Coal in million short tons, oil in million barrels, and natural gas in billion cubic feet.
SOURCE: Energy Information Administration.

Table 2.2   **Cost Performance Characteristics of Available Technology**

Technology Type	Overnight Cost	Heat Rate (Btu/Kwh)
Conventional Coal	$1,249	9,000
Natural Gas Combined-Cycle	$575	7,200
Nuclear	$1,500–$2,000	NA

SOURCE: EIA Assumptions to the Annual Energy Outlook, 2006.

Natural Gas Cost Advantage

The cost of coal is now estimated at $1,000 to $1,300 per kilowatt, whereas a new gas-fired combined-cycle plant is considered to cost nearly half that amount.

Compared to the soaring cost of just bringing new nuclear plants to market, capacity additions utilizing fossil fuel technology seem preferable, as demonstrated in Table 2.2. Especially in an environment where regulatory delays, required redesign, and construction impediments were likely, just based on overnight costs natural gas wins out. Of course, such large capital projects that incorporate huge labor and materials requirements can often yield a wide range of realized costs. The cost of coal is now estimated at $1,000 to $1,300 per kilowatt, whereas a new gas-fired combined-cycle plant is considered to cost nearly half that amount.

Regarding the competitiveness of coal versus natural gas, natural gas is clearly the cheaper technology and has an easier permitting process due to the perception that it is less polluting than burning coal. This made natural gas the fuel of first choice for many utilities and private companies throughout the 1990s. The increased efficiency gain with natural gas, which approaches 60 percent fuel efficiency versus nearly 30 percent for conventional coal, was also responsible for its strong popularity.

Selecting New Generation Assets

When considering new generation, fuel, costs and environmental considerations definitely shape the decision process. Since increasing power demand means increasing installed capacity domestically, the choices to develop new capacity are limited to the existing technology that can be deployed in the near term. Therefore, base-load solutions will continue to include coal, nuclear, and natural gas. To fulfill intermediate and peaking needs, new capacity most probably means natural gas, but might also include renewable sources of electricity.

The concerns with adding more fossil fuel base-load capacity are twofold, and really comprise essential reasons why nuclear power should be considered. Coal-fired technologies at 2.21 cents per kilowatt-hour do have readily available domestic supplies of fuel, which is cost advantaged on a Btu basis, as shown in Figure 2.7, versus the cost of other fossil fuel technologies such as with natural gas at 7.51 and oil at 8.09 cents per kilowatt-hour. However, existing coal technology is associated with considerable emissions issues. For coal-fired plants these issues include greenhouse gases (principally CO_2), sulfur dioxide, nitrogen dioxide, and mercury. The negative effects of all of these coal-derived emissions must be included in determining the total cost of relying on greater amounts of coal for this nation's electricity requirements.

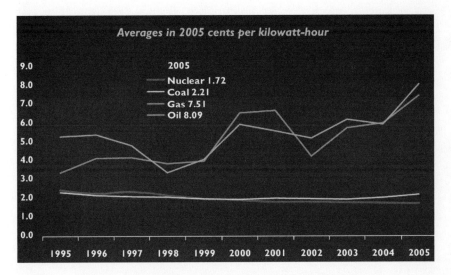

Figure 2.7 **U.S. Electricity Production Costs, 1995–2005**
SOURCE: Nuclear Energy Institute.

Fossil Fuel Price Volatility

Reliance on oil is having a detrimental effect on the U.S. economy, causing inflation, slowing growth, and endangering our nation's energy security.

All of the previously mentioned cost comparisons are susceptible to volatility in fossil fuel prices, which have dramatically increased over the past several decades. This is especially true for crude oil, now a global commodity. Figure 2.8 shows the annual price of West Texas Intermediate (WTI), one of the world's price benchmark crude oils, since 1983. Changing geopolitical supply-affecting events and increasing demand have ricocheted prices generally between $20 and $30 per barrel for most of this period, save the last few years when prices have climbed to unheard of levels in excess of $60 a barrel. At these elevated levels, further reliance on oil is having a detrimental effect on the U.S. economy, causing inflation, slowing growth, and endangering our nation's energy security.

U.S. prices for natural gas delivered to the city gate displayed considerably less volatility than crude oil for much of the same time period, with prices hovering around $3 per million Btu. Figure 2.9 shows that post-1999, natural gas prices began to show considerable volatility, spiking to an average of nearly $9 per million Btu during 2005 (this high was

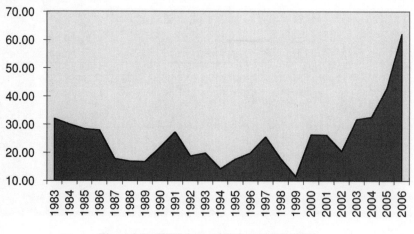

Figure 2.8   **WTI Annual Prices, 1983–2006**
SOURCE: Energy Information Administration.

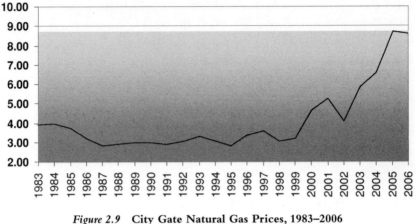

Figure 2.9 **City Gate Natural Gas Prices, 1983–2006**
SOURCE: Energy Information Administration.

skewed by Hurricane Katrina's impact on U.S. natural gas production). These recent price increases have led the way for alternative supplies of natural gas, such as increasing amounts of LNG imports, and have many power providers looking for more economical alternatives to the fuel.

The United States possesses enormous domestic reserves of various qualities of coal, and prices for the fuel steadily declined for almost 20 years. However, recent higher crude oil and natural gas prices have given coal producers pricing power to raise prices. Figure 2.10 shows that in

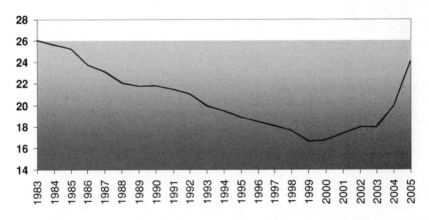

Figure 2.10 **U.S. Coal Prices, 1983–2005 (Dollars per Short Ton)**
SOURCE: Energy Information Administration.

2005, the average cost of a short ton of coal reached $24, a gain of approximately 50 percent since the year 2000. But even at current prices, the fuel remains an attractive option for power generation if environmental challenges associated with its use can be resolved.

The extreme price volatility of oil, natural gas, and even coal affects the cost effectiveness of conventional fossil fuel–fired generation assets and creates additional price uncertainty for both power suppliers and end-use electricity customers. Nuclear power, with its rather predictable cost structure, shields its customers from price volatility and supply uncertainties.

Emissions and the Kyoto Protocol

The Kyoto Protocol is an agreement among nations under the United Nations Framework on Climate Change, which seeks to address the anthropogenic emissions of carbon dioxide as a result of energy use. The ratification treaty covers more than two-thirds of total greenhouse gas (GHG) emissions sources, in more than 160 countries. The treaty became binding in February 2005, after Russia signed on in late 2004, helping to push coverage to more than 55 percent of 1990 levels of carbon dioxide output. The essential goal of the Kyoto Protocol is to have developed countries reduce their greenhouse gas emissions to 5 percent below the 1990 actual levels by 2008. In effect this would mean reducing emissions to 15 percent below expected 2008 output that would have occurred without mitigation. Target levels can be met with purchasing emissions reductions from outside the affected entity.

> *The essential goal of the Kyoto Protocol is to have developed countries reduce their greenhouse gas emissions to 5 percent below the 1990 actual levels by 2008. In effect this would mean reducing emissions to 15 percent below expected 2008 output that would have occurred without mitigation.*

The Protocol does not address obligations beyond the 2012 time period, but it is anticipated that GHG emissions limits of some type would be extend past the Protocol period. Although the United States was a signatory to the Protocol, it did not ratify the treaty. Support for GHG emissions mitigation has emerged at the state and city level within the United States, and it is anticipated that binding constraints will mean that the United States can fulfill a pledge to reduce carbon intensity (the amount of emissions are rising relative to overall economic growth) by 18 percent by 2012.

Despite the lack of ratification, U.S. cities, states, and regions have taken the initiative to reduce carbon dioxide emission levels at paces that set target levels by year and use the 1990 level as a common metric. Within the Northeast, the Regional Greenhouse Gas Initiative covers states from Delaware to Maine (without Massachusetts and Rhode Island, and with Pennsylvania and Maryland as observers only). This agreement would commence at the start of 2009, capping emissions at a set level through 2014, then seeking 10 percent reduction below that level by 2018. The initial cap is approximately the 1990 level. This program applies to all generators greater than 25 megawatts, and would allow the potential for trading and carbon sequestration outside of the electric power sector. Similarly, California has set an initiative to reach year 2000 levels by 2010 and year 1990 levels by 2020, with further reductions called for in the future.

While these efforts are centered in areas that have less coal-fired capacity than the interior states, individual city commitments increase the reach of this trend. It is clear that limits to carbon emissions are evolving domestically without the Kyoto efforts, and that various combinations of limits would directly impact the potential for growth of coal-fired generation, which creates substantial emissions unlike the other forms of fuel shown in Figure 2.11.

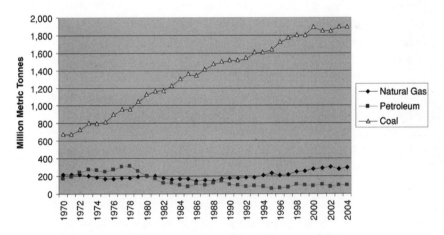

Figure 2.11 **Carbon Dioxide Emissions from Electric Power Sector**
SOURCE: Energy Information Administration.

Environmentally Friendly Renewable Energy

Renewable energy is energy obtained from sources that are essentially inexhaustible, unlike hydrocarbon-based fossil fuels, which are in finite supply. Types of renewable energy currently available in the United States include solar, wind, geothermal (heat energy extracted from reservoirs in the earth's interior), and biomass (organic materials, such as wood byproducts and agricultural wastes that can be burned to produce energy or converted into a gas and used for fuel).

Renewable energy (along with conservation) stands as a viable alternative to generating power with fossil fuels or nuclear technology. Mainly because of their perceived environmental friendliness or less intrusive nature, these technologies present an attractive method to meet power demand, on a limited basis. The current structure of electric power markets and the limitations inherent in each type of alternative fuel dictate that dramatic changes in the pattern of consumption or use of alternatives remains limited.

First, the sheer size of the installed fossil and nuclear capacity, complemented by hydropower resources, at first glance demonstrates that without massive reduction in consumption, switching even a limited amount of conventional power generation to alternatives is not feasible. Even if these resources were able to run at full utilization rates, the impact on fossil fuels would be to reduce current consumption patterns by only a few percentage points. In fact, the total increase in renewables output from 1990 to 2004 can be accounted for by less than 2 percent of just the coal-fired capacity (see Figure 2.12).

Second, the availability factor for these fuel sources is inconsistent, and they are often not available at times of peak need. To compare with coal- or nuclear-based technology, it is necessary to consider the alternative as capable of running in base-load operation. For nuclear, that means 24/7 during the complete fuel-load cycle, or 18 to 24 months flat-out. To compare with coal, that would mean availability at least through peak seasons—that is, from April to September and from October through March. Geothermal energy presents the best comparison, given its constant availability of fuel source, with maintenance of the generating plant the sole impediment to full-load operations. Biomass energy might be considered comparable to fossil technologies, as the operator is tasked with procuring

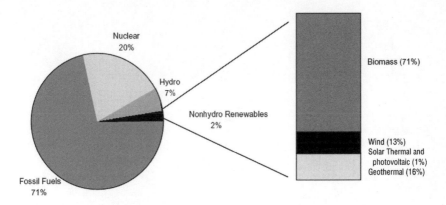

Figure 2.12   **U.S. Electricity Supply in 2004, Highlighting the Share of Renewables**
SOURCE: Energy Information Administration.

the fuel source in a similar fashion, and the balance of the generating cycle is considered the same.

Given the inability to store electricity on a large scale, generating technologies based on solar and wind present less comparable solutions. On larger scales and under average conditions, larger arrays of installed capacity can be considered equivalent to conventional generation. However, wind is not a constant during on-peak hours (8 A.M. to 11 P.M. weekdays) and can often be lacking during the hottest times of the summer, when the highest effective demand occurs, requiring the fullest utilization of resources. Solar power is not available in evening hours or during periods of extended cloudiness.

Further limitations can be inferred in the infrastructure required. For the solar and wind power potential (see Figures 2.13 and 2.14), the area of potential capacity is limited for development on a larger commercial scale, although small-scale units have a larger range for development. The size of potential projects thus limits their impact to supplemental status rather than replacement. Also limiting the potential development is the fact that the transmission and distribution grid is not as robust in areas where renewables are likely to be developed, thus delaying large-scale adoption of these technologies and implying additional costs.

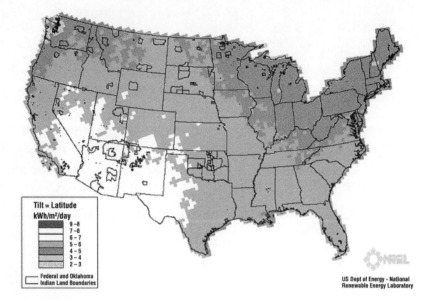

Figure 2.13   **Resource Potential for Renewable Technology: Solar**
SOURCE: National Renewable Energy Laboratory.

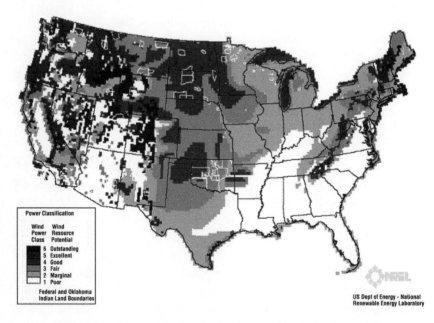

Figure 2.14   **Resource Potential for Renewable Technology: Wind**
SOURCE: National Renewable Energy Laboratory.

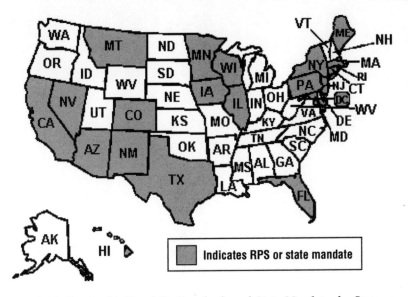

Figure 2.15 **Renewable Portfolio Standards and State Mandates by State, as of 2005**
SOURCE: Energy Information Administration

Working in favor of bringing renewables to the grid are state mandates that call for meeting generation portfolio standards under a certain time frame (see Figure 2.15). Combined with subsidies from state and federal sources, these programs insure that current marginal costs are not the only economic drivers that dictate which supply is utilized (see Table 2.3).

Rediscovering Nuclear Power

What the preceding information tells us is that while the United States possesses numerous energy options, there are definite drawbacks to each. Not one is a perfect solution. While the United States hasn't built a nuclear power plant for decades, the nation's economy continues to rely heavily on nuclear power for electricity generation as economic and environmental issues bring greater reliance on fossil fuels into serious question. While most of the nation's 103 commercial reactors have been

Table 2.3 Electricity Net Generation from Renewable Energy by Energy Use Sector and Energy Source, 2000–2004 (Thousand Kilowatt-Hours)

Sector/Source	2000	2001	2002	2003	2004[P]
Total	356,478,576	294,946,110	351,250,926	363,216,799	358,766,924
Biomass	60,726,183	56,964,468	61,621,675	61,264,772	60,042,172
Wood/Wood Waste	37,594,867	35,199,916	38,665,038	37,529,099	37,294,927
MSW/Landfill Gas	20,304,947	19,931,044	20,184,617	20,179,386	19,592,596
Other Biomass[a]	2,826,369	1,833,508	2,672,020	3,556,287	3,154,649
Geothermal	14,093,158	13,740,503	14,491,310	14,424,231	14,355,859
Conventional Hydroelectric	275,572,599	216,961,046	264,328,831	275,806,329	269,636,745
Solar	493,375	542,755	554,831	534,001	579,048
Wind	5,593,261	6,737,337	10,354,279	11,187,466	14,153,100
Commercial	2,111,621	1,548,109	1,597,472	1,966,052	1,882,280
Biomass	2,011,871	1,481,627	1,584,675	1,893,807	1,778,755
Wood/Wood Waste	26,958	17,626	12,505	13,049	12,751
MSW/Landfill Gas	1,601,153	1,181,827	1,267,615	1,455,294	1,454,433
Other Biomass[a]	383,760	282,174	304,555	425,464	311,571
Conventional Hydroelectric	99,750	66,482	12,797	72,245	103,525

Industrial	33,626,302	30,848,324	34,572,014	33,223,295	33,951,800
Biomass	29,491,148	27,703,056	30,747,367	29,000,871	28,915,566
Wood/Wood Waste	28,651,835	26,888,490	29,643,205	27,988,372	27,793,219
MSW/Landfill Gas	30,858	237,273	202,209	161,467	145,448
Other Biomass[a]	808,455	577,292	901,953	851,032	976,899
Conventional Hydroelectric	4,135,154	3,145,268	3,824,647	4,222,424	5,036,234
Electric Power[b]	320,740,653	262,549,676	315,081,440	328,027,452	322,932,844
Biomass	29,223,164	27,779,786	29,183,633	30,370,094	29,347,851
Wood/Wood Waste	8,916,074	18,293,800	9,009,328	19,527,678	9,488,957
MSW/Landfill Gas	18,672,936	18,511,944	18,714,793	18,562,625	17,992,715
Other Biomass[a]	1,634,154	974,042	1,465,512	2,279,791	1,866,179
Geothermal	14,093,158	13,740,503	14,491,310	14,424,231	14,355,859
Conventional Hydroelectric	271,337,695	213,749,293	260,491,387	271,511,660	264,496,986
Solar	493,375	542,755	554,831	534,001	579,048
Wind	5,593,261	6,737,337	10,354,279	11,187,466	14,153,100

[a]Agriculture byproducts/crops, sludge waste, tires, and other biomass solids, liquids and gases.

[b]The electric power sector comprises electricity-only and combined-heat-power (CHP) plants within North American Classification System (NAICS) 22 category whose primary business is to sell electricity, or electricity and heat, to the public.

P = Preliminary.

Note: Data revisions are discussed in Highlights section. Totals may not add due to independent rounding.

SOURCES: Energy Information Administration, Form EIA-759, "Monthly Power Plant Report," Form EIA-860B, "Annual Electric Generator Report—Nonutility," Form EIA-906, "Power Plant Report," and Form EIA-920, "Combined Heat and Power Plant Report."

SOURCE: Energy Information Administration, "Renewable Energy Trends 2004."

successfully operating for decades, these assets also have a limited life, operating under 40-year licenses. The 40-year licensing period was selected due to economic and antitrust considerations rather than the technical limitations of the nuclear facility. With many of these assets nearing the end of their 40-year operating lives, many utility operators are seeking 20-year license extensions from the NRC.

According to the NRC, the first U.S. nuclear operating license will expire in the year 2009; approximately 10 percent will expire by the end of 2010; and more than 40 percent will expire by 2015.

According to the NRC, the first U.S. nuclear operating license will expire in the year 2009; approximately 10 percent will expire by the end of 2010; and more than 40 percent will expire by 2015. In anticipation of this, by the start of 2006, 22 nuclear facilities had their licenses renewed for an additional 20 years. The status of these license renewal applications is shown in Table 2.4.

These nuclear unit license extensions have attracted little notice from the public, and there has been limited opposition to these license extensions. The relative ease of these license extensions, coupled with current market fundamentals, forecasted demand growth, and the limitations of conventional fossil fuel and renewable technologies, has U.S. utility executives again thinking about constructing new nuclear reactor capacity after a multiple-decade hiatus. This new nuclear capacity will be one of the foundations for this nation's energy security in the twenty-first century.

Table 2.4 Status of License Renewal Applications

Applicant	Plant Name and Units	Date Application Received by NRC	Date NRC Issued GEIS Supplement*	Date NRC Issued SER**	Date NRC Issued License
Baltimore Gas & Electric Co.	Calvert Cliffs 1 and 2	April 1998	November 1999	November 1999	March 2000
Duke Energy	Oconee 1, 2, and 3	July 1998	February 2000	February 2000	May 2000
Entergy Nuclear Operations	Arkansas Nuclear One 1	February 2000	April 2001	April 2001	June 2001
Southern Nuclear Operating Co.	Edwin I. Hatch 1 and 2	March 2000	May 2001	October 2001	January 2002
Florida Power & Light Co.	Turkey Point 3 and 4	September 2000	January 2002	February 2002	June 2002
Virginia Electric & Power	Surry 1 and 2, North Anna 1 and 2	May 2001	December 2002	November 2002	March 2003
Duke Energy	McGuire 1 and 2, Catawba 1 and 2	June 2001	December 2002	January 2003	December 2003
Exelon	Peach Bottom 2 and 3	July 2001	January 2003	February 2003	May 2003
Florida Power & Light Co.	St. Lucie 1 and 2	November 2001	May 2003	July 2003	October 2003
Omaha Public Power District	Fort Calhoun	January 2002	August 2003	September 2003	November 2003
Carolina Power & Light	Robinson 2	June 2002	December 2003	January 2004	April 2004
Rochester Gas & Electric Corp.	Ginna	August 2002	January 2004	March 2004	May 2004
SCE&G Exelon	Summer Dresden 2 and 3, Quad Cities 1 and 2	August 2002 January 2003	February 2004 June 2004	January 2004 July 2004	April 2004 October 2004
Southern Nuclear Operating Co.	Farley 1 and 2	September 2003	March 2005	March 2005	May 2005
Entergy Nuclear Operations	Arkansas Nuclear One 2	October 2003	April 2005	April 2005	June 2005

(Continued)

Table 2.4 *(Continued)*

Applicant	Plant Name and Units	Date Application Received by NRC	Date NRC Issued GEIS Supplement*	Date NRC Issued SER**	Date NRC Issued License
Indiana & Michigan Power Co.	D.C. Cook 1 and 2	November 2003	April 2005	May 2005	August 2005
Tennessee Valley Authority	Browns Ferry 1, 2, and 3	January 2004	June 2005	January 2006	May 2006
Dominion Nuclear Connecticut	Millstone 2 and 3	January 2004	July 2005	August 2005	November 2005
Nuclear Management Co.	Point Beach 1 and 2	February 2004	August 2005	October 2005	December 2005
Constellation Energy	Nine Mile Point 1 and 2***	May 2004	May 2006	June 2006	
Carolina Power & Light	Brunswick 1 and 2	October 2004	April 2006	March 2006	June 2006
Nuclear Management Co.	Monticello	March 2005		July 2006	
Nuclear Management Co.	Palisades	March 2005			
AmerGen Energy Co.	Oyster Creek	July 2005			
Entergy Nuclear Operations	Pilgrim	January 2006			
Entergy Nuclear Operations	Vermont Yankee	January 2006			
Entergy Nuclear Operations	FitzPatrick	August 2006			

*Plant-specific supplement to the Generic Environmental Impact Statement.
**Safety Evaluation Report.
***Plant-specific review schedule.
SOURCE: Nuclear Regulatory Commission.

3

A Call to Action

In recent years, increases in global oil production capacity have struggled to keep pace with rapidly growing demand, particularly in China, the other emerging economies in Asia, and the United States. That slower growth in productive capacity relative to growth in demand has resulted in a decline in global surplus capacity to produce crude oil. At the same time, perceived risks to supply posed by geopolitical instability and other uncertainties have grown.

> —Guy Caruso, administrator, U.S. Energy
> Information Administration, in a statement
> before the House of Representatives,
> Energy and Resources Subcommittee,
> June 7, 2006

The United States, the lone remaining world superpower and the wealthiest nation on earth, does not exist in a global vacuum. In an increasingly competitive world economy, the United States must have access to considerable and secure energy supplies, both domestic and foreign, to fuel its economy and comfortable way of life.

Many critics or skeptics of increased nuclear power usage in the United States point to the fact that the country possesses numerous domestic energy sources, whether these be traditional fossil fuels (oil, coal, natural gas) or newer technological advanced fuels (ethanol, hydrogen) and has yet to fully exploit renewable alternative fuels such as wind, solar, and geothermal. These nuclear power critics believe investment should be made in these alternative fuels instead of constructing new nuclear power plants that will produce radioactive waste.

Resource Nationalism

What nuclear power critics fail to realize is that we now live in a world of increased competition for energy resources. With a finite amount of non-renewable natural resources on earth, a type of resource nationalism has begun to emerge. As global industrialization forces countries to look for secure new energy supplies, in many instances the interests of both energy suppliers and consumers have begun to conflict.

There are greatly varying opinions regarding the exploitable quantities of oil and gas still available. On one end of the spectrum you have subscribers to the "peak oil" theory, which states that global oil production has or will shortly peak, and in the future the supply of oil will not be able to keep pace with demand. The other side of the argument, the position taken by most energy firms, states that technology will make available greater quantities of economically viable hydrocarbons to be used for fuel in the future.

Whether fossil fuels run out in 20 years or 200 years is not really important. Under each scenario, both industrializing and developed nations require greater amounts of energy on an annual basis. This will increase competition for energy sources, raise prices, and give energy suppliers greater power in the market.

Resource nationalism has begun to change traditional energy supply relationships between nations. For example, Venezuela, a principal crude oil supplier to the United States, supplying more than a million barrels per day for many decades, has taken steps to diversify its customer base for its oil and has reduced crude oil exports to the United States by about 25 percent over the past year. While the Chavez government may just be putting on a show to gain approval from its constituents, there are a number of countries, especially China, interested in purchasing this crude oil to fuel their drive to industrialize. This effectively limits the potential U.S. crude oil supply. With potentially fewer dedicated suppliers of crude oil, it would be unwise for the United States to turn its back on the greater utilization of nuclear power.

Captive Oil Consumers

After air, water, and food, energy is probably the most essential commodity for life. For much of the twentieth century, oil played an increasing role in fueling this country's economic growth. During the 1950s and 1960s the global oil industry was rather boring and predictable. There was plenty of cheap energy. Crude oil supplies were abundant and growing, and demand was rather modest by today's standards. The United States was the major consumer of oil, with crude oil imports used to supplement substantial domestic production. Oil was purchased under long-term contracts, and prices showed little movement for years on end. It was an industry built on relationships and long business lunches.

There was little financial management of the industry, whose revenues were purely commodity-based. In the 1970s the United States was highly dependent on oil to run its economy. A significant number of electricity-producing utilities on the U.S. East and Gulf Coasts burned millions of barrels of residual fuel oil (also known as Number 6 oil) to generate electricity. While many of these utilities now burn natural gas or coal, oil remains an important peaking or back-up fuel for these facilities.

The United States, with a crude oil consumption of approximately 20 million barrels per day, is the largest global oil consumer. The United States is also blessed with considerable crude oil assets. Its domestic oil production reached its apex in 1970 when 11.3 million barrels per day were pumped from the ground. Over the next 36 years, U.S. production fell to 6.8 million barrels per day, a decrease of 39 percent. This daily production now represents just 8 percent of the world's daily crude oil production.

Today the world consumes approximately 85 million barrels of oil per day, of which 30 million or 35 percent comes from nations in the Organization of Petroleum Exporting Countries (OPEC) cartel. Forecasts call for the world to consume 118 million barrels per day, a 39 percent increase over 2006 levels, in 2030 due to continued global industrialization and the rise of the Chinese and Indian economies. The challenge of meeting increases in oil demand is made even greater when one realizes that the world's existing oil fields tend to decline approximately 8 percent per year.

Global oil production is having great difficulties keeping pace with the world's demand for oil, and sizable, economically viable new oil discoveries are becoming harder to find. In 2005, only 5 billion barrels of crude oil were discovered. While this sounds like a large amount, it pales in comparison to the mid-1960s when discoveries totaled approximately 90 million barrels per day.

This increased pressure on supply has been reflected in the commodity's price. Since the year 2000 the price of crude oil has tripled to previously unheard of levels, above $60 per barrel. These higher crude prices have been reflected at the pump with U.S. consumers paying as much as $3.00 per gallon. In this environment, OPEC, with a large percentage of global production, has considerable market power.

The OPEC cartel has been in existence since September 1960 and controls 75 percent of the world's oil reserves. The organization's influence on world energy markets has waxed and waned over the past 46 years. At periodic production meetings OPEC sets daily output quotas for its 11 members. These quotas are determined by global economics and supply factors. Table 3.1 shows the cartel's current 28 million barrels per day production quotas on an individual member nation basis. Iraq, in the

Table 3.1 **OPEC Production Quotas**

	OPEC Quota (in Thousands of Barrels per day)	July 2006 Production
Algeria	894	1,360
Indonesia	1,451	890
Iran	4,110	3,750
Kuwait	2,247	2,550
Libya	1,500	1,700
Nigeria	2,306	2,100
Qatar	726	800
Saudi Arabia	9,099	9,200
United Arab Emirates	2,444	2,600
Venezuela	3,223	2,400
OPEC 10	28,000	27,350
Iraq	NA	2,100
Crude Oil Total		**29,450**

SOURCE: Energy Information Administration.

midst of rebuilding its oil infrastructure, with a daily production of approximately 2 million barrels per day, currently does not have an OPEC production quota.

Saudi Arabia, with current production of 9 to 10 million barrels per day, produces the lion's share of the cartel's daily output and, with its surplus production capacity, has traditionally taken on the role of "swing producer," making up any production shortfalls experienced by the other members and keeping prices within desired limits.

All of the cartel's members, save Venezuela, are Islamic nations. Following is a brief description of the current energy fundamentals of each of the Islamic members; Venezuela is considered in the next section.

Algeria

This North African nation, which has experienced years of civil war and continuing political unrest, possesses an estimated 11.8 billion barrels of proven oil reserves. Foreign companies control approximately 44 percent of Algeria's crude oil production. Algeria's average crude oil production, about 1.4 million barrels per day, is well above its current OPEC quota of 894,000 barrels per day (as of July 2005). The nation has a 2010 production goal of 2.0 million barrels per day, an increase of approximately 500,000 over current levels.

Indonesia

This Asia Pacific nation currently holds proven oil reserves of 4.7 billion barrels of oil. Indonesia has great difficulty meeting its 1.45 million barrel per day OPEC production quota and currently produces just 900,000 barrels per day. This total is 10 percent below its 2003 production levels of roughly 1 million barrels per day. The decline is due mainly to aging oil fields, a lack of new investment in exploration, and regulatory hurdles. The country's declining oil production could be turned around once its new 600 million barrel Cepu field in Java comes on line. The field is being developed by ExxonMobil in partnership with Pertamina, the state-run oil monopoly.

The Indonesia government continues to face regional challenges, such as a separatist movement in Aceh; an oil- and gas-rich province in north Sumatra; and Irian Jaya, a gas-rich province at the eastern end of the country. The government is also attempting to dilute threats posed by an al-Qaeda-linked terrorist group, called Jemaah Islamiyah.

Iran

The Persian nation's economy relies heavily on oil export revenues. Such revenues represent around 80 to 90 percent of total export earnings and 40 to 50 percent of the government's budget. The country has 132.5 billion barrels of proven oil reserves and in 2005 produced an average of 3.94 million barrels per day of crude oil, roughly 5 percent of world crude production. Iran's current sustainable crude oil production capacity is estimated at 3.8 million barrels per day, which is around 310,000 barrels below Iran's latest (July 2005) OPEC production quota of 4.11 million barrels per day.

Iran is one of the most hawkish nations within OPEC and has created tensions in the Middle East and Western nations with its desire to enrich uranium to produce nuclear energy. This endeavor has attracted suspicions that the actual goal of this research is to produce a nuclear weapon. Iran's course of action has put it on the path to conflict with the United Nations, and has resulted in sanctions being brought against the nation.

Iraq

The nation contains 115 billion barrels of proven oil reserves, the third largest in the world (behind Saudi Arabia and Canada). There is considerable instability in Iraq; some even go as far as to classify it as an ongoing civil war. Iraq was producing about 3 million barrels of crude oil per day in the late 1980s. Its crude production has suffered from a lack of spare parts and investment during the last two decades of the twentieth century, and today it produces approximately 2 million barrels per day. The nation currently does not have an OPEC production quota. Political instability continues to keep foreign investment away.

Kuwait

This nation contains 99 billion barrels of proven oil reserves, or roughly 8 percent of the world's total. Currently, Kuwait produces about 2.5 million barrels per day of crude oil, about 250,000 barrels per day above its

OPEC production quota. Liberated from Iraqi hands by the U.S.–led coalition in 1991, Kuwait is generally seen as a friend of the U.S., but some industry experts have suggested that the nation's petroleum reserves as are being overstated by Kuwaiti government.

Libya

Libyan oil production is currently at 1.7 million barrels per day. More than 90 percent of Libya's exports are sold to neighbors in Europe. Libya is interested in increasing its oil production to 2 million barrels per day by 2008–2010, and to 3 million barrels per day by 2015, and is attempting to attract additional foreign investment in its energy sector.

Nigeria

This north African nation is a challenging place for oil operations. There is significant corruption and tribal factions, which sabotage oil operations and in some cases kill foreign energy workers. Since the early days of oil production in the 1950s, Nigeria has also suffered environmental damage due to a lack of regulatory oversight. The country currently produces 2.1 million barrels per day. Its OPEC production quota is 2.3 million barrels per day.

Qatar

Qatar has proven recoverable oil reserves of 15.2 billion barrels. The nation exports almost all of its oil production to Asia, with Japan by far its largest customer. Qatar's oil production rose slightly in 2005, reaching 1.087 million barrels per day, but it had fallen back to 800,000 barrels per day in 2006, still above its OPEC production quota of 726,000 barrels.

Saudi Arabia

This nation, with 261.9 billion barrels of oil reserves, has one-fourth of the world's proven reserves and some of the lowest production costs. Saudi Arabia supplies the United States with about 1.5 million barrels per day of crude oil, or 15 percent of U.S. crude oil imports. Saudi Arabia maintains crude oil production capacity of around 10.5 to 11.0 million barrels per day, and claims that it is capable of producing up to 15 million barrels per day in the future and maintaining that production level for 50 years. The nation's current OPEC quota is 9.1 million barrels per day, and it produces just above that mark. The Saudi royal family has had some difficulties keeping Islamic fundamentalists, who are attempting to destabilize the Saudi government, in check.

United Arab Emirates

The United Arab Emirates (UAE) contains proven crude oil reserves of 97.8 billion barrels, or slightly less than 8 percent of the world total. Abu Dhabi holds 94 percent of this amount, or about 92.2 billion barrels. Dubai contains an estimated 4.0 billion barrels. The UAE's current OPEC production quota is 2.44 million barrels per day and its current crude oil production, as of July 2006, was 2.6 million bbl/dbarrels per day.

Threats to OPEC Production

Militant Islam is a growing force that has the potential to disrupt current world oil fundamentals. While in decades past, religious fundamentalism may not have been of any great importance or concern in today's post-9/11 world of growing Islamic militarism one must question just how wise it is to link our economic well-being and security to unstable oil-exporting nations.

Venezuela

Venezuela, the only South American member nation of OPEC and a founding member of OPEC, poses a geopolitical threat to U.S. energy security interests. Venezuela possesses 77.2 billion barrels of proven conventional oil reserves, the largest amount in the Western Hemisphere. In the past, Venezuela regularly exceeded its OPEC production quota. However, since his election in 1998, President Chavez has maintained a policy of strong adherence to the country's quota, seeking to increase oil revenues through higher world oil prices rather than increased production. In the past, in order to meet its quota, Venezuela occasionally shut in some production and delayed bringing new capacity on line. Venezuela is currently producing 2.4 million barrels per day, well below its OPEC quota of 3.22 million. This short-fall can be attributed to an industry-damaging strike in 2002–2003, which is believed to have damaged production.

While Venezuela is the number four crude oil supplier to the United States, in recent years the government of Hugo Chavez has created difficulties for the U.S. government, payback for the American support of an opposition government in 2004. The nation is currently aligned with Cuba and Iran and is looking to sell greater amounts of crude oil to China.

Spare Production Capacity

Since the year 2000, OPEC's spare production capacity has eroded as world demand has soared. At one time the cartel had spare production capacity of 6 million barrels per day; this has subsequently dwindled to 1.5 million barrels per day. Currently, Saudi Arabia is the only OPEC nation possessing meaningful amounts of surplus production capacity to offset any potential shortfalls in the world oil markets.

U.S. Domestic Oil Supply

The United States was a major world crude oil producer for much of the twentieth century. Its domestic production was even sufficient to meet most of the Allies' European World War II military requirements. After reaching a peak of 11 million barrels per day, U.S. domestic production has been on the decline.

The nation's Prodhoe Bay field on Alaska's North Slope is the largest oil field in the United States; however, current production is considerably smaller than its initial production. The field began to pump crude oil in 1977 and its daily production reached an apex in 1989 when 1.5 million barrels were produced. Since 1989, Prodhoe Bay production has fallen by 73 percent to 400,000 barrels per day.

The use of advanced drilling technology and reservoir management has reversed this downward trend to some degree. One of these recent success stories has been Chevron's discovery of a huge 3 to 15 billion barrel crude oil field in the U.S. Gulf, utilizing deepwater drilling technology and 3D seismology. But these finds are not expected to keep pace with U.S. demand growth.

Natural Gas—The Key
to U.S. Energy Independence?

We have a lot of natural gas in the United States. At one time this gas was an unwanted byproduct produced by those who were drilling for oil, and due to its low price and limited access to market the gas was flared off (burned away) at the well site. Today, natural gas is no longer thought to be the poor cousin of oil. Much of this nation's new generation capacity is natural gas–fired, and nuclear energy critics believe sizable new amounts of low-cost, quick-to-build, natural gas-fired electricity generation capacity could be built in the years to come, which would nullify the need to expand this nation's reliance on nuclear power.

U.S. annual demand for natural gas is about 23 trillion cubic feet and is projected to increase as much as 12 trillion cubic feet during the next 10 years as utilities rely more heavily on gas for electricity generation. In other words, gas currently accounts for roughly 24 percent of U.S. energy use, but by 2020 it is expected to rise to 36.5 percent.

In addition to power generation applications, industrial, commercial, and residential demand for natural gas continues to increase. This has placed considerable pressure on U.S. natural gas reserves, causing these reserves to deplete faster than anticipated. It now takes approximately 2.5 times more active rig capacity to produce the same amount of gas as it did eight years ago. Falling production is illustrated by the fact that for the last eight years, U.S. natural gas production averaged approximately 52 billion cubic feet per day. Figure 3.1 shows that minor gains have been made in U.S. natural gas production since 1990, but this growth clearly won't keep pace with the United States' future energy needs.

To help offset eroding domestic gas production, the United States has turned to Canada. Imports of Canadian gas via pipeline currently account for approximately 16 percent of the natural gas consumed in the United States. This total, while significant, is not expected to increase substantially in the near term due to declining field yields, pipeline delivery constraints, and increasing internal Canadian natural gas demand. The EIA projects that U.S. natural gas production will increase from 19 trillion cubic feet in 2003 to 24 trillion cubic feet by 2025. If domestic production and imports from Canada can't keep pace with demand, the United States must look overseas for additional supply.

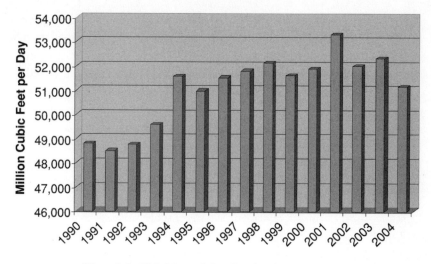

Figure 3.1   **U.S. Natural Gas Production, 1990–2004**
SOURCE: Energy Information Administration.

Is LNG the Answer?

In an attempt to diversify and wean the United States from being overly dependent on foreign sources of crude oil and to augment its North American natural gas supplies, a movement has been underway to increase this nation's use of liquefied natural gas (LNG). This is natural gas that is cooled to −160° degrees Celsius so that the gas transforms into a liquid state 1/600th of the size of the natural gas in its gaseous state. This liquefied gas is then transported to areas of demand in specialized LNG carriers, which are basically insulated thermos bottles designed to keep the LNG in its liquefied state. Upon arrival at an LNG receiving terminal, the LNG is then warmed and brought back to its gaseous state and then injected into a natural gas pipeline, where it is commingled with traditional, domestic natural gas supplies.

For many decades, LNG has been the primary fuel used for electricity generation in Japan, and until recently that island nation consumed the vast majority of this fuel. Rising oil and natural gas prices and greater efficiencies and economies of scale in the LNG industry have made the fuel a cost-effective import for other nations such as South Korea, China, and various nations in the Atlantic basin, such as the United States.

U.S. imports of LNG, anticipated to meet approximately 15 percent of U.S. natural gas consumption by the year 2025, will make up part of the domestic natural gas supply shortfall. The United States has begun to import greater quantities of LNG, mostly from the island of Trinidad. These imports are expected to break 1 trillion cubic feet per year in 2007 or 2008. To handle this increased capacity, efforts are underway to construct additional U.S. regasification terminals to augment the five currently in operation. Constructing these terminals is no simple task due to the well-known NIMBY syndrome. There are more than 60 different LNG receiving terminal projects proposed in North America, but the vast majority of these won't be built. The U.S. Department of Energy has high hopes for LNG imports; the agency expects these imports to increase six-fold in the coming decade.

The use of LNG to supply electric utilities' gas turbines sounds very promising. Opponents of nuclear power have asked, why build reactors when electricity can be generated with clean-burning natural gas, which can be obtained from overseas should domestic supplies one day prove to be inadequate? While natural gas is indeed a cleaner-burning alternative, this proposed solution presents a number of problems. First, liquefaction facilities are expensive to construct, perhaps as expensive as constructing a nuclear power plant. Second, in many instances, these liquefaction facilities are being proposed in politically unstable areas. The following nations currently liquify and export LNG:

- Indonesia
- Australia
- Nigeria
- Algeria
- Malaysia
- Oman
- Trinidad and Tobago
- Abu Dhabi
- Brunei
- Libya
- Qatar
- United States (limited amounts are exported to Japan from Alaska under long-term contract, making the United States the only nation to both import and export LNG)

In the next few years Angola, Norway, Egypt, and Russia are also expected to join the list of LNG exporters.

A Potential OPEC for LNG

The LNG market is quickly evolving from a regional market to a global
market. With 15 nations expected to be importing LNG in the year 2010,
there is a chance that a significant portion of the world's economy will be
increasingly subject to availability of this supply of gas. Under these cir-
cumstances, what is to stop the LNG exporting nations from organizing
their own cartel and operating in a similar manner to the OPEC cartel in
dictating supplies and prices? In fact, many of these LNG exporting nations are already members of OPEC. If the United States were to forgo
additional construction of nuclear power plants to generate electricity and
rely on LNG instead, wouldn't we simply be switching our energy dependence from the exporters of oil to the exporters of LNG?

The initial steps in forming an LNG cartel may have already taken
place. In 2001, the Gas Exporting Countries Forum (GECF) was founded.
The Forum is an informally structured group of some of the world's leading
gas producers aimed at representing and promoting their mutual interests.
Collectively, the GECF controls approximately 73 percent of the world's gas
reserves and 40 percent of production. The group is dedicated to exchanging
ideas, technology, and cost-cutting proposals. Membership of the GECF has
fluctuated since its formation and has consisted of Algeria, Bolivia, Brunei,
Egypt, Indonesia, Iran, Libya, Malaysia, Nigeria, Norway (as an observer),
Oman, Qatar, Russia, Trinidad and Tobago, the UAE, and Venezuela.

Is King Coal the Answer?

Coal is indeed the king of U.S. electricity generation, producing more
than 50 percent of the nation's electric power. In many instances coal
generation is inexpensive compared to other fossil fuels, but it's a relatively
dirty form of energy compared to natural gas and produces considerable
emissions, which is expected to limit its significant expansion.

On the positive side, the United States has more coal than any other
country in the world, with estimated recoverable reserves of 275 billion

tons. This represents approximately 25 percent of world supply and more than 250 years of supply for domestic consumption. This share of world coal reserves is in sharp contrast to the U.S. share of global oil and natural gas reserves, which are estimated to be less than 2 percent and 3 percent, respectively.

Power developers, currently faced with rising natural gas prices, increasingly restrictive emissions requirements, and a desire for fuel diversification, are reexamining their power-generation portfolios and are looking toward coal and clean coal technologies, such as coal gasification, as a means to alleviate these concerns by producing electricity using U.S. domestic coal resources. The coal gasification process chemically breaks down the coal into cleaner hydrogen gas, which can then be burned to generate electricity or produce other low-sulfur petroleum-related products.

To develop new energy technologies, the Bush administration introduced the Clean Coal Power Initiative (CCPI) in 2002. The program provides a forum for the testing of these new technologies prior to full-scale commercialization. Early CCPI demonstrations focused on technologies that apply to existing power plants and construction of new plants. Later demonstrations are expected to include systems comprising advanced turbines, membranes, fuel cells, gasification processes, hydrogen production, and other technologies.

President Bush's U.S. energy program calls for an additional $2 billion in funding over the next decade for another round of the government's 20-year-old Clean Coal Technology Program. This funding is particularly important when one considers that greater than half of the over 1,000 U.S. coal-fired power plants are more than 30 years old and will require replacement over the next 20 years.

One can see that the supply side of the United States' energy equation is indeed complex, and locating additional supplies of domestic and foreign sources of fossil fuels is becoming increasingly challenging. The demand side of the U.S. energy equation is equally as complex.

Power Supply

The U.S. power market is the largest in the world, as measured by total output and number of power plants. The dynamics of the power market, which include seasonal, weekly, and daily peak demands over the wide geographic and diverse customer base, necessitate a portfolio approach to serving end-users' demand, also known as *load*. The growth of the electric power market is dictated by coverage of the contiguous transmission grid and the power plants that supply electricity to any customers connected to it. This precludes importing power from any other country to the United States besides Canada and Mexico, both of which have interconnections with the U.S. power grid.

The development of regional power pools in the United States was built around geography, shared facilities, and the concept of central station power, with coal-fired steam boilers providing the generation for interconnected grids to reach customers over a predetermined market. The plentiful coal supply in the United States interior allowed coal power plants to dominate the electric utility system. However, individual regional markets around the country have varying mixes of generation capacity.

Table 3.2 shows the share of installed capacity by fuel type, with coal at 32 percent of just over 1 million megawatts, followed next by natural gas and dual-fired (essential generating capacity that can switch between natural gas and refined petroleum price, based on price and availability). Nuclear power only has a 10 percent share of the total generating base, as of year-end 2004. However, the rankings change when considering the actual output over the

Table 3.2 **Installed U.S. Capacity by Fuel Type**

Energy Source	Number of Generators	Nameplate Capacity (Megawatts)	Percent
Coal	1,526	335,243	32%
Petroleum	3,175	37,970	4%
Natural Gas	3,048	256,627	24%
Dual-Fired	3,003	193,115	18%
Other Gases	119	2,535	0%
Nuclear	104	105,560	10%
Hydroelectric Conventional	3,995	77,130	7%
Other Renewables	1,608	21,113	2%
Pumped Storage	150	19,569	2%
Other	42	754	0%
Total	**16,770**	**1,049,615**	**100%**

SOURCE: Energy Information Administration.

Table 3.3   U.S. 2004 Generation by Fuel Type

Energy Source	Net Generation (Thousand Megawatt-Hours)	Share
Coal	1,978,620	50%
Petroleum	120,646	3%
Natural Gas	708,979	18%
Other Gases	16,766	0%
Nuclear	788,528	20%
Hydro	268,417	7%
Renewables	90,408	2%
Pumped Storage	(8,488)	0%
Other	6,679	0%
Total	**3,970,555**	**100%**

SOURCE: Energy Information Administration.

year. Table 3.3 shows that in 2004 coal was 50 percent of total net generation, followed by nuclear at 20 percent and natural gas at 18 percent.

The difference in actual energy output versus the size of the installed capacity reflects the plant utilization, in turn determined by the technology type, unit availability, and fuel costs, and nonfuel operating and maintenance charges. In addition, plant owners elect to dispatch or run units based on their own business decisions, while independent grid operators may call on various resources for stability and security reasons, in addition to those already mentioned.

Given the growth of U.S. power demand, both total energy throughout the year and coincident peak hour for a given interconnected system during the season, power supply must be able to handle serving each hour of load as well as the absolute peak, based on extreme weather conditions, with additional capacity to spare. Power demand is relatively inelastic, as most customers have high expectations for service and demand nearly flawless and reliable delivery for computing or manufacturing processes. The vagaries of power plant operations, which include forced outages, as well as maintenance and refueling cycles, imply that all units cannot provide 100 percent availability. When taken in conjunction with transmission and distribution grid configurations, the need for stable and secure performance dictates that redundancies be pervasive in generation and transmission.

Power planners (at utility, state, regional, and federal levels) thus model unit performance and grid operations, and match with power demand trends, in order to best anticipate market balances on a current and forward basis. Most simply stated, the reserve margins for regional and subregional markets are derived, as the increment of net available capacity above the anticipated peak hour demand, as a percentage of total demand. Daily operating parameters include accommodating "first contingency" failure, meaning having enough supply online and available to cover losing the biggest single generating unit in a region (often nuclear units are the largest contingency). Forward planning means arranging to have enough power-generating capacity on line to cover expected peak load plus 12 percent additional at a minimum, per Federal Energy Regulatory Commission (FERC) Order RM01-12-000. More common guidelines suggest a reserve margin closer to 15 percent. During the price spikes of 2001 and 2002, reserve margins sagged to 10 percent and below in individual power pools, which greatly concerned regulatory authorities and plant operators.

The North American Electric Reliability Council (NERC) is the key organization that plans for regional reliability and ensures the integrity of the grid. The organization was established after the massive East Coast blackout of 1968 "to ensure that the bulk electric system in North America is reliable, adequate and secure." (See www.nerc.com/about/.) The NERC's seasonal assessments depict what expected margins will be, in the first year, and out to 10 years, assuming the system is operating within reasonable parameters. The most recent NERC assessment in 2005, shown in Figure 3.2, shows the

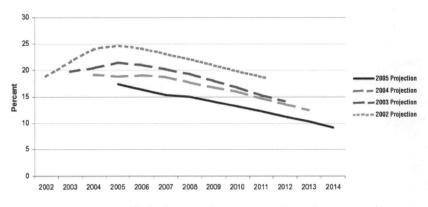

Figure 3.2 **United States Capacity Margins—Summer**
SOURCE: North American Electric Reliability Council.

United States will be approaching the 10 percent capacity margin soon after 2012, based on current modeling of demand resource development.

This leads to the primary issue confronting the power supply market: If new capacity must be built, what will this new capacity be, and how will it be built? The design of market structures that would create incentives to bring new capacity to the market are beyond the scope of this book. However, it is clear that different technologies can be brought to market under different time frames, and those market designers foisting a particular capacity-building regime on a system can influence or predetermine what type of generation capacity (and which fuel source) is used.

Of course, North American electrical capacity is not evenly distributed across the continent. Geography and population growth have been the principal forces shaping grid growth. In addition, power transmission cost and laws of physics indicate that limits exist to stringing high-voltage wire across the country, requiring generating capacity to be located in multiple locations. Regional power markets have also evolved around various reliability councils, each of which has unique characteristics. Suffice it to say, that each regional market has a different level of reserve margin, and the fuel mix is constantly evolving each year according to new build, retirements, and availability/utilization. Table 3.4. lists the demand and capacity for each region; Figure 3.3 displays the location of the regions.

Historical data show the dominant position that coal has maintained in U.S. electricity generation during the post-WWII era, as depicted in Figure 3.4, with nuclear power only garnering a significant share in the post-1980 period. However, since the 1990s, the dominant fuel contributing to growth of total capacity has been natural gas, which is found domestically in significant quantities or generally imported from Canada. While generation capacity growth has gone through waves of development (first with coal and hydro, then oil, then nuclear, and most recently natural gas), the need to stay in front of electric power demand has been the over-riding objective. Figure 3.5 shows that if we take the projected demand growth from the EIA base-case from 2005 out to 2025, new capacity development would need to average 10,000 to 15,000 megawatts each year, from the starting point of needing bringing new generation to market.

Table 3.4   Regional Capacity and Margins

Region	Net Internal Demand	Planned Capacity Resources	Reserve Margin
East Central Area Reliability Coordination Agreement (ECAR)	104,230	128,326	23.1
Florida Reliability Coordinating Council (FRCC)	41,934	51,106	21.9
Mid Atlantic Area Council (MAAC)	57,981	69,855	20.5
Mid-America Interconnected Network (MAIN)	56,731	66,729	17.6
Midwest Reliability Organization (MRO-U.S.)	30,442	35,965	18.1
Northeast Power Coordinating Council (NPCC-U.S.)	58,078	36,917	20.4
South East Reliability Corporation (SERC)	163,579	182,569	11.6
Southwest Power Pool (SPP)	41,262	48,710	18.1
Western Electricity Coordinating Council (WECC-U.S.)	128,692	166,946	29.7
Electric Reliability Council of Texas (ERCOT)	60,998	69,218	13.5
Total U.S.	**743,927**	**889,341**	**19.5**

SOURCE: North American Electric Reliability Council.

U.S. power plant development experienced a boom from 1998 to 2003 and has left many regions with excess generating capacity. Even so, Figure 3.6 shows that the outlook for near-term growth (before 2010) is heavily skewed toward natural gas technology (combined-cycle for base-load, combustion turbines for mid-merit and peaking use). Eventually, more coal capacity is modeled to come online; however, there may be some limits, from an environmental emissions perspective, to how much each of these fuels can contribute on a long-term basis.

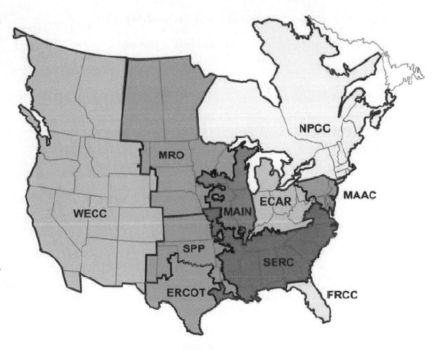

Figure 3.3   **NERC Regions**
SOURCE: North American Electric Reliability Council.

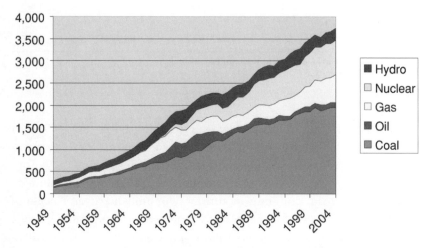

Figure 3.4   **U.S. Total Annual Generation by Fuel Type**
SOURCE: Energy Information Administration.

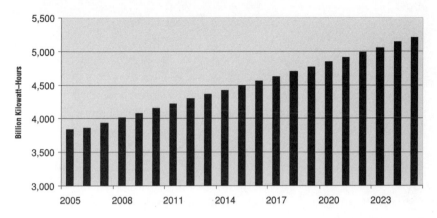

Figure 3.5 **Projected U.S. Electric Power Demand, 2005–2025**
SOURCE: Energy Information Administration.

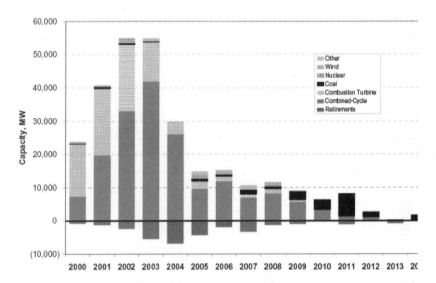

Figure 3.6 **Projected U.S. Capacity Additions by Sector**
SOURCE: Energy Information Administration.

U.S. Power Demand

Demand for electric power will continue to grow over the next two decades. As the national economy grows, electrical energy demand has demonstrated a growth pattern that is slightly slower, but steady nonetheless. To meet that demand, the United States and other countries have relied on a portfolio mix of fuels, generally optimizing least cost and local resources. Given our native coal resources and the development of steam turbine technology, the installed base of electric generating capacity has grown to keep up with domestic demand. Coal-fired plants now account for over 50 percent of the U.S. supply, followed by nuclear plants, then oil/gas and hydroelectric facilities.

Renewable resources are growing quickly but from a very small base, and their contribution to the macro balance will be limited over the next 10 years in relation to the aggregate demand, given constraints on technology and their cost competitiveness. With environmental limitations to increased coal-burn, and the apparent lack of consistent growth to domestic oil/gas production, the question emerges: How can we accommodate the growth of electric power demand with conventional technology and known, available resources?

In the 1990s, the market assumed that North American natural gas resources would be plentiful enough to cover entirely the incremental demand needs of the electric power sector. The growth of electric power capacity since then has been heavily skewed to gas-fired power plants. The last few years have indicated how difficult it is to maintain, let alone increase, production from the domestic reserve base. The realization that we need to accelerate imported supplies to supplement local resources has resulted in the prolific liquefied natural gas (LNG) project announcements. This then calls into consideration the security and stability of foreign sources of oil and gas, and the future potential for dislocated supplies from current as well as emerging exporters of hydrocarbons. Against this background, power supplied from domestic nuclear plants stands out as an obvious choice in which to invest, encourage, and develop.

What's Really behind Demand

In the post-World War II era, overall end-user energy demand has grown at a consistent pace, only showing three incidences of year-on-year declines (1974, 1982, and 2001), reflecting high fuel prices and weaker economic growth. (See Figure 3.7.) Since 1995, average annual energy consumption has increased by 1.9 percent. To be sure, in the short term (within a calendar year) power demand is more strongly influenced by weather trends, a hotter than normal summer or a colder than usual winter. The advent availability of air-conditioning made available to the general public grew quickly post-WWII. Prior to that time, the peak coincident hourly electricity usage within any given power pool occurred during the winter season. After the rise of air-conditioning, utilities transitioned to summer peaking—that is, generating the most power in a given hour—during the hottest time of the summer when many residential and commercial customers sought relief indoors from oppressive heat.

Aggregate demand, shown in Figure 3.8, should be measured in two ways: on a peak hourly demand basis, which is the highest coincident consumption during the year, and as the total consumption of energy basis, from each hour during the year. It is important to understand both metrics, as the different technology and fuels available for generating electric power also dictate what time of the year power plants are available, as

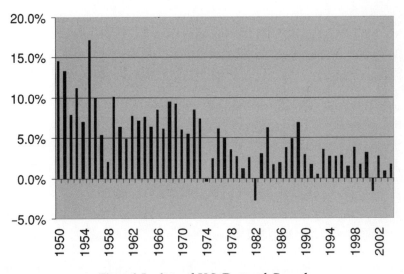

Figure 3.7   **Annual U.S. Demand Growth**
SOURCE: Energy Information Administration.

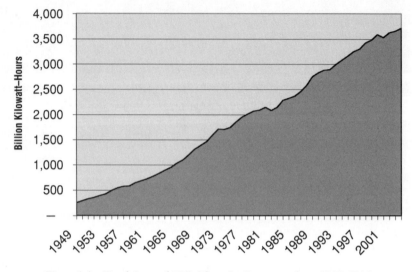

Figure 3.8 **Total Annual U.S. Electric Consumption, 1949–2001**
SOURCE: Energy Information Administration.

well as what time of the day the generating units are being utilized, either for energy or stand-by service.

Each broad sector of electric consumers has varying uses for power supplied, so an understanding of each allows better anticipation of future electric demand growth. The common practice is to classify or divide the customer base into four broad sectors: residential, commercial, industrial, and transportation. A fifth sector sometimes noted is direct-use; this refers to the electric consumption by larger customers (typically industrial facilities) that generate their own power supply within the plant premises or off the wholesale utility grid.

As shown in Figure 3.9, commercial entities have demonstrated the most consistent electric sales growth during the postwar era. Residential consumers are heavily influenced by seasonal weather patterns, cooling and heating homes to the extent dictated by temperature variations. Industrial demand growth is more closely associated with economic activity, as the larger facilities are the biggest single-point consumers of electric power demand and individual industrial trends (i.e., automobile production) will influence electric power consumption more directly than weather trends.

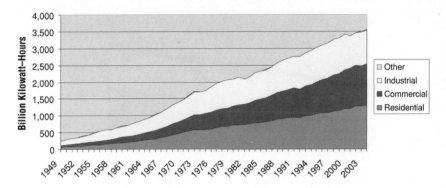

Figure 3.9 **U.S. Annual Retail Sales, by Sector**
SOURCE: Energy Information Administration.

Going forward, sector growth will be led by commercial customers who are expected to increase demand by more than 50 percent from 2005 to 2025. This will be followed by residential sector growth at 33 percent, and then the industrial users growing just 16 percent, during the 20 years, or less than 1 percent per year. The direct-use segment should match the percentage growth of commercial customers at over 50 percent, but their current scale is just 10 percent the size of the commercial sector. These growth estimates give the base-case, provided by the Energy Information Administration division of the Department of Energy. New model updates are released every year and provide the data used by the federal government for its work. The assumptions to this forecast include normal weather, 3.0 percent GDP growth, 2.5 percent chain-linked inflation, and 10-year Treasuries maintaining a yield between 5.0 and 7.0 percent during the period to 2030. Other assumptions and model cases may be found at www.eia.doe.gov.

Any one of these assumptions or others (such as fuel price spikes or adverse weather) can be altered to produce different outcomes over the next decade and beyond. However, the historic evidence is clear in showing that demand growth follows broad trends but is materially influenced in any given year by acute events. We can safely assume that electric power consumption will continue to grow over the forecast horizon, and sector demand will also trend upward (Figure 3.10), but may vary substantially from the base-case.

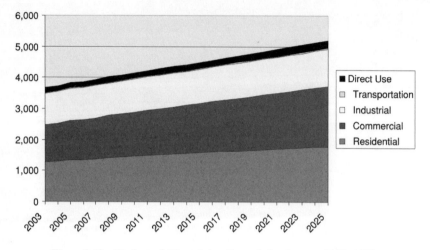

Figure 3.10 **Projected Electricity Growth by Sector, 2003–2025**
SOURCE: Energy Information Administration.

Limits to Capacity Growth, by Fuel

In the 1990s, the United States went through a period of significant deregulatory initiatives in both gas and power on a federal and state level (Energy Policy Act of 1994, Order 888, Order 636, all at FERC). These efforts, some more explicitly than others, positioned natural gas as the marginal fuel to meet demand growth. Price action during the period prior to the mid-1990s gave the impression that the average market value for natural gas held near $2.00 per million British thermal units (mmbtu), and mean reversion behavior meant price excursions were brief and limited in degree. With the assumption of cheap and plentiful domestic natural gas reserves, the increased call on production appeared without constraint. Deregulating natural gas markets meant merchant providers could sell gas, without ties to infrastructure or the production function.

Meanwhile, bringing competition to the supply function of wholesale power markets and removing the cost-of-service rate-making compact meant taking away the incentive for traditional integrated utilities to continue to add generating capacity on a regular basis to regional systems. Rather, to drive excess capacity out of the system, generating asset investments would be deferred. New capacity-owners would only come into the market in anticipation of tightening markets or when price signals dictated. The pressure would be to add capacity more cheaply, ideally lowering the cost of electricity for consumers, on a retail basis.

With new electric generating capacity owners entering the market in a merchant fashion, selling power on a wholesale basis, the immediate intention is to bring the newest, cheapest, and more risk-averse capacity on line first. By definition this was simple-cycle gas-fired capacity, followed by combined-cycle units. This more efficient configuration of steam and a combustion cycle, combined, increased efficiency and brought production costs lower. In most power pools, the generating capacity is a mix of base-load fuels, cheapest run-of-river hydro (if available), coal, nuclear, then oil and gas units (of various technologies), and renewable resources on an availability basis. The marginal cost of power then is determined by the type of fuel generating the last megawatt of power.

This marginal cost of power has become natural gas in many of the nation's power pools, as this fuel is dispatched after the lower cost units are put on line. Base-load units are usually on line at full utilization during summer and winter months, saving the low demand "shoulder seasons" for refueling and maintenance. When demand goes to seasonal peaks, typically the price is solely oil- and gas-based, with an upper limit set by power market regulators or by the inferred value of denying power service (i.e., rotating blackouts).

Since the late 1990s, new power plant capacity has been dominated by technology fueled by natural gas, for both base-load operations and peaking purposes. However, during this time the domestic productive capability of both gas and oil has demonstrated its challenges. In fact, Figure 3.11 shows, since 2001 the monthly output of natural gas in the lower 48 states has generally decreased, and has shown susceptibility to the impact of hurricanes on Gulf of Mexico production. Even if the 2005 hurricane season is taken as an anomaly, domestic production has been shown to decline, year-to-year.

With near record prices for natural gas at the benchmark Henry Hub, and elsewhere, domestic oil and gas producers have every incentive to increase production. Figure 3.12 shows that average prices of $1.00 to $2.00/mmbtu during the early 1990s and before have given way to current prices above $7.00. Future prices for natural gas remain strong. If one reviews the forward price curve for the commodity, as traded in the futures market, prices fail to drop below $7.00 before 2010.

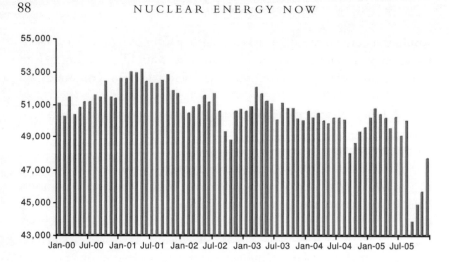

Figure 3.11 **U.S. Natural Gas Dry Production since 2000**
SOURCE: Energy Information Administration.

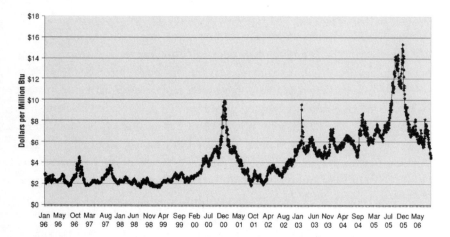

Figure 3.12 **U.S. Natural Gas Price, Spot Henry Hub Futures Contract**
SOURCE: Courtesy of the New York Mercantile Exchange, Inc.

In response to these fuel economics, some producers have been able to organize resources to increase production of existing natural gas fields or bring new production online from formerly uneconomic or unexploited regions. Much of this new production is nonconventional, and emanates from shale, tight sands, and coalbed methane reserves. Beyond the available proven reserves are reserves that are off-limits to development in ecologically or environmentally sensitive locations (e.g., Rocky Mountains, Pacific and Atlantic coasts), and thus is not available for development. The success in producing gas from accessible reserves is closely balanced by the decline rates encountered in existing producing fields, from which each year's supply declines. The curse of new and more efficient extractive technology has been that gas in reserve gets produced even quicker.

With an increasing price function, some end-use customers in the natural gas market have responded, electing to move offshore, curtail or shut-down consumption, or switch to less expensive fuels. Similar to the way the customer base in electric power markets treats demand for power as nearly inelastic in the short term, so to do customers of natural gas. In winter time, space-heating customers have little tolerance for interruptions to supply. Indeed, since natural gas fuels some electric power supply, the same inelasticity is transferred through the production chain. Figure 3.13 shows that gradually, the customer mix in the

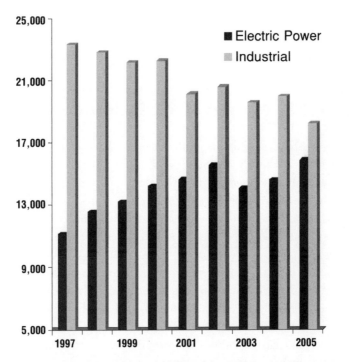

Figure 3.13 **U.S. Natural Gas Demand by Sector**
SOURCE: Energy Information Administration.

natural gas market is shifting to accommodate limited resources and higher prices. Industrial customers have moved production of fertilizer offshore of fertilizer, for example, to markets where natural gas still is priced at $2.00 or below. Growth of the industrial sector in natural gas will be limited, and challenged by the perceived growth to the electric power customer base.

The electric power customers for gas can no longer assume that domestic supply will cover their needs, either. The gas market has noted this mismatch of demand growth and supply stasis. The emerging trend is to develop gas import facilities, allowing the off-loading of LNG, which is produced in various countries around the world, then liquefied through extreme cooling, loaded into LNG carriers, and brought to consuming nations, where the liquid is gasified, and put into the local gas network. Demand trends could easily increase the consumption level of LNG to 6 or 8 billion cubic feet per day by the end of the decade, principally driven by growth in the electric power sector. The issues of security of supply are yet to be addressed, if only because the current supply of LNG is such a small component. Concerns about pricing and availability will continue to linger and will attract more attention as this form of natural gas grows.

The Answer: More Nuclear Power

Currently there is no "magic bullet" that will solve the energy supply challenges facing the United States and the rest of the world. Numerous fuels are available to power industry and generate electricity. These fuels range from low-tech solutions such as burning animal manure and wood, to utilizing traditional fossil fuels, using various forms of "green" energy, and unlocking the power of the atom. All of these fuels have their own inherent strengths and weaknesses.

Nuclear power, with its proven track record and its ability to economically produce tremendous amounts of energy from very modest amounts of relatively inexpensive fuel, should not be ignored. In recent decades, the rest of the world has continued to add to its nuclear generating capacity and has in some ways moved ahead of the United States in utilizing this technology. If the United States is to remain competitive in the twenty-first century, we have no choice, but to aggressively construct new nuclear generation assets.

The following chapters examine nuclear power's growing global footprint and will chronicle its current and past successes in Europe and the Far East. The technology's proven safety record and continuing safety upgrades will also be explored, along with current efforts to further expand this critically needed electricity-producing infrastructure.

4

Nuclear Power's Growing Global Footprint

The right to energy for all, even in the most far-reaching rural regions, was at the beginning of the last century a major source of economic and social progress in our country: our company was even established for this purpose. Today this is a global challenge that concerns 2 billion of the world's inhabitants.

—Francois Roussely, former CEO and Chairman of Electricite de France (EDF), statement during Global Compact French Business Leaders' Meeting, January 27, 2004

The United States, the first nation on earth to weaponize the atom and then harness its power for civilian use, has long since lost its monopoly on nuclear generation technology. There are currently 31 nations utilizing nuclear reactors to help meet their electricity generation requirements. A total of 443 commercial nuclear generating units operate on a global basis (see Appendix G) with a total capacity of about 364.9 gigawatts, producing approximately 16 percent of world's energy output. These units displace more than 2.5 billion metric tons of CO_2 per year and help minimize global greenhouse gas emission increases.

The world's reliance on nuclear power for electricity generation is expected to grow, with an additional 31 reactors slated for operation by the year 2013. The amount of electricity expected from this new nuclear generation is substantial. If each of these reactors produces 1,000 megawatts of power on average, another 31,000 megawatts of generating capacity will be added on a global basis by 2013. Assuming one megawatt of electricity is enough to power the needs of 1,000 U.S. homes, this 31,000 megawatts would be equivalent to the energy needed to supply power to 31 million U.S. homes. These new nuclear generation facilities are being sited around the globe. Three of these proposed reactors are to be placed in Iran and North Korea, and their development is being closely watched by both the U.S. government and the International Atomic Energy Agency (IAEA).

The potential for growth is even greater in the Far East, with China planning to spend $50 to $65 billion on nuclear energy–related construction by 2020.

This global nuclear power development trend contrasts greatly with the United States, which has not built a new nuclear reactor for approximately 30 years. Figure 4.1 shows that while there have been reactor capacity up-

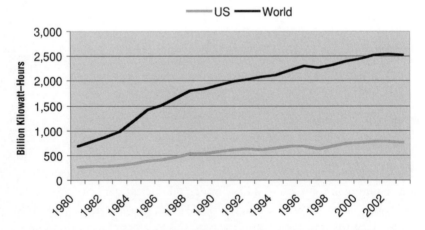

Figure 4.1   **U.S. versus Global Net Nuclear Power Generation, 1980–2003**
SOURCE: Energy Information Administration.

grades and efficiency gain in the United Stattes, these have only contributed modestly to U.S. generation growth. This contrasts greatly with global nuclear generation capacity development, which has more than tripled over the last two decades and now stands at 2,500 billion Kilowatt hours.

This imbalance is expected to widen over the next decade, as nuclear power construction resumes in Europe after a 15-year hiatus. The potential for growth is even greater in the Far East, with China planning to spend $50 to $65 billion on nuclear energy–related construction by 2020. This expenditure could fund the construction of 31 additional nuclear power stations, increasing China's total nuclear power generation capacity to 40 million kilowatts.

Vive la France

While nuclear power is a contentious issue in the United States, it has greater acceptance internationally, especially in France. To many nuclear energy proponents, France is a beacon for the nuclear power industry. The first French commercial nuclear power plant was commissioned in 1963; since then the nation has built an impressive and yet relatively young group of reactors. The average age of a French nuclear reactor is 18 years. With a nuclear facility's designed life expectancy of 40 years, the French are well positioned to utilize significant amounts of nuclear energy in the decades to come.

Over the past half-century, the French have overcome many of the same issues and challenges that face the U.S. nuclear industry today. These include regulatory oversight, waste disposal, and safety concerns. The French, motivated through their desire to remain energy independent, successfully met these challenges, thereby enabling their heavy reliance on nuclear energy. When the French began development of their first commercial nuclear reactors in the 1950s, they utilized a "fast breeder" reactor design fueled by uranium and plutonium. This type of reactor is capable of producing both electric power and weapons-grade nuclear material. This nuclear material later assisted France with its entry into the nuclear club in 1960 when the nation successfully tested its first nuclear weapon.

France has 59 nuclear reactors. These are operated by Electricite de France (EdF) and have a total capacity of over 63 gigawatts, supplying over 426 billion kilowatt-hours per year of electricity. France has the second-largest electricity sector in the European Union, behind Germany. In 2005, French electricity generation was 549 billion kilowatt-hours net and consumption was 482 billion kilowatt-hours, or 7,700 kilowatt-hours per person. The country depends on nuclear energy for almost 80 percent of its electricity. This figure is approximately four times greater than the percentage of electricity generated by nuclear power in the United States and approximately twice the percentage of electricity generated by Sweden, its closest nuclear generation competitor in Europe (see Figure 4.2).

France's increased use of nuclear energy has also helped curtail its dependence on imported oil and has had a dramatic effect on the amount of greenhouse gas emissions produced. France produces electricity more economically than other European countries and has become the largest net exporter of electricity in the EU. Over the last decade, France exported 60 to 70 billion kilowatt-hours net of electricity each year, also making it the world's largest net exporter of electricity. This is quite a dramatic change when one considers that for most of the 1970s France was a net electricity importer. This change in status is the direct result of the French nuclear industry, which has contributed to annual electricity sales revenues in excess of 3 billion euros. The largest recipients of France's electricity exports are Italy, Germany, and Belgium.

France is the world's largest nuclear power generator on a per capita basis and ranks second in total installed nuclear capacity behind the United States. Its ascent to its relative position of dominance in the field

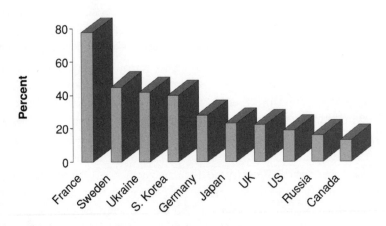

Figure 4.2   **Nuclear Power as a Percentage of Electricity Generation**
SOURCE: Energy Information Administration.

of generation was not by chance, but the result of a well-orchestrated effort on behalf of the French government.

The Drivers behind French Commercial Nuclear Development

France does not possess any sizable deposits of fossil fuels, and it relied mostly on imported oil to run its growing post–World War II economy. The French realized just how dependent and vulnerable their economy was to imported Middle East oil in 1956 when Egypt, after nationalizing the waterway, blocked transit through the Suez Canal, a major transit route for oil from the Middle East to Europe. The French government's fears were realized again less than two decades later, in 1973, with the effects of a global Arab oil embargo. To lessen their dependence on foreign sources of fossil fuels, the French enacted

> *The French realized just how dependent and vulnerable their economy was to imported Middle East oil in 1956 when Egypt blocked the Suez Canal.*

an ambitious nuclear power building program that called for the construction of six reactors per year. The national rallying cry for this initiative was the slogan, "France doesn't have oil, but it has ideas."

Such an ambitious nuclear generation development project costs billions and would have emptied the French coffers unless some creative financing was utilized. Instead of raising taxes and running the risk of a taxpayer revolt, the French devised an innovative strategy to offset part of its ambitious nuclear build program. To raise funds, the French made the decision to build fuel reprocessing facilities with surplus capacity to handle their own needs as well as international demand. As a global reprocessor of nuclear waste, France soon began to reprocess waste from European nations such as Germany and for countries as far away as Japan. While this waste reprocessing strategy resulted in relatively minor protests in France in the 1970s and 1980s, these protests failed to change the government's approach.

The French nuclear program is based on American technology. After experimenting with gas-cooled reactors in the 1960s, the French gave up and purchased American pressurized water reactors designed by Westinghouse. By purchasing just one type of reactor, the French were able to build their plants more economically than nuclear facilities built in the United States. Moreover, management of safety was much easier since the lessons learned from an incident at one nuclear facility could be quickly implemented by managers at another identical French reactor. This centralized planning and management have been critical to the success of France's nuclear industry, enabling it to operate safely and efficiently.

The U.S. nuclear industry has traditionally lacked this standardized approach championed by the French and instead utilized a variety of reactor types built by a number of competing, cost-conscious firms. This lack of standardization hindered efficient U.S. reactor training and negatively affected reactor performance. Today, taking a cue from the French, the U.S. nuclear industry is achieving a greater degree of standardization through the consolidation of operators and more thorough government regulations. The French, through their centrally controlled, standardized approach, have achieved a high degree of success with their nuclear industry. This has become a point of national pride, since it enables the nation to manage its dependence on imported fossil fuels.

The Waste Issue

As the saying goes, there is no such thing as a free lunch. This saying holds true whether it's a corned beef sandwich in the United States or foie gras in France.

In the late 1980s, the issue of nuclear waste came to the foreground in France. French policy is to reprocess spent nuclear fuel so as to recover uranium and plutonium for reuse and to reduce the volume of high-level wastes for disposal. Government officials never thought reprocessing would pose much of a problem, since it not only produced additional energy but also reduced the volume and longevity of French radioactive waste. Their plan called for the small quantity of high-level waste ultimately produced to be buried in underground geological storage, and French engineers began digging exploratory holes in France's rural regions.

This action, however, resulted in considerable opposition from the regions considered for waste disposal, and in some cases riots broke out. The same rural regions that had actively lobbied to become nuclear power plant sites were openly hostile to the idea of being selected as France's nuclear waste dump. In 1990, all underground storage activity was ceased and the matter was turned over to the French parliament for further review.

France's rural population held the view that urbanite Parisians were consuming the majority of the electricity produced, yet the nuclear waste would be permanently abandoned in rural community backyards. This view is very similar to the current U.S. opposition to the Yucca Mountain nuclear waste disposal site proposed in Nevada. The French have attempted to solve their waste disposal problem by introducing waste deposit reversibility and stocking. Under this proposal, the waste would not be buried permanently, but rather stocked in a way that made it accessible at some time in the future when it could potentially be removed and relocated.

Further, France's 1991 Waste Management Act called for the construction of three to four waste research laboratories at various sites, such as the Bure underground rock laboratory located in eastern France. These laboratories were charged with investigating various options, including deep geological storage, above-ground stocking, and transmutation and detoxification of nuclear waste. In 2006 the French parliament was to decide which of these laboratories will become their national waste-stocking center.

The costs of these reprocessing and waste management facilities are not insignificant; EdF sets aside 0.14 cents (European) per kilowatt-hour of nuclear electricity for waste management costs. Total provisions at the end of 2004 amounted to €13.4 billion—€9.6 billion for reprocessing (including decommissioning of facilities) and €3.8 billion for disposal of high-level and long-lived wastes. In the United States, the costs of managing and disposing of wastes from nuclear power plants represents about 5 percent of the total cost of electricity generated. U.S. nuclear utilities set aside 0.1 cent per kilowatt-hour to provide for the management and disposal of nuclear waste. These funds are obtained from the utility customer and thus far total more than $20 billion.

Why Nuclear Energy Works in France

How was France able to get its people to accept nuclear power when the citizens of other nations, especially the United States, have been so hostile to the concept? What can nuclear project developers learn from the French experience? The answer to the first question can be explained by the uniqueness of French culture and politics.

First, the French tend to place a high value on their independence as a nation. While this at times might make them a problematic ally (from the U.S. government's point of view) it has greatly benefited their nuclear industry development. To the French, the thought of being dependent on the volatile Middle East for their energy was quite disturbing. French citizens, perhaps sensing their diminished role as a superpower on the post–World War II stage, quickly accepted the notion that nuclear power might be a necessity since they, in their diminished role, could not adequately secure or protect their supply of imported oil. A popular French slogan at the time, "No oil, no gas, no coal, no choice" succinctly sums up their position.

Conversely, the United States had a totally opposite attitude toward energy independence following the conclusion of World War II. Being the most prosperous nation on earth and a global superpower that possessed huge energy assets (enough to supply most of the Allied war effort), the small amounts of energy imported were of little consequence and there was no public opposition to importing this inexpensive energy. It wasn't until 1973, the time of the first Middle East oil shock, that then–President Richard Nixon announced a goal of "energy independence" for the United States.

At the time of President Nixon's energy pronouncements, the United States was importing a third of its oil. In 2006, it imported 60 percent of its oil, and this percentage is expected to increase over time due to domestic production declines and increasing demand. For many years, President Nixon's goal of energy independence was forgotten, and Jimmy Carter's efforts at energy conservation at the end of the 1970s failed to have much of an impact on Americans, who have been called "drunk" on cheap energy.

By the middle of the first decade of the twenty-first century, small energy-efficient cars used by much of the world had been muscled off American roads by SUVs and other gas guzzlers. The United States now consumes 9.5 million barrels of gasoline each day, equal to 400 million gallons at the pump. Our staggering gasoline consumption alone represents about 10 percent of the world's daily crude oil production.

Recent price shocks and increasing geopolitical conflicts relating to energy supplies now have many Americans reconsidering their laissez-faire attitudes toward energy supply and its consumption. In June 2005, the Yale School of Forestry and Environmental Studies released poll results that illustrated the general public's changing opinion concerning U.S. energy policy. The telephone poll of 1,000 U.S. adults, conducted by Global Strategy

Group in May 2005, revealed that 92 percent of Americans are worried about dependence on foreign oil and that 93 percent want government to develop new energy technologies and require the auto industry to make cars and trucks that get better gas mileage. While now on the right track, the United States is still some 50 years behind the French in realizing that our security is jeopardized by our reliance on imported energy.

The success of nuclear energy in France has a lot to do with French culture. The French have a history of large, centrally managed technology projects that have been extremely popular with the public. The public's mostly positive response to the development of nuclear energy appears to follow the same pattern as its approval of the costly development of high-speed bullet trains and supersonic passenger jets. Part of the popularity of these large government projects probably stems from the fact that in France, scientists and engineers tend to have a higher status than in the United States and that many high-ranking French civil servants and government officials are trained as scientists and engineers, rather than lawyers as in the United States. The engineering experience of these French technocrats led them to develop a highly standardized, centrally planned nuclear industry that encourages efficiencies in training and operations. This has also contributed to the overall safety of the French nuclear industry.

Lastly, French authorities have worked hard to highlight the benefits of nuclear energy as well as the risks. Multimillion-dollar television advertising campaigns were implemented to reinforce the link between nuclear power and the electricity used by consumers. French nuclear plants also solicited the public to take tours, an invitation that 6 million Frenchman accepted, although this policy is probably a thing of the past due to recent concerns over the security of such installations.

French public opinion polls at times have shown that approximately two-thirds of the population is strongly in favor of nuclear power.

French public opinion polls at times have shown that approximately two-thirds of the population is strongly in favor of nuclear power. While French people have similar negative imagery and fears of radiation and disaster as Americans, the difference is that cultural, economic, and political forces in France appear to counteract these fears. French citizens cannot control nuclear technology any more than Americans can, but the fact that they trust their technocrats who do control it makes them feel more secure. Most French people know that life would be very difficult without nuclear energy. Because they need nuclear power more than the United States does, they tend to fear it less.

While a majority of the U.S. public, when polled, respond that they are in favor of nuclear power, they tend not to want this infrastructure anywhere near them. The public, until recently, has also failed to grasp the necessity for increased power generation from nonfossil sources of energy. It is here where a great contrast exists between French and U.S. nuclear efforts. When the French were threatened by the Arab oil embargo in 1973, their government, in addition to encouraging consumers to trim their energy consumption, also launched a massive pronuclear power campaign utilizing the slogan "En France, on n'a pas de petrole, mais on a des idees" ("France doesn't have oil, but it has ideas"). This advertisement ran on France's only state-run television station. The entities behind the campaign were two state-controlled companies: Cogema, now part of Areva SA, and Electricite de France, then the country's electricity monopoly.

While the French put forth a fairly sophisticated pronuclear campaign to win public opinion, the U.S. government has mostly neglected to use this approach and, as a result, the U.S. nuclear industry suffers. In recent years, the Nuclear Energy Institute, a private U.S. nuclear advocacy organization, has undertaken advertising campaigns on behalf of its membership in an attempt to help sway public opinion toward the expansion of nuclear energy. The French, to gain public acceptance for nuclear units, also offered incentives to local communities, such as providing steam produced from reactor operations free of charge to local businesses (commercial greenhouses) in exchange for the placement of nuclear generation assets. This has, in the past, prompted these communities to compete against each other to attract these facilities.

French Nuclear Economics

France's nuclear power program has cost hundreds of billions of francs. Half of this cost has been self-financed by Electricité de France, 8 percent has been invested by the state, and 42 percent has been financed through commercial loans. France has steadily grown its electricity exports and become the world's largest net electricity exporter. In fact, electricity has become France's fourth largest export. Italy, without any operating nuclear power plants, is Europe's largest importer of electricity, most coming ultimately from France. The United Kingdom has also become a major customer for French electricity.

Civaux 1 and 2, France's 57th and 58th operating nuclear power reactors, situated on the river Vienne, just south of Poitiers, are the third and fourth units of France's advanced 1,450-megawatt N4 reactor series. Civaux 1 began commercial operation in August 1999, and start-up for Civaux 2 occurred in late 1999.

Electricite de France has put the cost of the Civaux units at $4.1 billion. It claims other plants commissioned worldwide in recent years cost as much as 60 percent more than these new units. The Civaux figure works out to an impressive $1,349 per electrical kilowatt, which is much lower than several foreign nuclear projects, and even around the level of a few large coal projects. Further, EdF has stated that its nuclear operating costs are 10 centimes (2 cents) per kilowatt-hour, compared to its estimates of gas-fired operating costs of 15 centimes (2.9 cents) per kilowatt-hour and coal-fired costs of 13 centimes (2.5 cents) per kilowatt-hour. This has helped to make France's electricity among the cheapest in western Europe.

Decommissioning Costs

Eleven experimental and commercial power reactors are being decommissioned in France. Eight of these are first-generation gas-cooled, graphite-moderated types, of which six are very similar to the UK Magnox type. There are plans for dismantling these units, which have not operated since 1990 or before. However, progress is being constrained by the availability of sites for disposing of the intermediate-level wastes and the contaminated graphite from the early reactors. The remaining three reactors include the 1,200 electrical megawatt Super-Phenix fast reactor, the 1966 prototype 305 electrical megawatt pressurized water reactor at Chooz, and an experimental gas-cooled heavy-water reactor (GCHWR) at Brennilis.

Costs have also been incurred for the final decommissioning of reprocessing plants. Frances' UP1 reprocessing plant at Marcoule was decommissioned in 2004 and the site was given over to the Atomic Energy Commission (CEA). The total cost is expected to be some €5.6 billion. The plant was closed in 1997 after 39 years of operation, primarily for military purposes but also taking the spent fuel from EdF's early gas-cooled power reactors. It was operated under a partnership, Codem, with 45 percent share each by CEA and EdF and 10 percent share by Cogema. EdF and Areva (for Cogema) will pay CEA €1.5 billion and be clear of further liability. EdF puts aside European 0.14 cents per kilowatt-hour for decommissioning, and at the end of 2004 it carried provisions of €9.9 billion for this.

Decommissioning costs are also an issue of importance with the U.S. nuclear industry. The country's 103 commercially operating units have 40-year licenses from the NRC. As these licenses near expiration some of these units will apply for and receive 20-year operating extensions. The owners of other units might not apply for an extension or could possibly be denied. These reactors, and ultimately all reactors, will need to be decommissioned, and the costs associated with decommissioning will be covered by the aforementioned fund paid by utility customers in their monthly bill. Using this method to fund the decommissioning costs effectively protects the public from additional expenditures or unknown costs relating to decommission of U.S. nuclear units. This effectively eliminates one of the possible hurdles or challenges for the further expansion of nuclear generation assets in the United States.

French Nuclear Reactors

France's first eight power reactors were of gas-cooled design, but EdF then chose pressurized water reactor (PWR) types, supported by new enrichment capacity. Apart from one experimental fast breeder reactor, all French units are now PWRs of three standard types designed by Framatome (the first two derived from U.S. Westinghouse types): 900 MWe (34), 1300 MWe (20), and 1,450 MWe N4 type (4). A complete list of France's 59 nuclear reactors can be found in Table 4.1. This is a higher degree of standardization than anywhere else in the world. The 900 MWe reactors all had their lifetimes extended by 10 years in 2002, after their second 10-year review. Most started up in the late 1970s to early 1980s, and they are reviewed together in a process that takes four months at each unit. A review of the 1,300 MWe class followed, and in light of operating experience, EdF uprated its four Chooz and Civaux N4 reactors from 1,455 to 1,500 MWe each in 2003.

Table 4.1 **Operating French Commercial Reactors**

Reactor	MWe Net	Start Date
Belleville 1 and 2	1,310	6/88, 1/89
Blayais 1–4	910	12/81–10/83
Bugey 2–3, 4–5	910, 880	3/79–1/80
Cattenom 1–4	1,300	4/87–1/92
Chinon B 1–4	905	2/84–4/88
Chooz B 1–2	1,500	5/00, 9/00
Civaux 1–2	1,495	3/00, 9/00
Cruas 1–4	915	4/84–4/85
Dampierre 1–4	890	9/80–11/81
Fessenheim 1–2	880	12/77, 3/78
Flamanville 1–2	1,330	12/86, 3/87
Golfech 1–2	1,310	2/91, 3/94
Gravelines B 1–4	910	11/80–10/81
Gravelines C 5–6	910	1/85, 10/85
Nogent s/Seine 1–2	1,310	2/88, 5/89
Paluel 1–4	1,330	12/85–6/86
Penly 1–2	1,330	12/90, 1192
Saint-Alban 1–2	1,335	5/86, 3/87
Saint-Laurent B 1–2	915	8/83
Tricastin 1–4	915	12/80–11/81
Phenix	233	7/74
Total (59)	**63,363**	

SOURCE: World Nuclear Association.

France has exported its PWR reactor technology to Belgium, South Africa, South Korea, and China. There are two 900 MWe French reactors operating at Koeberg, near Capetown, in South Africa; two at Ulchin in South Korea; and four at Daya Bay and Lingao in China, near Hong Kong. Framatome, in conjunction with Siemens in Germany, then developed the European pressurized water reactor (EPR), based on the French N4 and the German Konvoi types, to meet the European Utility Requirements and also the U.S. Electric Power Research Institute (EPRI) Utility Requirements. This was confirmed in 1995 as the new standard design for France and it received French design approval in 2004.

French reactor development continued in mid-2004 when the board of EdF decided to build the first demonstration unit of an expected series of 1,600 MWe Framatome ANP EPRs. Construction of this unit is expected to start in 2007 at Flamanville on the Normandy coast, following public consultation and licensing, and a tentative start-up is set for 2012. EdF is aiming to firm up an industrial partnership with other European utilities or power users for its construction. (Finland is also building an EPR unit at Olkiluoto.) After experience with the initial EPR units, a decision would be made about 2015 on whether to build more of them over 30 years or so to replace the present EdF fleet, or switch to alternative designs such as Westinghouse's AP1000 or General Electric's advanced simplified boiling water reactor (ASBWR). However, in August 2005, EdF announced that it planned to replace its 59 present reactors with EPR nuclear reactors from 2020, at the rate of about one 1,600 MWe unit per year. It would require 40 of these to reach present capacity.

There have been two significant fast breeder reactors in France. Near Marcoule is the 233 MWe Phenix reactor, which started operation in 1974. It was shut down for modification from 1998 to 2003 and is expected to run for a further few years. A second unit was a 1,200 MWe Super-Phenix, which started up in 1996 but was closed down for political reasons at the end of 1998 and is now being decommissioned. The operation of Phenix is fundamental to France's research on waste disposal, particularly transmutation of actinides. Efforts by the French to continually improve their commercial nuclear technology and operations have prompted both GE and Westinghouse to enhance their reactor designs and operational capabilities.

Putting a Tiger in the Tank: Reactor Fuels

In order for nuclear power plants to operate, they must have a fuel source. For most nuclear reactors this source of fuel is uranium. Uranium is a relatively common metal, as common as tin and zinc, and typically found in rocks as well as in seawater. The world's known recoverable uranium reserves are primarily located in the 14 nations shown in Table 4.2. Half of the world's uranium reserves are located in just three countries: Australia, Kazakhstan, and Canada.

Half of the world's uranium reserves are located in just three countries: Australia, Kazakhstan, and Canada.

Table 4.2   **World's Recoverable Uranium Reserves**

	Tons Uranium	Percentage of World
Australia	1,143,000	24%
Kazakhstan	816,000	17%
Canada	444,000	9%
USA	342,000	7%
South Africa	341,000	7%
Namibia	282,000	6%
Brazil	279,000	6%
Niger	225,000	5%
Russian Fed.	172,000	4%
Uzbekistan	116,000	2%
Ukraine	90,000	2%
Jordan	79,000	2%
India	67,000	1%
China	60,000	1%
Other	287,000	6%
World total	**4,743,000**	

SOURCE: IAEA, *Uranium 2005: Resources, Production and Demand* (known as the "Red Book").

Nuclear Fuel Prices

The world's 443 nuclear reactors with combined capacity of approximately 365 gigawatts of electricity require about 68,000 tons of uranium fuel each year to operate. The price of the uranium that is used to generate approximately 16 percent of the world's electricity has jumped fivefold since 2001 to a record $47 a pound. Some analysts believe uranium prices might reach as high as $60 per pound by May 2007. In 2005, spot (nonterm contract) uranium sales transactions accounted for roughly 34 percent of the industry's supply; however, the bulk of industry fuel supply purchases are based upon three- to seven-year term contracts. According to the financial firm Merrill Lynch, uranium prices have risen 56 percent in 2006 as record oil prices spurred demand for alternate sources of energy, and uranium prices averaged $43 a pound, compared with the 2005 average of $28.

Like any other freely traded commodity, uranium prices fluctuate based on supply and demand. Many uranium producers have made forward sales of production in an effort to lock in these higher prices and estimates have been heard in the market that there might be unfulfilled uranium requirements of 50 million pounds as early as 2009. During low-price periods, high-production-cost operations, many of which were located in the United States, were forced to cease operations. Under today's economic conditions, Canada produces the largest share (28 percent) of mined uranium, followed by Australia (23 percent). These market shares have been unchanged for the past four years. (See Table 4.3.)

Production from the world's uranium mines supplies roughly 55 percent of the nuclear fuel requirements of power utilities. Another important source of nuclear fuel for commercial reactors is the decommissioning of nuclear weapons stockpiles, the result of nuclear disarmament treaties signed by the United States and countries of the

Table 4.3   **Uranium Production from Mines (Tons)**

Country	2002	2003	2004	2005
Canada	11,604	10,457	11,597	11,628
Australia	6,854	7,572	8,982	9,519
Kazakhstan	2,800	3,300	3,719	4,357
Russia (estimated)	2,900	3,150	3,200	3,431
Namibia	2,333	2,036	3,038	3,147
Niger	3,075	3,143	3,282	3,093
Uzbekistan	1,860	1,598	2,016	2,300
USA	919	779	846	1,039
Ukraine (estimated)	800	800	800	800
China (estimated)	730	750	750	750
South Africa	824	758	755	674
Czech Repub.	465	452	412	408
India (estimated)	230	230	230	230
Romania (estimated)	90	90	90	90
Germany	212	150	150	77
Pakistan (estimated)	38	45	45	45
France	20	0	7	7
Brazil	270	310	300	0
Total World	**36,063**	**35,613**	**40,219**	**41,595**

SOURCE: World Nuclear Association.

former USSR. These treaties are expected to reduce the nuclear arsenals of the treaty participants by approximately 80 percent, with the nuclear fuel recycled to meet commercial power applications. It should be noted that nuclear weapons contain uranium enriched to concentrations over 90 percent U-235, about 25 times the proportion typically seen in reactor fuel, which makes these weapons a significant source of radioactive fuel. In addition, some weapons possess plutonium-239, which has the flexibility to be used in diluted form in either conventional or fast breeder reactors.

Today, almost half of the uranium used in U.S. nuclear power plants comes from the "down-blending" of Russian weapons-grade military uranium from their decommissioned weapons.

The U.S. government has made available 174 tons of military high-enriched uranium surplus for civil power generation. Today, almost half of the uranium used in U.S. nuclear power plants comes from the "down-blending" of Russian weapons-grade military uranium from their decommissioned weapons. It is estimated that since the year 2000 the dilution of 30 tons of military grade, highly enriched uranium has displaced about 9,000 tons of uranium oxide per year from world mining operations; this represents about 11 percent of the world's reactor requirements.

After mining operations and using the fuel from decommissioned nuclear weapons, the balance of the world's commercial reactor fuel requirements are met from the reprocessing of spent nuclear fuel.

Fuel Reprocessing

Used nuclear reactor fuel still contains significant quantities of uranium, U-235 and U-238, as well as plutonium isotopes. These fuel concentrations account for some 96 percent of the original uranium and over half of the original energy content. Fuel reprocessing, currently done in Europe and Russia, separates uranium and plutonium from the waste fuel, enabling it to be recycled and reused in reactors as a mixed oxide fuel in what is known as a *closed fuel cycle*. Reprocessing plants in the UK, France, and Russia have an annual capacity of 5,000 tons. Besides domestic fuel, western European reprocessing facilities also reprocess used fuel from other nations, most notably Japan.

Managing Spent Fuel

There are over 250,000 tons of spent nuclear fuel in storage. Currently, most of this fuel is stored locally on the utility site in secure buildings isolated from the reactor site. Each year, the world's nuclear reactors create about 12,000 tons of spent fuel, and about 25 percent of this is reprocessed. Table 4.4 shows the global waste management practices currently employed by nations operating commercial nuclear reactors. Of the 15 nations, roughly half reprocess their waste while the other half currently use or are looking to employee long-term storage of their waste.

In France, the French company Cogema meets the nation's nuclear fuel needs. Cogema is an industrial group that is majority-owned by the French government. In fact, the French Atomic Energy Commission owns 82 percent of the shares of Cogema, with the other shares owned by

Table 4.4   Global Spent-Fuel Waste Management Practices

Country	Policy	Facilities and Progress toward Final Repositories
Belgium	Reprocessing	Centralized waste storage. Repository construction to begin about 2035.
Canada	Direct disposal	Underground repository laboratory established. Repository planned for use in 2025.
China	Reprocessing	Centralized used fuel storage in LanZhou.
Finland	Direct disposal	Low- and intermediate-level spent-fuel repositories in operation since 1992. Deep repository for used fuel under construction near Olkiluoto, expected to open 2020.
France	Reprocessing	Two short-lived waste facilities. Site selection studies underway for deep repository expected in 2020.
Germany	Reprocessing, but shifting to direct disposal	Low-level waste sites since 1975. Intermediate-level waste stored at Ahaus. Used fuel storage at Ahaus and Gorleben. High-level waste repository operational after 2010.
India	Reprocessing	Research on deep geological disposal for high-level waste.

Country	Policy	Facilities and Progress toward Final Repositories
Japan	Reprocessing	Low-level waste repository in operation. High-level waste storage facility at Rokkasho-mura since 1995. Investigations for deep geological repository site begun, expected operation post-2035.
Russia	Reprocessing	Sites for final disposal under investigation. Central repository for low- and intermediate-level wastes planned from 2008.
South Korea	Direct disposal	Central interim high-level waste storage planned for 2016. Central low-level waste repository planned from 2008. Investigating deep high-level waste repository sites.
Spain	Direct disposal	Low- and intermediate-level waste repository in operation. Final high-level waste repository site selection program for commissioning 2020.
Sweden	Direct disposal	Central used fuel storage facility in operation since 1985. Final repository for low to intermediate waste in operation since 1988. Underground research laboratory for high-level waste repository. Site selection for repository in two volunteered locations.
Switzerland	Reprocessing	Central interim storage for high-level wastes at Zwilag since 2001. Central low- and intermediate-level storages operating since 1993. Underground research laboratory for high-level waste repository, deep repository to be finished by 2020.
United Kingdom	Reprocessing	Low-level waste repository in operation since 1959. High-level waste vitrified and stored at Sellafiled. Underground high-level waste repository intended.
United States	Direct disposal	Three low-level waste sites in operation. Decision made in 2002 to proceed with geological repository at Yucca Mountain.

SOURCE: World Nuclear Association.

an oil company and an engineering firm. It services 25 percent of the world market for uranium enrichment and conversion, 50 percent of the world's fuel reprocessing facilities, and over 80 percent of the world's mixed oxide (MOX) fuel fabrication.

Cogema operates two plants in France for the conversion of yellow cake to uranium hexafluoride. In addition, Cogema owns the Georges Besses uranium enrichment plant in France, which has the capacity to enrich almost one-third of the world's annual uranium supply. Finally, Cogema and Framatome (the French nuclear reactor design and construction company) jointly own several fabrication plants. These Fragema plants have about one-third of the production capacity of the world's PWRs.

France uses some 12,400 tons of uranium oxide concentrate (10,500 tons of uranium) per year for its electricity generation. Much of this comes from Cogema in Canada (4,500 tons of uranium per year) and Niger (3,200 tons) together with other imports, principally from Australia, Kazakhstan, and Russia, mostly under long-term contracts. In its natural form, uranium is concentrated after mining as yellow cake, which is primarily uranium oxide (U_3O_8). For enrichment, it must then be converted into the form of uranium hexafluoride, UF_6. From this state, it must be enriched primarily by one of two methods, either gaseous diffusion or gaseous ultracentrifugation. This takes the 0.71 percent U–235 content of natural uranium and increases it to the 3 to 5 percent range that is necessary in order to run light-water reactors. After enrichment, the uranium must then be fabricated in UO_2 pellets, which are then made into fuel assemblies. It is these fuel assemblies that are loaded into nuclear power plants.

Since the beginning of the nuclear power era in France, the French have mined their own uranium, almost to the point of exhaustion. Currently, over 70,000 metric tons of uranium have been excavated in France. This leaves the French with uranium reserves of around 200,000 metric tons. However, this uranium ore is of very poor quality and is not economically feasible to excavate. The French nuclear power industry has thus turned to other sources around the world for uranium.

One of the closest and easiest places for the French to obtain uranium is from their former African colonies. Of particular interest are Niger and Gabon, both of which have extensive uranium deposits. In

Niger, Cogema owns 57 percent of the Somair mining operation and 34 percent of the Cominak mining operation. In Gabon, Cogema owns 68.4 percent of the Comuf mining operation. In addition, Cogema owns 100 percent of the Cluff mining operation in Canada, 71 percent of the Christensen Ranch mining operation in the United States, and 3.3 percent of the Ranger mining operation in Australia. Moreover, Cogema is also involved with new production at five different mining operations in Canada and is the primary motivator in some recent studies of the feasibility of uranium mining in Kazakhstan, Uzbekistan, Mongolia, and Madagascar. Through all of these various sources, Cogema permits France to obtain uranium for its nuclear power plants. The company's diversified uranium assets also make France less dependent on a particular foreign source for its energy needs.

Spent fuel from various reactors is sent to Cogema's 1,600 ton/year La Hague plant in Normandy for reprocessing. This extracts the plutonium and uranium, leaving high-level wastes that are vitrified and stored there for later disposal. The plutonium is shipped to the 120 ton/year Melox plant at Marcoule for prompt fabrication into MOX fuel, which can be used in about 30 reactors in Europe. The reprocessing of 1,150 tons of EdF's used fuel per year (about 15 years after discharge) produces 8.5 tons of plutonium (immediately recycled as MOX) and 815 tons of reprocessed uranium (repU). Of this about 650 tons is converted into stable oxide form for storage. Some of the repU has been reenriched at Pierrelatte and EdF has demonstrated its use of repU 900 MWe power plants. However, it is currently uneconomical due to conversion costing three times as much as that for fresh uranium, and enrichment needing to be separate because of U-232 and U-236 impurities (the former gives rise to gamma radiation, the latter means higher enrichment is required). However, EdF is reported to be planning increased use of repU.

All these fuel cycle facilities are operated commercially, with international customers. Together they comprise a significant export industry and France's major export to Japan. In August 2004 Areva announced a €4 billion contract to treat 5,250 tons of EdF's spent uranium fuel at La Hague. The deal covers also the provision of 100 tons of MOX fuel per year to EdF from the separated plutonium for seven years, and the packaging of the separated high-level wastes.

Keeping France Safe

The Nuclear Safety Authority (Autorite de Surete Nucleaire, or ASN) is the regulatory authority within France responsible for nuclear safety and radiological protection. It reports to the Minister of Environment, Industry and Health. The General Directorate for Nuclear Safety and Radiological Protection (DGSNR) was established in 2002 by merging the Directorate for Nuclear Installation Safety (DSIN) with the Office for Protection against Ionizing Radiation (OPRI) to integrate the regulatory functions and to draft and implement government policy. Research is undertaken by the Institute for Radiological Protection and Nuclear Safety (ISRN), also set up in 2002 from two older bodies. ISRN is the main technical support body for ASN and also advises DGSNR. The Atomic Energy Commission (Commissariat a l'Energie Atomique, or CEA) was set up in 1945 and is the public R&D corporation responsible for all aspects of nuclear research and development.

All uranium supplied to France is covered by both IAEA safeguards and bilateral safeguards which ensure that it cannot be used for weapons. Euratom safeguards also apply in France and cover all civil nuclear facilities and materials. France, being a state with nuclear weapons capability, is party to the Nuclear Non-Proliferation Treaty (NPT), which it ratified in 1992 and under which a safeguards agreement has been in place since 1981. It undertook nuclear weapons tests in 1960 through 1996 and ceased production of weapons-grade fissile materials in 1996. Since then it has ratified the Comprehensive Test Ban Treaty. Similar nuclear fuel safety regulations are in place with the Nuclear Regulatory Commission (NRC) in the United States, which is responsible for ensuring that nuclear fuel and materials are secure and that their use is limited to approved power applications.

The Future of French Nuclear Power

France's commitment to and reliance on nuclear power did not happen by accident; it was a well-thought-out strategy created by the nation's government that has cost approximately $120 billion through 2005. Its march to nuclear-based energy independence has not been free from setbacks and adverse developments. The French have experienced an occasional low-level radiation leak, but have never experienced a major nuclear accident like Chernobyl or Three Mile Island.

While France benefits greatly from its decision to construct and operate a fleet of standardized nuclear power plants, the nation has not managed to completely shake off the shackles of fossil fuels. Even at current nuclear-based generation capacity, oil represents approximately 50 percent of France's energy consumption, and this percentage is on the rise due to increased demand for refined transportation fuels. This number, however, is considerably below 1973 levels when fossil fuels accounted for 65 percent of the country's energy usage. To prevent further increases in fossil fuel usage, France plans to further develop its nuclear power capacity.

> *The French have experienced an occasional low-level radiation leak, but have never experienced a major nuclear accident like Chernobyl or Three Mile Island.*

This goes against the trend seen in most other European countries, although that has begun to slowly change. France continues to develop a new generation of nuclear reactors and is upgrading its existing plants. The French believe their nuclear expansion efforts will put them on the path to greater energy security, which, along with radioactive waste management and respect for the environment, is an integral part of their energy policy for the new millennium.

Other European Markets

In recent years, France has stood alone as the bastion of nuclear power in Europe. Its neighbors Belgium and Germany have made commitments to close their nuclear power stations within the next two decades. Both countries have also banned new nuclear reactors while making increased use of solar, wind, and other renewable energy resources. In addition, the UK has no plans to replace the current generation of nuclear power stations, and Italy is dismantling its four generating plants. The last of these four Italian plants was closed in 1990 shortly after a 1987 referendum vote against nuclear power. Lastly, Spain also has a moratorium on construction of new plants.

While these developments might appear to be bearish for the industry in Europe, recent events such as the Russian natural gas curtailment have prompted many nations to reexamine the use of nuclear power to reduce dependence on oil and natural gas imports. Recent developments around Europe include the following:

- Finland is constructing a third-generation pressurized water reactor, designed by the French company Areva. The facility is due to come on line in 2009.
- The Bulgarian government is looking to construct two new nuclear units.
- Romania has restarted building a power station that was mothballed 15 years ago.
- The Czech Republic's energy plan foresees the construction of two more nuclear plants by the end of the decade.
- The Swiss parliament has ended a moratorium on building nuclear power plants and extended the operating lifetime of the country's five existing units.
- The British government has promised an energy review this year that might favor the construction of new nuclear assets.

Throughout Europe, nuclear supporters have sought to deflect attention away from the problem of nuclear waste by highlighting the problems associated with fossil fuels, most notably foreign dependence on supply and greenhouse-gas emissions. This strategy has yielded some success. A 2005 EU poll on the subject reported that some 62 percent of respondents agreed that nuclear power was advantageous in terms of cutting greenhouse gases—up from just 41 percent four years earlier. How ironic that the green movement, once a staunch opponent of nuclear power, might end up being one of its strongest advocates in Europe and around the world.

Nuclear Power's Role in the Developing World

The substantial international growth of commercial nuclear power creates competition for nuclear fuel and increases the importance of nuclear waste management and fuel reprocessing operations. Two rapidly industrializing nations, China and India, are planning to increasingly rely on nuclear power to meet their growing energy needs in the decades to come.

China's Economic Emergence

Many pundits predict that the twenty-first century will belong to the Chinese. With 1.3 billion people, the Chinese are an economic force with which to be reckoned. China's development, however, is highly dependent on being able to obtain sufficient quantities of commodities and natural resources, especially energy. The Chinese are aggressively pursuing new supplies of fossil fuels, have attempted to purchase Western oil firms (Unocal), and are interested in purchasing crude oil and refined products from new suppliers such as the Venezuelans. In addition, the Chinese have most recently shown interest in partnering with the island nation of Cuba to explore for oil offshore in the Florida Straights, a course of action which is raising the eyebrows of U.S. government officials and environmentalists. The Chinese are also aggressively looking to expand their domestic nuclear generation capabilities.

> *China and India are planning to increasingly rely on nuclear power to meet their growing energy needs in the decades to come.*

Most of China's electricity (about 80 percent) is produced from fossil fuels, mainly coal and some amounts of hydroelectric power. The Chinese have about 508 gigawatts of installed generation capacity. In 2005, nuclear generation accounted for 7.6 gigawatts of this capacity and provided 52.3 billion kilowatt-hours of electricity, 2.1 percent of the total. The Chinese are projecting their electricity consumption to grow at an average of 4.3 percent per year through 2025. To help meet this substantial demand, the Chinese government plans to increase nuclear generating capacity to 40 gigawatts by 2020, a fivefold increase from current levels, requiring an average of 2 gigawatts per year being added, but even with this large capacity expansion, nuclear power will account for less than 5 percent of China's installed capacity.

Mainland China currently possesses nine commercial nuclear reactors and six others in various stages of construction (see Tables 4.5 and 4.6). In addition, the island nation of Taiwan (territory under rebel control, according to the Communist Chinese) has six operational nuclear power reactors (see Table 4.7) and two advanced reactors under construction.

In Taiwan, nuclear power supplies almost 40 percent of the country's base electric load and 20 percent of its overall load, but only makes up 14 percent of the nation's 36.3 GWe installed capacity. The Taiwanese use six

Table 4.5   Operating Chinese Mainland Reactors

Units	Type	Net Capacity	Start-Up Date
Daya Bay 1 and 2	PWR	944 MWe	1994
Qinshan 1	PWR	279 MWe	April 1994
Qinshan 2 and 3	PWR	610 MWe	2002, 2004
Lingao 1 and 2	PWR	935 MWe	2002, 2003
Qinshan 4 and 5	PHWR	665 MWe	2002, 2003

SOURCE: World Nuclear Association.

Table 4.6   Chinese Reactors under Construction

Units	Type	Net Capacity	Start-Up Date
Tianwan 1	PWR (VVER)	1,000 MWe	2007
Tianwan 2	PWR (VVER)	1,000 MWe	2007
Lingao 3	PWR	935 MWe	2010
Lingao 4	PWR	935 MWe	2011
Qinshan 6	PWR	610 MWe	2010
Qinshan 7	PWR	610 MWe	2010

SOURCE: World Nuclear Association.

Table 4.7   Taiwanese Operating Reactors

Units	Type	Net Capacity	Start-Up Date
Chinshan 1 and 2	BWR	604 MWe	1978, 1979
Kuosheng 1 and 2	BWR	948 MWe	1981, 1983
Maanshan 1 and 2	PWR	890 MWe	1984, 1985

SOURCE: World Nuclear Association.

reactors, of both GE and Westinghouse design, and there are two additional advanced boiling water reactors under construction.

Mainland China's centrally planned economy has and will continue to dedicate considerable resources to the expansion of nuclear power in the decades to come. During the nation's Tenth Economic Plan (2001–2005), the China National Nuclear Corporation (CNNC)—an agency that controls most Chinese nuclear sector business including R&D, engineering design, uranium exploration and mining, enrichment, fuel fabrication, re-

Table 4.8 **Potential Power Output of Chinese Reactors under Construction**

Plant	Province	MWe Gross
Lingao 2	Guangdong	2 × 1,000
Qinshan 4	Zhejiang	2 × 650
Sanmen 1	Zhejiang	2 × 1,100/1,500
Yangjiang 1	Guangdong	2 × 1,100/1,500

SOURCE: World Nuclear Association.

processing, and waste disposal within China—applied to build eight new reactors (four pairs) that could potentially generate upwards of 9,300 gross MWe of power. (See Table 4.8.)

Under the nation's eleventh five-year plan (2006–2010), another eight nuclear units are planned, and in China's twelfth five-year plan more than 16 provinces, regions, and municipalities have announced intentions to build nuclear power plants.

Chinese Reactor Technology One of China's goals is to aggressively develop its indigenous nuclear power capabilities. They are not interested in just purchasing foreign technology, but rather are striving to develop their own technology with input from foreign firms. This self-sufficient strategy holds true whether the Chinese are looking to develop nuclear reactors or less technical, more mundane items such as commercial or residential elevators for their growing cities.

The key elements in China's nuclear energy development strategy include:

- Relying primarily on pressure water reactors.
- Domestically fabricating and supplying nuclear fuel assemblies.
- Maximizing the domestic manufacturing of the nuclear plant and equipment.

China has not yet selected the type of reactor technology for its next generation of reactors. CNNC has been working with both Westinghouse and the French firm Areva to develop a Chinese standard design PWR reactor and possess the associated intellectual property rights. In September 2005, Atomic Energy of Canada Ltd. signed a technology development agreement with CNNC that might create an opportunity for the supply of additional Candu-6 reactors. Another reactor manufacturer, General Electric, has approached the Chinese with its new boiling water reactor designs; however, the Chinese has expressed interest only in pressurized water reactors.

Chinese Fuel Cycle   China has known uranium resources of 70,000 tons and currently produces 840 tons per year, about half of its current requirements. China uses a closed fuel cycle reprocessing strategy. The Chinese began construction of a centralized spent-fuel storage facility at the Lanzhou Nuclear Fuel Complex in 1994. The initial stage of that project has a storage capacity of 550 tons and has the potential to be expanded. At this planned storage complex, high-level wastes will be vitrified (using heat fusion to change or make into glass or a glassy substance), encapsulated, and put into a geological repository some 500 meters deep. Six candidate locations for this facility are said to be under review.

Nuclear Expansion in India

Over the decades, India has vacillated about its policy regarding foreign investment in its industries. After many years of pursuing policies based on import substitution and state ownership of critical industries, the Indian government began a series of economic reforms in the mid-1990s to relax restrictions on foreign ownership in some sectors, and privatization of some industrial enterprises. However, nuclear power remains beyond the scope of the current ownership regulations.

India is struggling to expand electric power generation capacity, which is seriously below peak demand at the present time. Although about 80 percent of the population has access to electricity, power reliability continues to be a problem. This hinders the nation's economic development. The government has targeted capacity increases totaling 100,000 megawatts over the next 10 years. As of January 2003, total installed Indian power-generating capacity was 126,000 megawatts.

India has a large and growing nuclear power program and expects to have 20,000 megawatts of nuclear generating capacity on line by 2020. Electricity demand in India has been increasing rapidly, with 534 billion kilowatt-hours produced in 2002, almost double the nation's 1990 generation. Currently, coal provides over half of India's electricity, but the nation's coal reserves are limited. In 2005, nuclear power supplied 15.7

billion kilowatt-hours, or 2.8 percent of India's electricity, but Indian officials are looking to increase that contribution to 25 percent by 2050. India has 14 small and one mid-sized nuclear power reactors in commercial operation (see Table 4.9), and seven under construction, including two large ones and a fast breeder reactor (see Table 4.10).

The nation seeks to be completely independent in the nuclear fuel cycle. India has modest uranium reserves, about 54,000 tons. Mining and processing of uranium is carried out by Uranium Corporation of India. Radioactive wastes from its nuclear reactors and reprocessing plants are treated and stored on site. Research on final disposal of high-level and long-lived wastes in a geological repository is in progress.

> *India expects to have 20,000 megawatts of nuclear generating capacity on line by 2020.*

Table 4.9 Operating Indian Reactors

Reactor	Type	Net MWe	Start Date
Tarapur 1 and 2	BWR	150	1969
Kaiga 1 and 2	PHWR	202	1999–2000
Kakrapar 1 and 2	PHWR	202	1993–1995
Kalpakkam 1 and 2 (MAPS)	PHWR	202	1984–1986
Narora 1 and 2	PHWR	202	1991–1992
Rawatbhata 1	PHWR	90	1973
Rawatbhata 2	PHWR	187	1981
Rawatbhata 3 and 4	PHWR	202	1999–2000
Tarapur 3	PHWR	490	2005

SOURCE: World Nuclear Association.

Table 4.10 Indian Reactors under Construction

Reactor	Type	Net MWe	Start Date
Kaiga 3 and 4	PHWR	202	2007
Rawatbhata 5 and 6	PHWR	202	2007, 2008
Kudankulam 1 and 2	PWR (VVER)	905	2007, 2008
Kalpakkam PFBR	FBR	470	2010

SOURCE: World Nuclear Association.

In July 2005, the United States and India signed an agreement to facilitate cooperation in the field of nuclear power generation. The agreement has the backing of the executive branch of the U.S. government and the bill was passed by the U.S. House of Representatives and Senate and signed into law on December 19, 2006. This law could pave the way for U.S. sales of nuclear fuels and nuclear reactors to India, which could help India increase the nuclear share of electricity generation.

This agreement offers India access to U.S. nuclear technology after it separates its nuclear facilities into military and civilian, and opens its civilian facilities to international safeguards.

The U.S. Fuel Cycle—A Work in Progress

While the United States was an early pioneer in civilian nuclear operations and technology, in the areas of uranium mining and spent-fuel reprocessing it has fallen sharply behind the efforts of other nations. In the 1950s U.S. federal subsidies heavily supported the U.S. uranium mining sector; however, economics today have greatly reduced domestic U.S. uranium production. Table 4.11 shows that this production was estimated at 3 million pounds or 1,500 tons per year in 2005, well below 1970 peak production of around 20,000 tons per year.

Current U.S. policy forbids the reprocessing of spent nuclear fuel due to security and proliferation issues. As a result, all spent fuel is treated as high-level waste. Electric utilities operating nuclear units are responsible for storing this spent fuel on site until it is taken over by the Department of Energy for final geological repository disposal in Yucca Mountain. This repository, while recommended by the DOE and signed into law by the executive branch in 2002, has yet to be approved by the Nuclear Regulatory Commission and is currently not in service.

Current U.S. policy forbids the reprocessing of spent nuclear fuel. As a result, all spent fuel is treated as high-level waste.

Plans call for the 70,000 ton high-level waste repository at Yucca Mountain in Nevada to be operating around 2010. This facility would be designed to accept 63,000 tons of spent reactor fuel, 2,333 tons of naval

Table 4.11 U.S. Uranium Production Statistics, 1993–2005

Items	1993	1994	1995	1996	1997	1998	1999	2000	2001	2002	2003	2004	2005[E]
Exploration and Development													
Surface drilling (million feet)	1.1	0.7	1.3	3	4.9	4.6	2.5	1	0.7	W	W	1.2	1.7
Drilling expenditures[a] (million dollars)	5.7	1.1	2.6	7.2	20	18.1	7.9	5.6	2.7	W	W	10.6	16.4
Mine Production of Uranium (million pounds U_3O_8)	2.1	2.5	3.5	4.7	4.7	4.8	4.5	3.1	2.6	2.4	E 2.2	2.5	3
Uranium Concentrate Production (million pounds U_3O_8)	3.1	3.4	6	6.3	5.6	4.7	4.6	4	2.6	E 2.3	E 2.0	2.3	2.7
Uranium Concentrate Shipments (million pounds U_3O_8)	3.4	6.3	5.5	6	5.8	4.9	5.5	3.2	2.2	3.8	E 1.6	2.3	2.7
Employment (person–years)	871	980	1,107	1,118	1,097	1,120	848	627	423	426	321	420	638

[a]Expenditures are in nominal U.S. dollars.
W = Data withheld to avoid disclosure. E = Estimate—the 2003 annual amounts were estimated by rounding to the nearest 200,000 pounds to avoid disclosure of individual company data. The 2005 annual amounts contain limited imputation for missing data.
SOURCE: Energy Information Administration.

and DOE spent fuel, and 4,667 tons of other high-level wastes, all from 126 sites in 39 states. As of early 2004, there were approximately 50,000 tons of civil spent fuel awaiting disposal and about 8,000 tons of government spent fuel and separated high-level wastes. Industry studies now claim that the repository could hold at least 286,000 tons and possibly 628,000 tons of used fuel and high-level wastes, rather than the 70,000 ton figure set by Congress in 1982.

Despite U.S. policy forbidding reprocessing, it is again being reconsidered as a way to limit the amount of fuel held in Yucca Mountain. In order for the United States to jump-start the development of its nuclear industry, lessons should be learned from successful world fuel reprocessing operations. Such operations, if initiated here, would create further efficiencies in the U.S. fuel cycle and would significantly lesson the amount of waste held in storage.

Summary

The U.S. public has many different perceptions, opinions, concerns, and misconceptions relating to the nuclear industry. Recent concerns over energy supply adequacy have some in favor of its expansion, while others see nuclear generation as a necessary evil that must be tolerated. There are also still substantial numbers who oppose its expansion in any form whatsoever. No matter what their position is, most are not aware that these assets already generate approximately 20 percent of the nation's growing demand for electricity.

Aside from improving its operating efficiency, the United States has done little to add to its nuclear generation base over the last few decades. This lack of development can be mostly attributed to safety concerns and unfavorable economics. While the United States has stood relatively still, other nations, both industrialized and developing, have and plan to utilize greater amounts of nuclear power to help meet their electricity needs. The French in particular have achieved considerable success with their nuclear industry and are now less dependent on imported oil than are other western European nations and the United States. Both China and India are aggressively pursuing all forms of energy to supply their growing economies and are putting considerable resources toward expanding their nuclear power generation.

In the wake of these commercial nuclear developments and increasing global competition over tightening supplies of fossil fuels, the United States must adopt fuel storage and processing innovations and learn operational lessons to greatly enhance its efforts to expand its fleet of commercial nuclear reactors. This fleet of reactors will play a critical role in producing significant amounts of relatively inexpensive and environmentally friendly electricity.

5

No Need to Wear a Lead Suit: Nuclear Safety Works

A commercial nuclear reactor, essentially a large and very complex teakettle, boils water to produce steam through a controlled chain reaction of fissionable material. This steam spins turbines to generate electricity. Safely controlling this chain reaction is essential since an uncontrolled, runaway fissionable reaction is basically a bomb.

Over the past 60 years the U.S. nuclear power industry has successfully controlled this reaction to produce trillions of hours of low-cost electricity in an environmentally friendly manner. While some critics may point to relatively minor operating accidents and fear more significant events, safety measures have always been in place and have even been augmented in recent years to ensure safe operation of these critical assets. These safety measures have made the U.S. nuclear industry one of the safest industries in the world. While one can easily count scores of workers who have been killed in refinery, petrochemical plant, and coal mining operations over the decades, not a single U.S. nuclear worker has been killed in the workplace or in incidents relating to workplace conditions. This is truly an enviable record, a record that the rest of the energy community would like to own.

In this chapter we outline the reactor safety development process and identify the improvements planned for the next generation of U.S. reactors, highlighting the steps being taken to ensure even greater safety performance for one of the safest industries in the world.

Reactor Theory 101

To better grasp the nuclear safety issue, one must have a rudimentary knowledge of atomic theory and radioactive isotopes. Uranium, a naturally occurring element 1.7 times denser than lead, consists of 92 positively charged protons and about 140 neutrons. Isotopes of uranium—atoms with different numbers of neutrons and the same number of protons—can be used as a fuel to generate electricity via a nuclear reactor or, in much more concentrated amounts, used to produce nuclear weapons. U-235, an isotope of uranium with 143 neutrons, is naturally unstable on a subatomic basis and decays by emitting low-level alpha particle radiation (this type of radiation has low penetrating power and a short range and generally fails to penetrate human skin).

Uranium is also one of the few materials that can be manipulated by man to undergo an induced fission (splitting) reaction. Should a free neutron strike a U-235 nucleus, the nucleus absorbs the neutron, becomes unstable and splits immediately into two lighter atoms. This process is depicted in Figure 5.1.

The splitting of the uranium atom then throws off two or three new

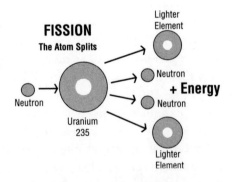

Figure 5.1 **Fission Diagram**

neutrons, depending on how the U-235 atom happens to split. Should there be a sufficient concentration of uranium atoms present and an available source of neutrons, an energy-producing chain reaction will result. The two new atoms produced then emit more powerful gamma radiation (which easily penetrates the human body and has negative effects on a submolecular level) as they settle into their new states. This induced fission process is capable of producing significant amounts of power for the following reasons:

- There is a high probability of a U-235 atom being split by neutrons, creating a sustainable reaction.
- The process of splitting the nucleus is incredibly fast, taking place in picoseconds (1×10^{-12} seconds), allowing great amounts of energy to be released in an incredibly short time.
- An enormous amount of energy is released, in the form of heat and gamma radiation. The energy released through fission results from the fact that the fission products and the neutrons resulting from the reaction weigh less than the original U-235 atom. The difference in weight is converted directly to energy at a rate governed by Einstein's famous equation $E = MC^2$: Energy is equal to mass times the speed of light squared.

Quantitative studies have shown that the fission of one U-235 nucleus will release 50 million times more energy than the combustion of a single carbon atom, approximately 200 million electron volts (MeV). To quantify this amount of energy in more concrete terms, a pound of enriched uranium, which is smaller than the size of a baseball, has the energy potential equivalent to approximately a million gallons of gasoline.

> *A pound of enriched uranium, which is smaller than the size of a baseball, has the energy potential equivalent to approximately a million gallons of gasoline.*

A sample of U-235 must be enriched to a concentration of at least 2 to 3 percent to be viable as fuel for civilian nuclear reactors in the production of electricity, while weapons-grade uranium is generally composed of 90 percent or more of U-235 (these greater concentrations are achieved through very complex, large-scale uranium enrichment operations). In commercial reactors, the uranium is generally formed into one-inch-long pellets approximately the diameter of a dime. These pellets are then configured into long rods, and the rods are collected together into bundles. The bundles are then typically submerged in water inside a reactor pressure vessel with the water acting as a cooling medium. In order for the reactor to work, the submerged bundle must become slightly supercritical. Without the operators controlling the reactor and the reaction, the uranium would eventually overheat and melt.

The other main isotope of natural uranium, U–238, is not itself fissionable in conventional reactors, but each atom can capture a neutron, indirectly becoming plutonium–239, another source of reactor fuel.

Controlling the Reaction

In a nuclear reactor, the fission process is successfully controlled by only allowing one neutron to produce another fission. Control rods (made from neutron-absorbing material such as cadmium) prevent the number of neutrons in a nuclear reactor from growing too large by absorbing excess neutrons. When the control rods are pushed in the reactor they absorb neutrons and slow down the reaction; when the rods are removed, the energy-producing chain reaction accelerates.

Using this approach, the chain reaction inside a nuclear reactor is effectively controlled. If more heat/steam for electricity generation is required from the reactor, the control rods are raised out of the uranium bundle. To create less heat/steam and reduce power output, the rods are lowered into the uranium bundle. The rods can also be lowered completely into the uranium bundle to shut the reactor down in the case of an emergency or to change the fuel.

The Evolution of Nuclear Reactor Safety

Over the past seven decades, the power of the atom has evolved from purely a theatrical concept to a proven and reliable source of energy. From the first major investigations in the 1940s to the operation of utility-owned electricity-producing reactors, safety has always been a top priority among nuclear researchers and operators to ensure the commercial power-producing viability of these generation assets.

Early Atomic Research

One of the pioneers of early atomic research was Enrico Fermi, who was awarded the Nobel Prize in 1935 for his research in the field of artificial radioactivity. Fermi left Italy and immigrated to the United States prior to the start of World War II and continued his nuclear physics research first at Columbia University in New York and then at the University of Chicago. It was at the University of Chicago in 1942 that Fermi conducted the first major experiments into controlled nuclear fission.

Safety played an important role in Fermi's pioneering nuclear fission experiments. With few standards to guide him, Fermi erred on the sign of caution as he conducted his research and incorporated multiple, by today's standards low-tech, safeguards.

The nuclear pile of Fermi's primitive reactor contained three sets of control rods. The pile's primary rod set was designed for fine control of the fission chain reaction. The other two control rods comprised the redundant safety systems for the experiment. One set of rods was automatically operated by an electric motor and responded to readings from a radiation measurement counter. Attached to one end of another control rod was a rope running through the pile and weighted heavily on the opposite end. During Fermi's reactor tests, this rod was withdrawn from the pile and tied down by another rope. If his primitive reactor had not operated the way mathematical models had predicted and if a failure occurred in the primary control rod, Fermi planned to have a "safety control rod axe man" (SCRAM) cut the rope with an axe.

The acronym SCRAM is still used today; however there are no axe-wielding reactor personnel in control rooms. Instead, control rods are held in place by devices that resemble claws which are held closed by electric current. The SCRAM switches are circuit breakers that immediately open the circuit to the claws holding the control rods, which results in the rapid insertion of the neutron-absorbing control rod and the termination of the fission reaction.

Not wanting to rely solely on mechanical rod control devices, Fermi also utilized a "liquid-control squad," people who stood on a platform above the reactor pile and were expected to use gravity to respond to a mechanical failure of the control rods by pouring a cadmium solution over the experiment, which would absorb the neutrons required for a fission reaction within the uranium.

On December 2, 1942, Fermi and his team successfully produced the first man-made self-sustaining nuclear chain reaction. This eventually led to his participation in the "Manhattan Project," the code name for the development of the atomic bomb, which played a critical role in ending the Second World War in the Pacific.

The Sole Member of the Nuclear Club   The U.S. government had a monopoly on atomic power until 1949, when the Soviet Union detonated its own nuclear device. To protect its status in the nuclear club, the U.S. government maintained strict control over existing and developing atomic technology. The government justified this control by citing national security issues and directed all initial research efforts toward military applications.

Nuclear reactor safety concerns in the postwar period were initially directed toward the siting of government facilities and the containment of any radiation potentially released from the operation of these facilities. There was no need to regulate the private sector due to the fact that the Atomic Energy Act of 1946 did not permit the privatization or commercial use of nuclear power. In 1948, the U.S. Atomic Energy Commission (AEC) established the Advisory Committee on Reactor Safeguards (ACRS). This committee was strictly an advisory body and it lacked statutory authority, although it was eventually given greater powers when the Atomic Energy Act was amended in 1954. The ACRS's mission was to prevent any loss of life related to the development of nuclear energy. Therefore, the committee exercised extreme caution with its reviews since a single accident in a proposed industrial nuclear reactor would destroy the potential for the future development of the peaceful use of nuclear power.

In reviewing each proposal for a reactor, the ACRS sought to answer two questions: What is the maximum potential accident? What are the consequences of such an accident?

One of the ACRS's most noteworthy proposals was its recommendation that the AEC establish, in a deserted location, an experimental facility for the study of nuclear reactor malfunction. In 1949, in response to these recommendations, the AEC established the National Reactor Testing Station.

Commercializing the Atom   If the U.S. government's strategy for nuclear development continued along its original 1940s path, the power of the atom would probably now be relegated to military applications. Postwar economic optimism and the enormous energy potential of atomic fission prompted the Eisenhower administration to alter U.S. atomic policy. On December 8, 1953, President Dwight Eisenhower gave his famous "Atoms for Peace" speech to the United Nations General Assembly. In this speech he proposed the establishment of the International Atomic Energy Agency, an organization within the United Nations, founded in 1957 and still in existence and operating some 50 years later, for the purpose of devising "methods whereby this fissionable material would be allocated to serve the peaceful pursuits of mankind. Experts would be mobilized to apply atomic energy to the needs of agriculture, medicine and other peaceful activities. A special purpose would be to provide abundant electrical energy in the power-starved areas of the world." (www.atomicinsights.com/FTROU/AtomsForPeace.pdf)

Less than a year after Eisenhower's speech, the U.S. Congress passed the 1954 Atomic Energy Act. This Act is one of the fundamental laws governing the peaceful uses of atomic energy and permitted the extensive use of atomic energy for commercial purposes. The Act ended the government's exclusive monopoly on atomic technical data and research and was the catalyst behind new efforts to support the growth of a private commercial nuclear industry. Specifically, the Act was passed "to encourage widespread participation in the development and utilization of atomic energy for peaceful purposes" and "promote world peace, improve the general welfare, increase the standard of living, and strengthen free competition in private enterprise." (See the Nuclear Regulatory Commission Web site, www.nrc.gov/.) The Act also assigned the AEC the responsibility to continue the nation's nuclear weapons program and protect the public's health and safety from the potential hazards of commercial nuclear power.

Less than a year after the 1954 Atomic Energy Act went into effect, Pittsburgh-based Duquesne Light Company was awarded a contract to design and construct the first commercial central station nuclear power plant in the United States at Shippingport, Pennsylvania. Construction of this facility began in September 1954 and Westinghouse, leveraging its experience from its previous U.S. naval nuclear projects, was the project contractor. The 60-megawatt pilot reactor, sponsored by the AEC, began commercial operations in 1957 and operated until 1982. This facility was quickly followed by the first full-scale commercial plant built in the United States, a 200-megawatt boiling water plant ordered in 1955 by Illinois's Commonwealth Edison. The reactor began operation in 1960 and operated until it was decommissioned in 1979. Table 5.1 outlines these and other projects of the 1950s.

Table 5.1 **Significant Reactor Safety Development Projects in the 1950s**

Reactor Type	Date	Description
Experimental Breeder 1	December 1951	First usable electricity from nuclear power.
Zero Power Reactor	June 1952	First reactor criticality accident.
MTR	March 1952	First reactor core and fuel test reactor.
Mark 1	March 1953	First reactor used in U.S. nuclear submarine, the *Nautilus*.
BORAX 1	July 1954	First destructive test of a reactor results in a partial core melt.
BORAX 2	Autumn 1954	Tests performance of boiling water power reactors.
BORAX 3	June 1955	Destructive tests continue. Reactor produces electricity for Arco, Idaho.
BORAX 4		Built for experience with operating power plant.
BORAX 5		Built for experience with operating power plant.
SPERT 1	June 1955	Built to follow up BORAX experiments.
SPERT 2		
SPERT 3		
Experimental Boiling Water	December 1956	Reactor achieves criticality.
Transient Reactor	February 1959	Criticality tests to simulate accidents on fuel/ components.

Lessons Learned from Early 1950s Nuclear Incidents   In the early 1950s, the experimental breeder reactor (EBR-I) was designed principally to study the "breeding" performance (the manufacture of more fissionable isotopes than are consumed) and behavior of reactors of this general type. It was also the first reactor to produce electric power.

One of the primary safety lessons learned from the EBR-I occurred in November 1955 when the unit suffered an accident that melted nearly 50 percent of its reactor core when automatic control systems did not function properly and a manual SCRAM was initiated after the reactor's power more than doubled. The reactor came within a second of exploding. However, this incident posed no real threat since the EBR-I core was very small, about 1/4 cubic foot, and the power level was small—specifically, 1.4 megawatts of heat output. (Source: Richard E. Webb, *The Accident Hazards of Nuclear Power Plants*, University of Massachusetts Press, 1976.)

It was later determined that the unit's control rods were prone to bowing and that the clamping of rods was required in subsequent designs to prevent this from occurring.

Another reactor, the zero power reactor (ZPR-I) at Argonne National Labs, a low-power experimental facility, suffered a "criticality" accident on June 2, 1952. An investigation later determined that the accident was the result of four procedural mistakes made by the project supervisor:

1. He was determined to complete an experiment even though he had not understood the behavior of the reactor immediately before the accident occurred.

2. Four persons violated the rule against entering the reactor chamber while there was water in the reactor. The reactor was safe when the water was absent, and was equipped with interlocks that prevented anyone from entering until no water remained with it. These interlocks were removed in a conscious violation of this necessary safeguard.

3. After the people entered the reactor chamber, they proceeded to change the configuration of the reactor.

4. The control rod was lifted out manually. (SOURCE: Robert Martin, "The History of Nuclear Power Safety," http://users.owt.com/ smsrpm/nksafe/)

These procedural failures reinforced the need for exact standards and practices to be implemented when working with nuclear reactors.

The two leading nuclear vendors of the day, General Electric and Westinghouse, benefited greatly from the safety lessons learned from these first nuclear reactors in the 1950s. By the end of this decade, the U.S. Navy had recruited Westinghouse into providing technical expertise and establishing a laboratory for developing a nuclear engine for navel vessel propulsion. This led to the development of the submarine thermal reactor in Idaho Falls, Idaho. The reactor, jointly developed by Westinghouse Electric and the Argonne National Laboratory, led to the deployment of the *U.S.S. Nautilus* in January 1954. The Nautilus, built for the U.S. government by the Electric Boat Company of Groton, Connecticut, became America's first nuclear-powered submarine capable of circumnavigating the earth while submerged. This dramatically increased the vessel's capacity to evade detection and enhanced the United States' security in the post–World War II world. General Electric was later awarded a government contract to develop similar nuclear technology at the Knolls Atomic Power Laboratory (KAPL) near Schenectady, New York.

Similar to the way that the Boeing Company—through its government sponsored WWII efforts—was responsible for the United States' dominance in the postwar field of aviation, Westinghouse and GE's work for the U.S. Navy led to their early dominance in the field of nuclear power development. In an effort to successfully commercialize their product and gain market share, both General Electric and Westinghouse aggressively offered electric utilities turnkey nuclear power plants at an investment loss during the 1950s and 1960s.

> *Westinghouse and GE's work for the U.S. Navy led to their early dominance in the field of nuclear power development.*

The 1960s: Standardization Is the Key to Safety

U.S. interest in nuclear power increased during the 1960s as the public and private sectors became increasingly aware of pollution resulting from coal- and oil-fired power plants. However, the AEC, the approval body for the new nuclear plants at the time, lacked a standardized approach to safety and permitting issues and evaluated each reactor proposal on a case-by-case basis. This process hindered development and had to be modified in order to facilitate the further commercial development of the U.S. nuclear power sector.

For example, in the late 1950s, the AEC received proposals for the construction of four nuclear power plants: Shippingport, Dresden 1, Indian Point 1, and Enrico Fermi. All of these proposed reactors were located within 25 miles of major metropolitan areas (Pittsburgh, Chicago, New York, and Detroit, respectively). To demonstrate the safety of these proposed facilities, the issuers of all licensing proposals had to present technical arguments for their specific design that:

- Recognized all possible accidents that could release unsafe amounts of radioactive materials.
- Included operation procedures reducing the probability of accidents to an acceptable minimum.
- Through the appropriate combination of containment and isolation, protected the public from the consequences of such an accident, should it occur.

This approach to plant safety turned out to be a rather tedious exercise as the applicant and the AEC both attempted to assess the degree of total designed safety using many parameters, some of which were extremely qualitative in nature. This created wordy, complicated, and confusing judgments that lacked consistency between various licensing proposal reviews.

In 1961, the AEC began to standardize the licensing process. The reactor siting issue was the first subject addressed with the new standardized guidelines. This new procedure created a baseline for what would be the required elements in a reactor site. These included the following:

- The probability of a major accident would be relatively small.
- An upper limit of fission product release could be estimated.
- Reactors were expected to be in inhabited areas.
- The containment building would hold any radiation.

Toward the end of the 1960s, the AEC's attention shifted from general reactor siting issues to containment integrity issues since the reactor's containment building was seen as the final independent line of defense against the release of radiation into the atmosphere. It was generally accepted by the AEC and others that this containment-building strategy would prevent the release of radiation during a severe accident and that the consequences of such an accident would only be felt within the immediate containment building area.

The AEC's safety focus continued to evolve as the 1960s progressed, and in 1967 a special task force was commissioned by the committee to look into the potential problem of core melting. The task force's findings showed that under certain severe accident conditions the integrity of the containment structure could be breached by a superheated liquefied reactor core. This finding forever changed the U.S. government's approach to nuclear power plant regulations, and regulatory focus began to shift from containment design to preventing accidents severe enough to threaten containment.

The 1970s: The Three Mile Island Decade

To many Americans, the nation's honeymoon with nuclear power ended on March 28, 1979, when the Three Mile Island (TMI) nuclear incident occurred. While the accident did not result in the loss of any lives, and relatively small amounts of radiation were released into the atmosphere, it did involve the total loss of the recently commissioned number two nuclear reactor at the facility, which had cost the utility billions of dollars to construct. Perhaps more importantly, the accident rattled the confidence of many individuals who previously had not questioned the safety of nuclear facilities.

While the focus was rightfully on the negative aspects of the Three Mile Island accident, there were positive takeaways. The facility's concrete containment structure did perform as designed, and the incident was the catalyst for considerable amounts of ongoing nuclear safety research from which the industry has benefited.

The TMI-2 reactor, a standard Babcock and Wilcox pressurized water reactor (PWR) design, consists of a reactor vessel, a pressurizer, four coolant pumps, and two once-through steam generators. The reactor's safety systems included control rods, high-pressure injection (from the emergency core cooling system), a borated water storage tank, and the building sump for recirculating the water supply.

The TMI incident occurred when a combination of mechanical failures and human errors deprived the plant's reactor core of essential coolant. This caused approximately half of the unit's fuel to become unstable and melt. The accident occurred when a pressure relief value associated with the unit's pressurizer became stuck in an open position and a large amount of reactor coolant was allowed to escape the closed system. The negative consequences of the reactor malfunction were then compounded when plant operators received conflicting data regarding the event and they subsequently failed to recognize the reactor's loss of coolant. Plant operators then mistakenly turned off the reactor's emergency cooling system that had automatically turned on as designed. By the time the operators recognized the actual nature of the accident, considerable reactor damage had already resulted.

Following is the approximate timeline for the first critical 15 hours of the TMI incident.

0:00:00	Pumps feeding water to the secondary loop shut down. Alarms sound.
0:00:01	The alarm is disregarded by plant operators; water pressure and temperature in reactor core rises.
0:00:02	The secondary loop pump fails, stopping the transfer of heat from the primary loop. The pressure relief valve (PORV) automatically opens.
0:00:03	Steam pressure in the reactor core rises above safe limits; backup pumps for secondary loop water system automatically turn on.
0:00:04	Operators are not aware that the pumps have been disconnected. Boron and silver control rods are lowered into the reactor; PORV light goes out, indicating valve is closed.
0:00:09	Reactor heat output lowered, PORV light goes out. The operators incorrectly assume that the valve is closed, but it is open and releasing steam and water from the core. Emergency water injection is initiated.
0:02:00	Operators observe that the water level in the primary system is rising while the pressure is decreasing.
0:04:30	Operators incorrectly interpret the rising water level in the core and shut off the EIW system, creating additional steam and pressure in core.
0:08:00	Secondary water-cooling loop pumps are turned on.
0:45:00	Primary loop pumps start to shake violently.
1:20:00	Cooling loop pumps are shut down.
2:15:00	Reactor core is exposed; the steam is converted to super-heated steam. This reacts with the control rods and

produces hydrogen and radioactive gases, which are vented through a value.

2:20:00　Reactor personnel on next shift shut valve venting gas.

2:20:30　Radiation alarm sounds and a site emergency is declared.

2:45:00　The core is uncovered and the radiation level of the water in the primary loop is 350 times its normal level.

3:00:00　Confusion is present as to whether the core is uncovered or not.

7:30:00　Operators pump water into the primary loop and open the backup valve to lower the pressure; hydrogen within the containment structure explodes.

9:00:00　Explosion is dismissed as just being a spike caused by an electrical malfunction.

15:00:00　A large portion of the core has melted; hydrogen is present in the primary loop. Water from the primary loop pumps is circulated and the core temperature is finally brought under control.

While bringing the malfunctioning reactor core back under control ended the TMI incident, it was just the start of the investigation to follow. Both utilities involved, Metropolitan Edison and General Public Utilities, had a considerable number of questions to answer to public officials, state and federal regulators, and the general public. Actions such as better training were immediately implemented by the nuclear industry to reduce the likelihood of further accidents in reactors of the same and different designs, and a wide range of government investigations, including the President's commission on the accident (also called the Kemeny Commission), commenced.

The Kemeny Commission's final report was made public just seven months after the accident on October 31, 1979. The report's findings chastised the reactor operators, the utility, the nuclear industry, and especially the Nuclear Regulatory Commission. Their recommendations called for broad changes in the operation and regulation of U.S. nuclear reactors. The committee's report included the following observations and recommendations:

- The NRC had a number of inadequacies and should be restructured to concentrate the agency's responsibilities more on reactor safety.

- The utility must dramatically change its attitudes toward safety and regulations and set and police its own standards to ensure the effective management and safe operation of nuclear power plants.
- Training of operating personnel requires the establishment of accredited training institutions with utility and NRC responsibility for adequate reactor-specific training.
- Utilities must improve the person-machine interface with the assistance of greater numbers of computers.
- Utilities must conduct advance planning for emergency radiation response.
- With regard to emergency planning and response, utilities must detail the actions public officials should take in the event of a release of radioactivity.
- Federal and state agencies, as well as the utilities, should make adequate preparations for a public information program so that during radiation-related emergencies timely, understandable, and accurate information can be provided to media outlets and the public.

Following the thorough investigation, it became apparent that the accident at the TMI number 2 reactor didn't have to happen. A very similar accident occurred at a sister plant 18 months earlier while operating at very low power. Following an investigation of the first accident, safety engineers for Babcock and Wilcox realized that improper operator response could cause a serious accident.

Following the thorough investigation, it became apparent that the accident at the TMI number 2 reactor didn't have to happen.

The TMI-2 accident was caused by human error as plant operators incorrectly interpreted plant data presented in the reactor control room. A detailed analysis of the incident showed that the reactor performed as designed and expected. Even with a substantial amount of core meltdown, the reactor's containment vessel was not breached and the amount of radioactivity released into the environment was minimal. As a result of the incident at TMI, human error would become the new focus for the industry with regard to safety during the 1980s.

The 1980s: The Call for Additional Reactor Design Refinement

The Three Mile Island accident was a wake-up call for many. The incident prompted the NRC to reexamine the adequacy of existing safety protocols and to impose new regulations to correct deficiencies. The regulations defined new requirements for operator training, testing, and licensing, and for shift scheduling and overtime. The NRC also began to emphasize the importance of the human element in operating these facilities, due to the fact that in several instances Three Mile Island personnel either ignored their training or misinterpreted or dismissed critical reactor monitoring equipment, which greatly magnified the gravity of the situation. To correct perceived deficiencies, the NRC recommended the increased use of reactor simulators and safety drills, along with assessments and upgrades of existing reactor control rooms and instrumentation, which were found to be suboptimal in many instances. While these hard-won lessons were being implemented in the United States, mismanagement would result in a much more serious nuclear reactor accident in the then Soviet Union.

In April 1986, a severe accident at the Chernobyl nuclear reactor in the former Soviet Union was caused by a mismanaged electrical engineering experiment. In conducting this experiment, the reactor staff bypassed multiple layers of safety protocols. It was subsequently determined that an unfavorable safety culture in which operating protocols were circumvented to meet politically motivated objectives was the primary cause of the accident and that a number of design factors contributed to the extensiveness of the fallout. Western-styled light water reactors are thermal reactors that use ordinary water instead of heavy water as a neutron moderator and coolant and are fueled by low-concentration enriched uranium, about 3 percent U-235. By contrast, Chernobyl's RBMK (an acronym for the Russian Reaktor Bolshoy Moshchnosti Kanalniy, which means "reactor of high power of the channel type") reactor design contained several recognized design flaws. These units:

- Are unstable under loss-of-coolant conditions.
- Can be unstable at elevated temperatures.
- Lack sufficient containment.

The Incident   On April 28, 1986, prior to a routine maintenance shutdown, the reactor staff at the Chernobyl-4 reactor was directed to perform a test to determine how long the unit's turbines would generate critically needed power following the loss of the unit's main electrical power supply. Similar tests were previously done at Chernobyl and at other nuclear facilities with similar design, despite the fact that this type of reactor is known to be unstable at low power settings.

As part of this test, Chernobyl plant operators deliberately disabled the unit's automatic shutdown mechanisms, and as the flow of coolant diminished, the reactor's power output increased. When operators attempted to halt the fission reaction and shut down the reactor from this unstable condition, a dramatic power spike resulted. This power spike prompted the reactor's fuel elements to rupture, and the resultant explosive force of released steam lifted off the reactor's cover plate, sending radioactive particles into the atmosphere. A second explosion soon followed and radioactive fragments of fuel and graphite from the reactor's core were released into the atmosphere. Furthermore, as air rushed into the core, the reactor's graphite moderator, the unit that controls the fission reaction by absorbing available neutrons burst into flames.

It has been estimated that all of the xenon gas (a neutron absorber that controls the reactor's fission reaction), about half of the radioactive iodine and cesium, and at least 5 percent of the remaining radioactive material in the Chernobyl-4 reactor core was released in the accident. The heavier particles of the material released landed close to the facility as dust and debris, but the lighter material entered the atmosphere and was carried by wind over the rest of the Ukraine, Belarus, Russia, and to some extent over Scandinavia and Europe, where it was found in high enough concentrations to be picked up by environmental monitoring stations.

Health Effects   First responders to the scene, primarily firefighters who extinguished small fires on the roof of the turbine building, received doses of radiation ranging up to 20,000 millisieverts (mSv). This group had an exceptionally high mortality rate, experiencing 28 deaths in the following four months and 19 additional deaths subsequently (source: Uranium Information Centre, http://www.uic.com.au/). Their mortality rate was exceptionally high due to the fact that authorities failed to immediately disclose to these individuals the hazardous conditions present. This failure to disclose negative news was a chronic problem of the former Soviet regime and drew them much criticism in the past.

The Soviet Union's subsequent efforts dealt with cleaning up the radioactivity at the site so that the remaining three Chernobyl reactors could be brought back in service, and that the damaged and now radioactive reactor could be more permanently encased in concrete. About 200,000 people, given the tag *liquidators*, were shipped in from all over the Soviet Union and were involved in the recovery and cleanup efforts during the remainder of 1986 and into 1987. These individuals were given no formal training or safety equipment other than leather aprons, and in many cases they moved shovels of highly radioactive material while standing directly on the exposed reactor core. These poorly informed individuals received high doses of radiation, averaging around 100 mSv. Some 20,000, or 10 percent of the liquidators, received about 250 mSv and a few received 500 mSv. The number of on-site liquidators eventually swelled to over 600,000, but most of these later arrivals received relatively low doses of radiation. The highest doses of radiation were received by about 1,000 emergency workers and on-site personnel on the first day of the accident.

Initial radiation exposure in contaminated areas around Chernobyl was due to iodine-131, which has a relatively short half-life; later the radioactive isotope caesium-137 was the main hazard. (Iodine-131 and caesium-137 have half-lives of 8 days and 30 years, respectively.) About 5 million Russians lived in areas contaminated by this fallout, and about 400,000 lived in more contaminated areas placed under strict control by authorities.

On May 2 and 3, 1986, some five days after the accident, 45,000 residents living within a 10-kilometer radius of the plant were finally evacuated to a safer location. The following day those living within a 30-kilometer radius were evacuated, and an additional 116,000 people from the more contaminated areas were evacuated and later relocated. Of these, about 1,000 have since returned without government approval to live within the contaminated zone, which has essentially become a ghost town. Most of the individuals evacuated received some radiation, but generally in doses of less than 50 mSv.

Subsequent studies conducted in the Ukraine, Russia, and Belarus put the number of people affected by the Chernobyl incident at over 1 million. By the year 2000 about 4,000 cases of thyroid cancer had been diagnosed in exposed children and among these nine deaths have been attributed to the released radiation. The exact numbers, however, of people who died because of the Chernobyl nuclear reactor explosion remains highly in dispute. The World Health Organization estimated up to 9,000 people died or will die of cancer because of the incident. Greenpeace International, which opposes nuclear power, in its own report estimated the death toll between 93,000 and 200,000, including cancer deaths and other illnesses like immunity disorders.

Safety Improvements   In the early 1990s some $400 million (U.S.) was spent on safety improvements to the remaining three reactors at Chernobyl, which continued to operate for a number of years due to severe energy shortages within the former Soviet Union. Chernobyl's unit number 3 operated until December 2000. Officials decided to shut down unit number 2 after it experienced a turbine fire in 1991, and unit 1 ceased operations at the end of 1997. Today, Chernobyl unit 4 is enclosed in a large, leaky concrete structure quickly erected to allow continuing operation of the remaining reactor at the facility. This concrete structure has some integrity problems and is not considered to be strong or durable enough to safely contain the radiation. Efforts are currently being made to reinforce this containment vessel, and there are additional plans for its reconstruction.

Since the Chernobyl accident, safety procedures at all Soviet-designed reactors have been significantly upgraded. This is due largely to the removal of operations from Communist party politics and agendas; the development of a safety-minded culture, which has been encouraged through increased interaction with Western nuclear power officials; and a significant investment in improving reactor quality. Modifications have been made to overcome deficiencies of Soviet RBMK reactors still operating. These deficiencies included the reactor's tendency to increase power output if cooling water were lost or turned to steam. This operating characteristic contrasts greatly with most Western reactor designs and resulted in the power surge that lead to the Chernobyl debacle.

Since the Chernobyl accident, safety procedures at all Soviet-designed reactors have been significantly upgraded.

Over the past decade, modifications have been made to all RBMK reactors still operating in the former Soviet Union. These modifications have included changes to the reactor's control rods. Additional neutron absorbers have been added to these rods and the reactor's fuel has been enriched from 1.8 to 2.4 percent U-235. Both of these modifications make the RBMK much more stable when operating at low power. In addition, the unit's automatic shutdown mechanisms are now tripped at a much faster rate, and other safety mechanisms and inspection equipment have been upgraded to ensure proper operation.

Greater former Soviet Republic reactor operating safety has also been achieved through a free exchange of ideas with the West, something that did not happen before the fall of the Soviet Union. Since 1989 over 1,000 nuclear engineers from the former Soviet Union have visited Western nuclear power plants, and Western engineers have made reciprocal visits to former Soviet reactors. This has resulted in over 50 "twinning arrangements" between East and West nuclear plants, enacted under the auspices of the World Association of Nuclear Operators, a body formed in 1989 to link more than 130 nuclear power operators in more than 30 countries.

The political fallout from the Chernobyl incident clearly put pressure on the global nuclear industry to further scrutinize its safety procedures and the mechanisms in place to prevent severe accidents. In response, governments and the private sector sponsored research into new and safer advanced reactor designs, safety systems, and refined regulation, activities that were first set in motion by the Three Mile Island incident just seven years earlier.

All of these efforts raised the universal safety standards of the global nuclear industry. A critical part of these new safety standards was the creation of a global regulatory body, the International Nuclear Safety Program (INSP), which offers reactor training to countries with developing commercial nuclear sectors.

Both Three Mile Island and Chernobyl demonstrated the potential for severe reactor accidents to occur. In the case of Three Mile Island, the effect of such an accident was greatly minimized due to the presence of effective containment systems, something that was lacking at Chernobyl. In fact, a post-accident analysis of the Chernobyl facility and the accident have led many to speculate that had there had been a U.S.-style containment infrastructure in place around the RBMK reactor, no radioactivity would have been released and there would not have been any injuries or deaths.

The 1990s and the New Millennium

The last decade of the twentieth century saw the rise of numerous INSP programs designed to ensure global safety and reliability of the commercial nuclear sector and to ensure that nuclear fuel remains within the hands of authorized organizations. Currently, the U.S. Department of Energy participates in cooperative efforts to continue safety improvements at Soviet-designed nuclear power plants, plants with designs similar to Chernobyl, and has initiatives with eight partnering countries—Russia, Ukraine, Armenia, Bulgaria, the Czech Republic, Hungary, Lithuania, and Slovakia—to correct major safety deficiencies and to establish self-sustaining nuclear safety infrastructures and regulatory agencies within these nations.

These joint safety enhancement efforts originated from U.S. commitments made during the G-7 Summit held in Munich, Germany, in July 1992. At this conference the leaders from the world's seven largest industrialized nations agreed to collaborate with host countries to reduce safety risks associated with older Soviet-designed reactors, many of which have checkered operating histories. Over the past 14 years, U.S.–backed reactor safety initiatives have expanded to include activities at 20 nuclear power plants that contain a total of 64 operating reactors. This work is being conducted in cooperation with similar initiatives put forth by Western European countries, Canada, and Japan, as well as the Nuclear Energy Agency, International Atomic Energy Agency, and the European Bank for Reconstruction and Development. All of these organizations are looking to:

- Reduce the likelihood of a nuclear accident in the new republics of Russia, Ukraine, and Eurasia, which tend to have less well-defined regulatory and safety guidelines and procedures.
- Promote a stable business climate for international nuclear investments in these countries.
- Provide greater protection for nearby population centers in Europe, which would be vulnerable to any releases of radioactive material.

New Passive versus Redundant Safety Designs

Even though the United States has not built a new reactor for decades, reactor technology has continued to evolve. Both U.S. and international reactor designers and manufacturers strived to produced newer reactor designs in the 1990s that feature greater operating reliability and will have lower costs of operation when they are expected to come online around the year 2015.

While safety has always been a primary concern with reactor development, the latest generation of nuclear reactor designs faces an even greater safety challenge in the post-9/11 world. With several U.S. utilities desiring to build and operate new nuclear reactors within the decade, reactor development, certification, and ultimate selection are all critical issues.

Safety perceptions are the primary hurdle affecting the acceptance of nuclear power, and manufacturers have taken two distinctly different paths to solve the safety problem. One approach, used by Westinghouse and GE, centers on passive safety system technology, which relies on gravity instead of a series of pumps and values that could malfunction. Another approach, championed by the firm Areva, relies on multiple redundant safety systems.

Westinghouse AP600 and AP1000 Reactors   Westinghouse and its licensees have approximately 50 percent of the world's largest installed base of operating nuclear plants. The company has continuously sought to improve their reactors over the past 50 years of commercial operations and in response to growing safety concerns has introduced new passive safety systems in its AP600 and more powerful AP1000 reactor lines.

The Westinghouse AP600 and the larger 1,117 to 1,154 megawatt AP1000 reactors utilize modular construction and a primarily passive safety system to ensure reliable, low-cost construction and a high degree of operational safety.

The Westinghouse AP600 and the larger 1,117 to 1,154 megawatt AP1000 reactors utilize modular construction and a primarily passive safety system to ensure reliable, low-cost construction and a high degree of operational safety. According to Westinghouse, compared with reactors currently in service, its new generation of reactors is expected to have a passive design containing:

- 50 percent fewer valves.
- 80 percent less safety-grade piping.
- 35 percent fewer pumps.
- 70 to 80 percent less control cable.

These efficiencies, including its modular design, are expected to reduce construction time to three years or less. In these new Westinghouse units, passive safety features dominate both the emergency core cooling system and the containment cooling system. These systems use only natural forces, such as gravity, natural circulation, and compressed gas, instead of relying on pumps, fans, diesel engines, chillers, or other rotating machinery in safety subsystems. These passive safety systems are significantly simpler than traditional PRW safety systems since they do not require a network of safety support systems, such as AC power, HVAC, water-cooling water systems, and seismic-rated buildings to house these various components.

Westinghouse's AP600 reactor was certified for operation by the NRC on December 16, 1999, and on February 27, 2006, NRC certification for the company's AP1000 went into effect, clearing the way for its eventual U.S. operation.

General Electric Economic Simplified Boiling Water Reactor
General Electric's economic simplified boiling water reactor (ESBWR) is a new, next-generation reactor design that attempts to combine improvements in safety with a simplified design and standardized components to produce a new nuclear power plant at a lower projected construction cost than other plants currently in operation. The ESBWR program had its origins in the early 1990s, when GE was developing its simplified boiling water reactor (SBWR). The ESBWR incorporates numerous passive safety features developed for the SBWR. Its design also takes into account the lessons learned by the firm in constructing and operating its advanced boiling water reactor (ABWR), a reactor with four units operating in Japan and another three units under construction in Taiwan and Japan. The key attributes of the ESBWR program are listed in Table 5.2; a cutaway diagram of the reactor is shown in Figure 5.2.

The ESBWR plant design relies on natural, gravity-based circulation and passive safety features to enhance plant performance and simplify its design. The simplified design of this new reactor is achieved through a significant reduction in its number of systems and components. General Electric's ESBWR design is rather innovative since it combines the shutdown cooling and reactor water cleanup systems, eliminating the need for 11 systems and reducing the number of required systems by 25 percent.

Table 5.2   **Key Attributes of the ESBWR Program**

Key Attribute	Elements of Attribute	Example Design Feature
Simplification	Reduced systems and structures	Passive safety systems
	Simpler operation	Natural circulation, elimination of recirculation pumps
		Passive isolation condensers
Standardized design	Standardized construction design	Seismic design envelops all site conditions
		Standardized components
Operational flexibility	Increased operating margins	Larger vessel with larger mass of water and steam
		No regions of thermal hydraulic instability
Improved economics	Low plant cost	Reduced materials and buildings
	Low development cost	Legacy features used
	Reduced licensing costs	Reduced and simpler systems
	Reduced O&M costs	Reduced construction time

SOURCE: Hines and Maslak, *Nuclear News,* January 2006.

Simply put, GE believes that in this design with fewer moving parts, there is less opportunity for something to go wrong.

The unit's passive safety systems are also expected to further enhance plant safety. In the ESBWR, the gravity-driven cooling system is designed to respond to all reactor loss–of–coolant situations. Should the reactor experience a coolant loss, additional water will flow into the reactor vessel, utilizing ever-present gravity instead of relying on pumps, which have the potential to fail. This natural, gravity-based circulation eliminates the need for electric grid AC-powered safety systems and on-site emergency electrical backup systems. With the use of natural circulation and passive safety features, safety diesel generators are no longer required to be on site.

Similarly, the reactor's passive containment cooling system also relies

Figure 5.2 Economic Simplified Boiling Water Reactor (ESBWR) Cutaway
SOURCE: GE Energy.

on natural features such as convection and conduction. The cooling system contains six safety-related passive, low-pressure loops. The water contained within them is available for 72 hours with no operator actions required following an accident, since the hard-piped connections present permit refill of water from on-site or off-site resources. The natural circulation used in the reactor is achieved through an increase in vessel height and a decrease in active fuel height.

To further reduce any potential security risk, many of the ESBWR's critical systems are also located below ground level. These subterranean systems include the unit's control room, spent-fuel pool, radioactive waste collection, and sample tanks. These various facilities can only be accessed by approved personnel via a series of secure tunnels and are thought to be secure even from an attack by a commercial airliner. The facility's simplified footprint also results in fewer buildings to patrol, further reducing the overall security risk.

Cost   The ESBWR's passive systems and standardized construction de-sign reduces both the unit's construction and operating costs. The facility, with fewer required manufactured components and reduced building size, requires less time for construction. At the same time, the ESBWR design is expected to improve operational reliability and reduce operational costs. The unit's fewer active components are also expected to reduce op-erator exposure to low-level radioactive waste because fewer maintenance functions will be required to safely operate the plant.

Status   General Electric's ESBWR was officially docketed by the Nu-clear Regulatory Commission on December 1, 2005, for design certifica-tion review. General Electric estimates completion of a preliminary safety evaluation report (SER) by 2007, and final design approval is expected about 15 months later in December 2008. Formal reactor design certifica-tion is typically granted 12 months after that time, which would be De-cember 2009. Should these approval dates be met, the ESBWR reactor is expected to be constructed and operational by 2014 or 2015.

General Electric's ESBWR Marketing Efforts   General Electric is partici-pating in the Department of Energy's Nuclear Power 2010 program along with NuStart Energy (a limited liability company formed in 2004 with nine member companies plus the Tennessee Valley Authority and two reactor vendors) and Dominion Resources, both of which have selected ESBWR technology for future implementation. This program was established by the DOE to act as a catalyst for new-build nuclear energy in the United States, thereby helping the United States meet long-term demand for electrical power generation. A number of utilities will be preparing ESBWR com-bined operating and licensing applications (COL) for submittal in 2007 and 2008. Once approved, a COL allows a utility to commence construc-tion, followed by plant start-up and commercial operation.

Areva   Newly designed passive safety systems are not the only approach proposed to successfully meet regulators' and the public's demand for even greater levels of reactor safety. Another firm, Areva, is championing an-other approach: multiple redundant safety systems.

Areva was created in 2001 through a merger of CEA-Industrie, Co-gema, Framatome-ANP, and FCI. The company is owned by the French government. The firm's 1,500 to 1,600 megawatt European pressurized water reactor (EPR) is being jointly developed between Siemens and Framatome-ANP.

Competing with passive reactor offerings, Areva's reactor relies on four separate, individually operating, and redundant traditional safety systems in an attempt to create an in-depth defense against any possible safety system mishap.

The U.S. EPR reactor design is relatively simple, using 47 percent fewer valves, 16 percent fewer pumps, and 50 percent fewer tanks as compared to a typical plant (four-loop reactor system) of comparable power output. It is designed to be 10 percent less costly to operate than most modern nuclear power plants and more than 20 percent less costly than the largest high-efficiency advanced combined-cycle gas plants currently under development.

The U.S. EPR is designed to use 17 percent less uranium per kilowatt-hour than current light water reactors. It can accommodate recycled fuel, and it features a flexible operating cycle—from 12 to 24 months. In addition, as a result of the reactor's design, many maintenance and inspection tasks can be completed while the U.S. EPR is operating.

Enhanced Safety   The U.S. EPR reactor, shown in the schematic in Figure 5.3, includes the following elements:

- It features four separate, redundant safety systems, each capable of performing the entire safety function for the reactor independently.
- It has a containment building that incorporates two cylindrical walls with separate domes—an inner wall that is four feet thick, made of prestressed concrete with a steel liner, and an outer wall of reinforced concrete more than four feet thick. The outer wall can withstand postulated external hazards.
- It is designed to withstand severe earthquakes. The base is composed of reinforced concrete; building height is minimized; and the heaviest components are located as low as possible.

U.S. Marketing Efforts   On September 15, 2005, Constellation Energy and Areva Inc. announced the formation of UniStar Nuclear, a joint enterprise to provide a business framework for the development and deployment of a fleet of advanced nuclear power plants in America. The new firm intends to offer a one-stop approach to design, build, license,

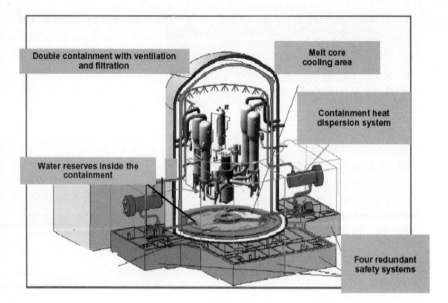

Double containment with ventilation and filtration

Melt core cooling area

Containment heat dispersion system

Water reserves inside the containment

Four redundant safety systems

Figure 5.3   **U.S. European Pressurized Water Reactor**
SOURCE: Areva.

and operate a fleet of nuclear power plants. UniStar Nuclear will market the U.S. EPR. Areva, as prime contractor to any potential new nuclear project under the UniStar model, will provide the nuclear reactor and all support, instrumentation, and control systems, as well as the initial load of nuclear fuel.

The Goal of Reactor Operational Safety

Ultimately, the goal of reactor safety is to reduce the likelihood of an adverse or threatening situation caused by the inadequate or faulty operation of a nuclear power plant. For reactors to operate safely the following four conditions must be met:

1. There must be no release of radioactive material in dangerous quantities from a nuclear facility to the general public.
2. Every reasonable effort should be made to eliminate accidents involving plant employees. The frequency of such events should be reduced

to the lowest possible level, certainly lower than that of other comparable industries.

3. The likelihood of a serious accident that would result in severe damage to the nuclear facility should be kept as small as possible.

4. System malfunctions and deviations from normal behavior should be reduced to a minimum.

Historically, governments have been primarily concerned with public and personnel safety; hence, nuclear safety research sponsored by government agencies is likely to address these issues. Operating groups—utilities and vendors—support a broad sponsorship in all four areas. While the two design approaches to safety (passive and redundant) are innovative and different, the question remains which will gain favor with utilities and firms looking to construct nuclear power facilities in the United States.

Historically, governments have been primarily concerned with public and personnel safety.

For the industry to survive and grow, nuclear advocates must dedicate themselves to restoring the public's faith in the industry's safety record. While the implementation of new technologies is expected to result in operational gains and efficiencies, none of these would be possible without the significant role played by reactor safety systems.

Safety in Response to Geopolitical Events

The U.S. Government Accountability Office (GAO) says that five years after 9/11, nuclear facilities have beefed up their security, but that these measures would fall short of protecting against an all-out attack. Others in the public and private sector disagree with this statement. Whether you agree or disagree with the current state of the nuclear industry's degree of preparedness from external threats, the following facts are known.

The industry has thus far spent approximately $1.25 billion on security since the September 11 attacks and has increased the number of ground security personnel from 5,000 to 8,000, as well as implementing other measures such as the installation of concrete security barriers. Critics, however, complain that it is not enough to insulate nuclear plants from attacks similar to the ones perpetrated on the World Trade Towers and the Pentagon.

The nuclear safety stakes are extremely high, with more than half of the nation's 103 nuclear reactors located near population centers, including two near Washington, D.C., and two close to New York City.

The nuclear safety stakes are extremely high, with more than half of the nation's 103 nuclear reactors located near population centers, including two near Washington, D.C., and two close to New York City. All of these facilities are required to possess security in depth, including integrated alarms and sensors, physical barriers, special nuclear material detectors, and metal detectors. These facilities also have armed security forces equipped with automatic weapons, night vision equipment, body armor, and chemical protective gear.

While threats to nuclear facilities may be real, damaging such a facility is not an easy task. Operators could quickly shut down and secure a nuclear reactor in the wake of a conventional ground attack. When considering a possible air attack similar to what occurred on September 11, one must remember that nuclear reactors are rather small targets. To have a chance of hitting such as structure, a plane would have to cut its speed. Recalling high school physics, specifically Newton's second law of motion, the force of an object is equal to its mass multiplied by its acceleration ($F = MA$). By cutting its speed, an airliner would have less force when it hit a nuclear facility, and the strength of a reactor's containment building, according to many experts, could withstand that kind of strike.

NRC Safety Operations in a Post-9/11 World

Since its founding in 1974, the Nuclear Regulatory Commission has had the responsibility for ensuring the peaceful use of nuclear energy and that nuclear power makes the maximum contribution to the security of the United States.

NRC responsibilities include:

- Granting nuclear licensees.
- Implementing accounting and auditing systems for nuclear materials.
- Implementing security programs and contingency plans for dealing with threats, thefts, and sabotage of nuclear material, high-level radioactive wastes, nuclear facilities, and other radioactive materials and activities that the NRC regulates.

The NRC has enacted a "domestic safeguards program" to ensure that special nuclear material within the United States is not stolen or diverted from civilian facilities. This safeguard programs has many features, including those outlined in the following sections.

Protection of Nuclear Facilities

Nuclear facilities require physical protection. These assets include nuclear reactors, fuel cycle facilities, and spent-fuel storage and disposal facilities. The vast majority of these assets are not centrally located but, rather, dispersed across the nation. Key features of NRC physical protection programs for these facilities include:

- The creation of a defense in depth using graded physical protection areas.
- The utilization of intrusion detection equipment.
- Plans created for intrusion response.
- Obtaining off-site assistance from local, state, and federal agencies.

When the NRC grants a nuclear license, the licensee must take a graded approach to physical protection of the assets through the use of specifically defined areas with increasing levels of security. These four areas are:

1. An exclusion zone.
2. Protected areas.
3. Vital areas.
4. Material access areas.

In the *exclusion* area the licensee has the authority to determine all activities including the exclusion or removal of personnel and property from the area. Fences and guard posts to limit access to an exclusion area are not required so long as the licensee has control over the area. The area may be traversed by a highway, railroad, or waterway, provided the utility is able to control traffic on these arteries should an emergency be declared.

A *protected* area under NRC regulations is located within the exclusion area and encompassed by physical barriers, such as multiple chain-link fences. Access to this protected area is controlled at designated gate entryways. All attempts to gain access to the facility through the barrier are detected by the constantly monitored perimeter intrusion detection system, and authorization for any unescorted access within the protected area is based on criminal history and other background checks.

Vital areas located within protected areas are required to have additional barriers and alarms to protect critical equipment. Additional authorization is required for all unescorted access to these areas. This authorization is granted by an authorized entry card that is inserted into a card reader or presented to a security guard outside controlled doors.

Material access areas are similar to vital areas, but these areas control all access to types of nuclear material that must be protected from theft. All physical protection protocols for these areas are similar to those of the vital areas but require two additional conditions:

1. No single person can be alone in a nuclear material access area. A minimum of two persons is required (two-person rule).
2. In addition to standard card-reader or security guard–controlled doors, volumetric intrusion detection systems must be employed when the area is not occupied.

Following the September 11 terrorist attacks, the NRC immediately advised all U.S. nuclear facilities to go to the highest level of security available at the time. Since then, additional security measures have been implemented to further strengthen security at all NRC-licensed facilities. These facilities include power reactors, decommissioning reactors, independent spent-fuel storage installations, research and test reactors, uranium conversion facilities, gaseous diffusion plants, fuel fabrication facilities, certain users of radioactive materials, and transporters of spent fuel and radioactive materials.

To further upgrade security at power reactors and fuel fabrication facilities possessing significant quantities of nuclear material, in April 2003 the NRC required facility owners to revise their physical security and contingency plans. After NRC review, these plans were implemented by October 2004.

Security Exercises

The NRC temporarily suspended commando-style mock attacks on nuclear facilities immediately following the terrorist attacks of September 2001 due to concerns over their psychological impact on personnel and the public during a heightened threat environment. However, in February 2003, the NRC resumed these security exercises as part of a pilot project to evaluate threat characteristics and promote security enhancements. In 2004 these exercises were expanded in order for the NRC to evaluate each plant site once every three years instead of every eight years, the standard used prior to the September 11 attacks.

Security Personnel

In efforts to further strengthen security at U.S. commercial reactors, the NRC issued orders on April 29, 2003, to reactor owners to enhance training and qualifications requirements for security personnel protecting these assets. These orders included more frequent weapons practice, more realistic training under a varying number of conditions, and firing against moving as well as fixed targets. In addition, the NRC also issued orders to ensure security personnel fitness for duty and that the number of hours worked does not compromise personnel's effectiveness in performing their duties.

Comprehensive Security Evaluation and Vulnerability Studies

Shortly after September 11, 2001, the NRC undertook a comprehensive reevaluation of the agency's safeguards and security program, regulations, and procedures, which resulted in numerous security improvements and ultimately led the agency to revise its adversary attributes in the design basis threats (DBTs) for radiological sabotage and theft of nuclear material.

The DBT identifies theoretical adversary force composition and characteristics against which the nuclear facility must be able to defend. The DBT applies to both nuclear power plants and certain nuclear fuel fabrication facilities.

Aircraft Attacks   Following the deadly World Trade Center and Pentagon attacks in September 2001, the NRC conducted an extensive analysis of the potential threat to nuclear facilities from aircraft attacks. While much of this analysis has been labeled as classified information, the NRC study reportedly confirmed that the likelihood of such a scenario damaging the reactor core and releasing radioactivity into the atmosphere is low. Furthermore, NRC studies confirmed that even in the unlikely event of a radiological release due to terrorist use of commercial aircraft, there would be time to take actions for protecting the public since nuclear reactors are not designed to spontaneously explode. Also, it is very unlikely that there would be a significant release of radiation from a deliberate attack of a large commercial aircraft on a spent-fuel pool at a reactor site.

> *While much of this analysis has been labeled as classified information, the NRC study reportedly confirmed that the likelihood of such a scenario damaging the reactor core and releasing radioactivity into the atmosphere is low.*

Cyber Security   The NRC also has taken steps to enhance cyber security at nuclear power plants. Since September 11, 2001, the NRC has issued a series of safeguard advisories and orders requiring nuclear power plant licensees to address the issue of cyber security in order to prevent any unauthorized remote access of systems. Additional measures to enhance cyber security are being considered as part of the comprehensive review of the NRC's security program.

Security Against Dirty Bombs   A radiological dispersal device (RDD) or "dirty bomb" is a conventional explosive, such as dynamite, accompanied by radioactive material. When such a device is detonated, the radioactive material would be spread to the surrounding area. Although these devices would be unlikely to cause serious health effects beyond those caused by the detonation of the explosive, they are designed to have a significant psychological impact on the public by causing fear, panic, and disruption.

The NRC has been working with the U.S. Department of Energy (DOE), the Federal Bureau of Investigation (FBI), the International Atomic Energy Agency (IAEA) and others to enhance physical protection and control of sources of radioactive material that present the highest risk if used by a terrorist in an RDD. In June 2003 this coalition formed a Materials Security Working Group and a related steering committee to work with the States to enhance security for high-risk sources.

Coordination and Communications   The NRC has expanded its involvement with the FBI; other federal intelligence and law enforcement agencies; NRC licensees; and military, state, and local authorities to better protect the public. Communications have also been expanded with the Department of Homeland Security (DHS), the Department of Defense, the Federal Aviation Administration, and others. The NRC also maintains close communications with nuclear regulators in Canada and Mexico, and has discussed security enhancements with nuclear regulatory bodies in other countries, including the United Kingdom, France, Germany, Japan, and Romania.

In February 2003, the NRC established a protected server system to facilitate the exchange of sensitive information between the NRC, licensees, and authorized state officials.

NRC Emergency Operations Center and Emergency Plans

The NRC has increased staffing of its 24-hour Emergency Operations Center to assist in the prompt dissemination of pertinent information to all concerned parties. In 2004, the NRC completed a major overhaul of the communications and computer systems in the Operations Center headquarters. The new design is expected to enhance communications, provide greater access to information, and assist in the coordination of teams with response duties during emergencies.

Other Security Actions

To consolidate security, safeguards, and responsibilities in the event of an incident, the NRC established an Office of Nuclear Security and Incident Response in April 2002. This office serves to streamline decision making, improve information dissemination, and provide a more visible point of contact and effective counterpart to the DHS as well as other federal agencies. In June 2003 the agency established the position of Deputy Executive Director for Homeland Protection and Preparedness in order to increase the agency's attention to crosscutting issues that affect security, incident response, emergency preparedness, vulnerability assessments and mitigation strategies, and external integration of comprehensive strategies for these areas.

Protection of Nuclear Material in Transit

The transportation of spent nuclear fuel requires physical protection to ensure the safe arrival of the material as well as the public's safety. Procedures for the physical protection of these assets includes:

- Use of NRC-certified, structurally rugged, shipment overpacks and canisters.
- Advance planning and coordination with local law enforcement along routes.
- Protection of information about schedules.
- Regular communication between transports and control centers.
- Armed escorts within heavily populated areas.
- Vehicle immobility measures to protect against movement of a hijacked shipment before response forces arrive.

Threat Assessment

In order to determine how much physical protection is enough to protect nuclear material, the NRC monitors intelligence sources to keep abreast of foreign and domestic events and remains aware of the capabilities of potential adversaries.

Conclusion

Nuclear safety is extremely important. The consequences of a reactor failure, whether a result of mechanical problems or human error, can be catastrophic. Over the past 65 years there has been a constant effort to improve reactor safety operations and the systems that operate these very complex machines. These advances will help ensure that reactor accidents such as those at Three Mile Island and Chernobyl don't happen again, and will help pave the way for a greater number of electricity-producing commercial nuclear reactors that will help supply the United States' and the world's growing energy demand.

6

Nuclear Power: Low-Cost Portal to U.S. Energy Security

It is not too much to expect that our children will enjoy in their homes electrical energy too cheap to meter, will know of great periodic regional famines in the world only as matters of history, will travel effortlessly over the seas and under them and through the air with a minimum of danger and at great speeds, and will experience a lifespan far longer than ours as disease yields and man comes to understand what causes him to age.

> —Lewis L. Strauss, Chairman, Atomic Energy Commission, in a speech to the National Association of Science Writers, New York City, September 16, 1954

The unstated reference in the speech given by Lewis Strauss was to the coming age of nuclear power. Obviously, electric utilities have not reached the point of giving away power for free, and utility bills have continued to rise over time despite utility deregulation initiatives. The price of electricity has continued to increase, partly due to higher fossil fuel costs. These higher fuel costs make the case for nuclear power even stronger now than in the past.

The operation of nuclear power plants over the past 30 years has provided a comprehensive track record for gauging the technology's economic viability, and gives a strong indication of how well this source of energy compares on an economic basis to energy generated from conventional fossil fuels and alternative fuel sources. The outstanding operating characteristic of nuclear plants is the low cost associated with the uranium fuel used in generating power, which in turn allows for low total production costs for electricity. On fuel cost alone, nuclear power compares favorably with the cheapest fossil fuel electricity generation. It also resembles the cost structure of hydroelectric and alternative resources wherein the nonfuel operating and maintenance charges make up the greatest share, with uranium fuel commonly accounting for just one-third of total production costs from nuclear power plants. Because the nuclear fuel cycle is not associated with hydrocarbon extraction or beholden to the drilling process, nor does it have multiple and competing end-use demands, nuclear energy provides an attractive alternative to the volatile market cycles of oil and gas, whose price formation is well disseminated in the press and is highlighted by fluctuating weather and geopolitical concerns.

The industry's ability to operate power plants using nuclear technology has improved significantly over time. The accumulated knowledge regarding the successful operation of these units has grown in North America to the point that nuclear plants are the most available and highest utilized of any generating technology. Operating costs are continually improving with each fuel cycle as better techniques are developed and deployed. While no new U.S. nuclear reactors have come on line since 1996, significant investments have been made in the existing operating plants, increasing their capacity size as well as improving their structure to ensure full use of the 40-year license life, if not beyond.

Deregulation and consolidation of the U.S. nuclear industry have allowed further cost cutting, principally through larger plant portfolios for each operator. This reduces personnel requirements and also increases the common knowledge base; experience gets shared internationally as well. These improvements are necessary to offset the high sunk capital or "overnight" financing costs that evolved during the reactors' construction years, the 1960s and 1970s. During that period, the heterogeneity of nuclear unit design, and the slowdown in construction resulting from the nation reconsidering the growth of this new generating capacity, meant that finance and construction costs soared. These higher costs were countered by the cheaper cost of fuel on a forward basis. But these cheaper fuel costs were not well known, and nuclear units developed a perception of being too expensive to build and unable to recoup greatly expanded up-front costs.

As nuclear plants paid down these costs and improved operations (after canceling or retiring poorly constructed projects), their greater economic competitiveness emerged. When compared against fossil fuel technologies and alternatives, their financial standing is clearly advantageous. As the United States considers the role of electric power generation in an age of volatile oil and gas prices, as well as carbon awareness, the argument for nuclear power is only enhanced, given its negligible CO_2 emissions.

Why Electricity Costs What It Does

The cost of electric power to the residential consumer is an average system cost, which reflects not only the cost of power generation, incorporating fuel, and other operating costs, but also the charges for transmission and distribution of the energy to the consumer. In addition, different state and local jurisdictions have additional tax rates. The final, typical bill for a residential electricity consumer is shown in Figure 6.1.

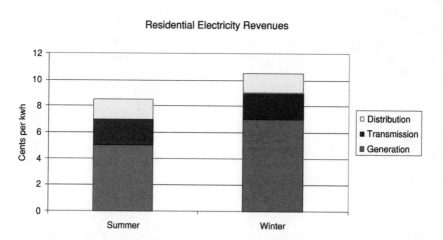

Figure 6.1 Typical Residential Electricity Charges by Component Type
SOURCE: Energy Information Administration.

The generation component of a typical residential electricity bill is the blended cost of all the different sources for electric energy utilized by the host utility, including varying fuel sources as well as imports from neighboring electric systems. Winter electric generation costs are at a premium to those of summer reflecting higher fuel prices, commonly due to higher oil and natural gas prices during the season, when the demand for these fossil fuels surges to heat homes. This tightens the market and increases power prices. These higher costs are typically offset by lower usage because air conditioners, the largest power-consuming appliance, are not in use during the winter months. For utility systems with a large percentage of generating capacity based on natural gas or residual fuel oil, these generation costs will be higher than the national average shown in Figure 6.2. Other utility systems with larger shares of generating capacity from coal, hydro, or nuclear will have rates below the national average.

These electricity prices are in constant flux. Changes in demand, rising fuel costs, and tariff rate changes create the relative geographic differ-

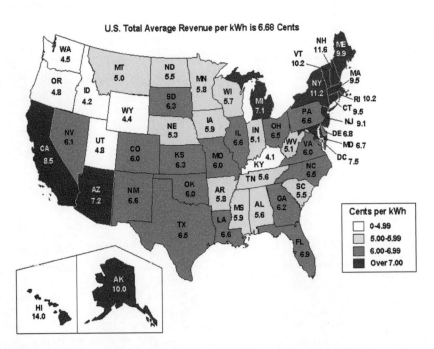

Figure 6.2   Estimated Average Revenue per Kilowatt-Hour for All Sectors at Electric Utilities, 2000
SOURCE: Energy Information Administration.

ence in costs that consumers pay. Hydro–dominated systems of the Pacific northwest have cheaper electricity. U.S. states heavily dependent on coal or nuclear, especially in the Midwest, also have less expensive electricity rates whereas northeastern states that utilize greater shares of oil- and gas-fired generation show higher retail electricity rates. This context provides a reference with which to gauge the performance of electricity produced from nuclear plants.

Emerging from a building phase that stretched from the 1960s until the 1980s, nuclear power is characterized by a general decline in production costs, both in fuel and nonfuel expenses. In Table 6.1, average U.S. nuclear power production costs are bifurcated into these general categories, with snapshots taken at intervals over the past 25 years. From their height in the mid-1980s, total nuclear operating costs have dropped by almost half. The decline has been commensurate in both fuel cycle and plant operations. Having completed new capacity development mostly by the early 1980s, given the slowdown pre- and post-TMI, utilities were left to grapple with operating this newer technology. One of the principal operating challenges was staffing reactor facilities with enough adequately trained personnel to comply with new government oversight aimed at preventing future operating problems.

These nonfuel issues persisted from the mid-1980s through the 1990s, at which point federal deregulation efforts, pushed by the Federal Energy Policy Act of 1992, forced the issue to electric utilities (also the only owners of nuclear capacity). Deregulation mandated that utilities must either operate their plants (of all types) in a cost-efficient manner, or the new market entrants, newly allowed nonutility generators, would take their market share. To be sure, some states were not given such a choice, as state regulators (in California and New England) demanded that utilities

Table 6.1   **Average U.S. Electricity Production Costs from Nuclear Plants, 2003 (Cents/kWh)**

Nuclear	1981	1985	1990	1995	2000	2003
Operations and Maintenance Costs	1.41	1.93	2.07	1.73	1.37	1.28
Fuel Costs	1.06	1.28	1.01	0.69	0.52	0.44
Total	**2.47**	**3.21**	**3.08**	**2.42**	**1.89**	**1.72**

SOURCE: World Nuclear Association, Federal Energy Regulatory Commission.

divest at least fossil generating capacity, leaving hydro and nuclear with their original owners, for the time being.

Given the reduction of operating costs, which have held at lower levels since 2003, future strides in cost reduction, while still feasible, may come in increasingly smaller increments. However, the most important feature of this cost profile is that its largest component relates to the existing structure and the personnel required to run the facility. Fuel issues can be significant, on a relative basis, but at this point comprise only 25 percent of the total power production cost. Going forward, continued improvements in plant management and physical capacity will help further reduce average costs. As older, less efficient plants get retired, the national average cost of nuclear power should continue to improve, provided that the remaining generating stock keeps up with required maintenance.

With these cost levels defined, it is possible to make comparisons to other fuel types used in generating electricity. However, it must first be noted that various technologies are used in different ways to bring power to the electric grid. For nuclear power, base-load operation is considered the exclusive mode—that is, generation facilities that operate at full utilization most of the time, or when not shut down for refueling or maintenance. This is most closely comparable to other steam technology, like coal-fired plants as well as gas- and oil-fired facilities. Combined-cycle plants, the most typical newly built natural gas units, also operate in base-load mode, but can operate in less available modes, or as required during low-electricity-demand periods, like overnight or during the spring and fall shoulder months.

In making energy cost comparisons, typically the all-in costs are divided between (1) electricity, the energy consumed by retail customers, and (2) capacity, the physical facilities installed to produce power. A third category of costs would be externalities, composed of, but not limited to the back end of the fuel cycle—waste product disposal, plant decommissioning, and so on. Also significant is the lack of emissions that nuclear power provides, in stark contrast to coal-fired electricity, which is the center of attention for the carbon-aware society. This cost component is becoming of greater importance with the identification of carbon emissions and the greater realization of linkages between greenhouse gases and global warming. Where to draw the line on this last category remains open for debate, but most of these extra items associated with cost of electric energy production are easily identified and quantified, and thus can be ascribed a value per megawatt-hour of energy consumed.

Nuclear Generation Costs

The evidence is clear, based on energy cost data filed with state and federal regulators, that the majority of well-run nuclear plants in the United States are comparable to the lowest-cost coal plants, on a consistent basis. For large nuclear and coal units, energy production costs of $20 per megawatt-hour are common, but they have somewhat different emphases on each line item expense. Of course, for coal plants, the largest cost component is the cost of coal, which is typically cheaper than the cost of other fossil fuels (e.g., natural gas or petroleum products) on an energy content basis, measured in British thermal units (Btu). These fossil fuels have also experienced a rising and/or volatile price path during the last few years. Increasingly, the market consensus is building for a fossil fuel price outlook that calls for sustained higher price levels, with any period of return to lower prices perceived as anomalous and short-lived.

In contrast, for nuclear power plants, the largest cost components are the nonfuel operating and maintenance charges—essentially personnel costs, and items related to maintaining the high level of regulatory adherence, given the higher standards that apply to nuclear power plants. Fuel costs average 25 percent of the total noncapital operating cost, or $5 per megawatt-hour if the total is $20 per megawatt-hour. Capital costs would add another $9 to $10 per megawatt-hour. This leaves $15 of nonfuel operating and maintenance charges, for a fully functional average nuclear power plant. The subset costs are broadly categorized as labor and materials, pensions and insurance, regulatory fees, property taxes, and general and administrative.

Nuclear Cost Variables

The two essential factors that result from this cost structure are that nearly the same magnitude of expenses will occur whether the plant is large or small, and whether the plant is operating or not. The operation of nuclear plants is optimized over the fuel cycle, meaning that near–100 percent availability and operation is expected in between outages for fuel loading. Of course, during the operating year, a number of different factors can yield variance to the average costs previously laid out. Most importantly, the cycle time for refueling and typical maintenance will determine the number of operating hours a per-unit cost of energy can be computed.

Refueling cycles originally varied between 12 and 18 months, ideally taking place during the shoulder months (spring and fall), at a time when the replacement cost of power was usually at its lowest point of the year. The duration of refueling time varies between 20 and 40 days on average, with shorter outages necessarily including acute or general maintenance activities. In addition, older plants can have issues that are commonly identified with aging materials and components. These older units can witness higher costs, even as the experience factor of the long-time owner/operator has allowed minimization of cost and outage time with each successive refueling performed.

Ultimately, some of these chronic issues with regard to aging plants can result in the need for one-time large component repair or replacements. The steam generator and reactor pressure vessels are two of the most expensive and often-replaced parts of the plant. The costs associated with these maintenance activities start in the tens of millions and can easily rise above $100 million for each replacement operation. However, amortized over the remaining life span of a fully functioning plant, these additional costs are substantial. Apart from the material cost, the outage time and the cost of replacement power to the utility can be the most significant depending on market conditions. An outage duration of three months is typical for replacement of these parts; thus, on an annual basis, the average production costs will spike upward, according to length of time out, compared to a normal operating year.

Table 6.2 gives a numeric comparison among different types of electric utility plant technologies. Fossil steam plants at 23.85 mills per kilowatt-hour are dominated by coal-fired economics, but also contain a much smaller proportion of gas- and oil-steam fired plants, which skews the aggregate number a little higher than coal alone. The gas turbines at 50.1 reflect peaking plants, those units that are required but only at the highest point of the demand cycle, sometimes not more than a few hours of the year. This combustion process is much more readily available but not as efficient. These plants are fired by natural gas and light fuel oil.

Table 6.2 Average Operating Expenses for Major U.S. Investor-Owned Electric Utilities, 1993–2004 (Mills/kWh)

Plant Type Operation	2004	2003	2002	2001	2000	1999	1998	1997	1996	1995	1994	1993
Nuclear	8.3	8.86	8.54	8.3	8.41	8.93	9.98	11.02	9.47	9.43	9.79	10.2
Fossil Steam	2.68	2.5	2.54	2.4	2.31	2.21	2.17	2.22	2.25	2.38	2.32	2.37
Hydroelectric	5.05	4.5	5.07	5.79	4.74	4.17	3.85	3.29	3.87	3.69	4.53	3.82
Gas Turbine	2.73	2.76	2.72	3.15	4.57	5.16	3.85	4.43	5.08	3.57	4.58	6.47
Maintenance												
Nuclear	5.38	5.23	5.04	5.01	4.93	5.13	5.79	6.9	5.68	5.21	5.2	5.73
Fossil Steam	2.96	2.73	2.68	2.61	2.45	2.38	2.41	2.43	2.49	2.65	2.82	2.96
Hydroelectric	3.64	3.01	3.58	3.97	2.99	2.6	2	2.49	2.08	2.19	2.9	2.65
Gas Turbine	2.16	2.26	2.38	3.33	3.5	4.8	3.43	3.43	4.98	4.28	5.39	7.52
Fuel												
Nuclear	4.58	4.6	4.6	4.67	4.95	5.17	5.39	5.42	5.50	5.75	5.87	5.88
Fossil Steam	18.21	17.35	16.11	18.13	17.69	15.62	15.94	16.8	16.51	16.07	16.67	17.65
Hydroelectric	—	—	—	—	—	—	—	—	—	—	—	—
Gas Turbine	45.20	43.91	31.82	43.56	39.19	28.72	23.02	24.94	30.58	20.83	22.19	26.39
Total												
Nuclear	18.26	18.69	18.18	17.98	18.28	19.23	21.16	23.33	20.65	20.39	20.86	21.80
Fossil Steam	23.85	22.59	21.32	23.14	22.44	20.22	20.52	21.45	21.25	21.11	21.8	22.97
Hydroelectric	8.69	7.51	8.65	9.76	7.73	6.77	5.86	5.78	5.95	5.89	7.43	6.47
Gas Turbine	50.10	48.93	36.93	50.04	47.26	38.68	30.3	32.8	40.64	28.67	32.16	40.38

SOURCE: Energy Information Administration.

For nuclear energy, the largest cost components are operation, at 8.3, followed by maintenance at 5.38, with fuel charges comprising the smallest share only 4.58. The opposite holds for fossil steam with fuel costs at 18.21, while hydroelectric is deemed to have no fuel costs.

The principal reason behind cost structure improvement from the 1990s to the present is the emphasis on improving the condition of plant structures and optimizing plant operations. Additionally, if these summary statistics reflect the industry as a whole, then taking out the worst performances will directly yield better average appearance for the industry. This is especially true when the retired units shown in Table 6.3 are removed from the list of industry plants. These tend to be much smaller than the average unit, were running less than rate typically desired, and had more money spent on ameliorating structures to come back into compliance with the NRC.

The average size of U.S. retired nuclear units is much smaller, just 510 megawatts, compared to the average capacity size of the remaining plants online, 900 megawatts. In addition, these retired units were generally older, with operating owners that sometimes did not possess a larger fleet of nuclear plants. That meant that the personnel required to operate one or two units resulted in higher unit cost, since larger fleets of nuclear units could benefit from a more highly optimized staff overseeing the same function across multiple units.

Increasing the productivity of the existing plant base, if the total output had been somewhat less than 100 percent, also improves the attractiveness of plant operations and helps lower the average cost components, as more megawatt-hours are produced with seemingly the same amount of installed megawatt base. The process of improving output, shown in Figure 6.3, required demonstrating a long-term commitment to the nuclear business, which many plant-owning utilities did during the 1990s. By combining better personnel management with improved or upgraded plant structures, higher output was achieved.

As U.S. nuclear capacity utilization approaches and surpasses 90 percent, as shown in Figure 6.4, prospects for further improvement are much diminished. Given that operating plants require taking the system into cold standby for refuelling and maintenance at least once every two years and that many plants do so every 18 months, 100 percent utilization is not feasible with the installed capacity.

Table 6.3 Retired U.S. Nuclear Units

Reactor Facility	Location	Type	MW	Status	Operating
Fermi 1	Monroe, MI	LMFBR	61	SAFSTOR	8/66–11/72
Indian Point 1	Buchanan, NY	PWR	265	SAFSTOR	1/63–10/74
Peach Bottom 1	Peach Bottom, PA	HTGR	40	SAFSTOR	6/67–11/74
Humboldt Bay	Eureka, CA	BWR	65	SAFSTOR to DECON	8/63–7/76
Dresden 1	Morris, IL	BWR	200	SAFSTOR	7/60–10/78
Three Mile Island 2	Harrisburg, PA	PWR	926	SAFSTOR	12/78–3/79
Shippingport	Shippingport, PA	PWR	72	Dismantled	12/57–10/82
Fort St. Vrain	Platteville, CO	HTGR	330	Converted	1/79–8/89
Rancho Seco	Herald, CA	PWR	913	DECON	4/75–6/89
Shoreham	Brookhaven, NY	BWR	820	Dismantled	5/89–5/89
Yankee Rowe	Rowe, MA	PWR	167	DECON	7/61–9/91
San Onofre 1	San Clemente, CA	PWR	436	DECON	1/68–11/92
Trojan	Prescott, OR	PWR	1,130	DECON	5/76–11/92
Millstone 1	Waterford, CT	BWR	660	SAFSTOR Prep	3/71–11/95
CT Yankee	Haddam Neck, CT	PWR	590	DECON Prep	1/68–12/96
Maine Yankee	Wiscasset, ME	PWR	860	DECON Prep	12/72–12/96
Big Rock Point	Charlevoix, MI	BWR	67	DECON Prep	11/65–8/97
Zion 1	Zion, IL	PWR	1,040	SAFSTOR Prep	9/74–1/98
Zion 2	Zion, IL	PWR	1,040	SAFSTOR Prep	9/74–1/98

SAFSTOR = Cold shutdown and safe storage.
DECON = Immediate dismantling.
SOURCE: TLG Services, Nuclear Regulatory Commission.

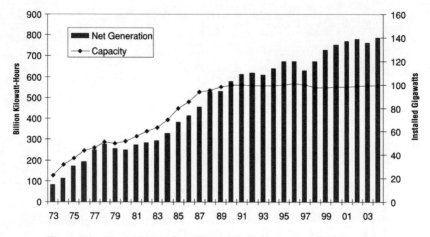

Figure 6.3   **Net U.S. Nuclear Generation versus Installed Capacity**
SOURCE: Nuclear Regulatory Commission.

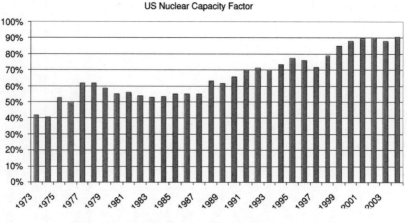

Figure 6.4   **U.S. Nuclear Operating Capacity Factor**
SOURCE: Energy Information Administration.

Fuel Costs

Almost by definition, any analysis of nuclear power production costs must consider spent-fuel management, end-of-license plant decommissioning, and disposal of waste fuel as essential components to the total costs. Deriving similar costs for other generating technologies is certainly feasible, but these items are not typically added onto total production costs for comparison purposes.

First consideration is what to do with the spent-fuel rods, once they are removed from service in the reactor core. There are currently two methods in practice to deal with reactive materials no longer required for power production: on-site storage or disposal in regional depositories. The third alternative, envisioned by the industry and federal government for decades, but still not in place, is a main repository that would provide long-term storage. The principal effort to make that solution viable is the Yucca Mountain Repository in Nevada. The current timeline for allowing receipts at Yucca Mountain is the first half of 2017.

The current method for storing spent nuclear fuel involves removing fuel from the reactor and placing it in a special pool of water, which is held in a steel-lined concrete basin, on the reactor site. The use of water provides a cooling element for the fuel itself, and also prevents airborne release of radiation to the ambient environment. After adequate cooling has taken place, the radioactive waste is removed from the pool and placed in dry-cask storage, also made of steel and concrete. This can either be on site or at regional depositories. Currently, there are 125 temporary waste storage sites in 41 states around the country. See Figure 6.5. More than 160 million U.S. residents live within 75 miles of a storage facility; thus, maintaining their integrity during this temporary storage phase is paramount. However, the cost of constructing and maintaining these facilities is dwarfed by the other expenses at the plant site.

Construction costs for on-site storage of spent nuclear fuel vary markedly from site to site, given the unique characteristics of each plant, and also the needs of each operator. In general, rough estimates in current dollars range from $50 to $100 million or more. On a per-megawatt basis, for a standard 1,000 megawatt plant, this amounts to $100 per kilowatt, or half that amount for a twin 1,000 megawatt plant. Against total plant construction costs of $1,500 per kilowatt and up, this amount amortized over the 40-year life of the plant becomes quite small.

More pressing is the issue that this on-site storage was foreseen as temporary, and thus not designed to hold 100 percent of the spent-fuel rods over the life of the plant. In fact, some facilities have begun to store more fuel on site than was originally envisioned, begging the question of when the federal storage solution will be ready for waste receipt. The operation of nuclear plants already has a self-funding feature for the federal

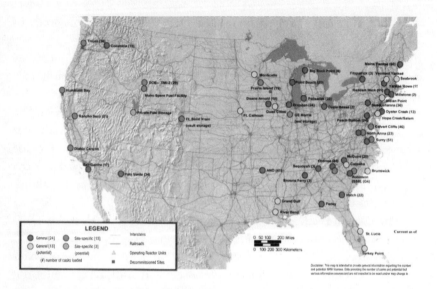

Figure 6.5   **Current and Potential Independent Spent-Fuel Storage Installations**
SOURCE: Federal Energy Regulatory Commission.

storage site, in the 0.1 cent per kilowatt-hour generated from these facilities that is being held in a trust fund to go toward site development and operation.

The cost structure of nuclear power is indeed complex. However, when all variables are accounted for, nuclear generation is extremely competitive against other fuels and has definite cost advantages in long-term operational costs due to the inexpensive nature of nuclear fuel.

Where We Stand Today

There is much renewed discussion regarding the rebirth of nuclear power in the United States. New reactors are being planned, and plans are being made to construct a centralized spent-fuel facility.

New Reactor Plans

According to U.S. Energy Secretary Samuel Bodman, 12 U.S. utilities are expected to file papers with the NRC over the next three years to build

18 nuclear reactors in an effort to meet the United States' growing demand for electricity. According to the North American Electric Reliability Council, of the 15 sites identified by various utilities, 13 are located in the southern part of the United States, where electricity demand is expected to grow by 30 percent in the next 15 years.

Because of the decade or more it takes to plan, design, and build a nuclear plant, many utilities are now pursuing preliminary plans to increase the number of functioning nuclear generation assets scheduled to operate in the years 2015 and 2025. One of the first steps in this process in applying for and obtaining an early site permit (ESP) from the NRC. The ESP is part of the NRC's new, streamlined licensing process designed to reduce various regulatory uncertainties by completing the involved application process in stages. Once received, the permit does not commit utility owners to build new nuclear units. It is just one of the initial steps in the licensing process should they desire to move forward in constructing a nuclear power plant.

Current Utility-Based Nuclear Expansion Efforts

After decades of little interest in expanding their nuclear generation assets, U.S. utilities have taken initial steps to construct new nuclear assets. These initial stages are summarized in the paragraphs that follow.

Tennessee Valley Authority   The nation's largest public utility, the Tennessee Valley Authority (TVA), provides electricity to 158 distributors serving about 8.6 million consumers in Tennessee and parts of Kentucky, Alabama, Mississippi, North Carolina, Georgia, and Virginia.

The TVA is considering completing a second nuclear reactor at its Watts Bar station located in Spring City, Tennessee, about 50 miles south of Knoxville. Watts Bar Unit 1 was the last reactor to begin operation in the United States. The utility is now considering spending $20 million for a detailed engineering study to determine the cost of completing the half-finished 1,160 megawatt Watts Bar Unit 2.

Construction on the Watts Bar reactors was halted in 1985 with the rest of TVA's nuclear program because of safety concerns. Construction eventually resumed on Watts Bar 1, which came on line in 1996, 23 years and $7 billion after its inception.

The TVA has three operating nuclear facilities in Tennessee and Alabama with five electricity-producing reactors. A sixth reactor is currently undergoing a $1.8 billion modernization project and is slated to return to service in May 2007 at the Browns Ferry station near Athens, Georgia. If completed, this would be the United States' 104th operating commercial reactor.

The TVA is also working with a group of utilities as part of a consortium called NuStart, which is looking to use the TVA's unfinished Bellefonte nuclear reactor site in Alabama to build a modern nuclear reactor. The TVA plans to submit combined construction and operating license application for two new reactors at the Bellefonte site by October 2007. The TVA and the NuStart consortium plan to ask the NRC for approval to build two Westinghouse AP1000 reactors. If their request is approved, TVA could begin construction on Bellefonte by 2010 and electricity production could be added as soon as 2015.

Southern Company   In August 2006, Southern Nuclear Operating Company, a subsidiary of Southern Company, filed an application with the NRC for an ESP to add more reactors to the Vogtle Electric Generating Plant in Waynesboro, Georgia. The Vogtle plant is owned by Georgia Power Company, Oglethorpe Power Corporation, the Municipal Electric Authority of Georgia, and the City of Dalton.

The Vogtle ESP will allow the NRC to review and preapprove the plant site for future construction of new nuclear units and allow Southern Nuclear to conduct design, construction, and other site-specific evaluations before the owners make the decision to build. The facility will also need approval from the Georgia Public Service Commission before a final decision is made to build the new units.

Southern Nuclear, which also operates the Hatch Nuclear Plant in Baxley, Georgia, and the Farley Nuclear Plant in Dothan, Alabama, is expected to prepare and file a combined construction and operating license (COL) in 2008 for the two proposed units at Vogtle. Southern Nuclear is also part of the NuStart Energy Development consortium mentioned earlier.

Duke Energy   In March 2006, Duke Energy Corporation selected a site in Cherokee County, South Carolina, for a possible nuclear power plant. The utility is expected to file an application with the NRC to build the plant in late 2007 or early 2008. A decision will be made after the application is approved whether to proceed with the construction of the plant.

Duke Energy is also considering building a nuclear reactor on the Yadkin River in Davie County, North Carolina, and is considering applying to the NRC for early permission to develop plans for the Davie County site and one in Oconee County, South Carolina. This would allow environmental and site-suitability reviews to be completed in advance of requesting licenses to build.

Officials with Duke Energy Carolinas, the electricity generating subsidiary of Duke Energy Corporation, have commented that their generating capacity must be increased to accommodate as many as 60,000 new customers a year in their North Carolina and South Carolina service territory. The company currently serves about 2.1 million customers in the two states.

Dominion Power   Dominion Virginia Power applied for an early site permit for its North Anna, Virginia, nuclear site in 2003. This permit, if approved, would give the company permission to use the site for two or more new nuclear reactors.

North Anna is located 40 miles northwest of Richmond on the North Anna River. The river is dammed to form Lake Anna, which provides cooling water for the power plants. The facility currently has two reactors. Unit 1 started in 1978, Unit 2 in 1980, and they generate a total of 1,786 megawatts of electricity.

Dominion Power plans to submit a license application for a new nuclear unit at North Anna by November 2007. The utility estimates the additional reactor would cost between $2 billion and $3 billion to construct. Construction is expected to take four years and Dominion expects the unit to commence operations in 2015.

South Carolina Electric & Gas   Southern Carolina Electric & Gas (SCE&G) is a regulated public utility engaged in the generation, transmission, distribution, and sale of electricity to approximately 610,000 customers in 24 counties in the central, southern, and southwestern portions of South Carolina. The company also provides natural gas service to approximately 292,000 customers in 34 counties in the state.

In December 2005, SCE&G and Santee Cooper notified the NRC of their intention to submit a joint application for a COL for a new nuclear facility. Development of the COL application began in early 2006 for two reactors in Summer, South Carolina. The utility expects to file the application in October 2007. Following an approximately three-year-long review process, the NRC could issue the COL during 2010, and if construction begins immediately after, a reactor would have an in-service date of around 2015.

In February 2006, SCE&G and Santee Cooper announced that they have selected a preferred site and reactor design should they go forward with a new nuclear facility. The companies selected the Westinghouse AP1000 pressurized water reactor technology, which would be built on the V.C. Summer Nuclear Station site near Jenkinsville, South Carolina. SCE&G and Santee Cooper are joint owners and share operating costs and generating output of the 1,000-megawatt V.C. Summer Nuclear Station, which began commercial operation in 1984; SCE&G is the plant operator.

SCE&G is also in the process of joining a consortium of utilities and reactor vendors called NuStart Energy Development, which will work cooperatively to facilitate the COL application process and complete the engineering design for these advanced plants.

Entergy   Entergy Corporation is an integrated energy company engaged primarily in electric power production and retail distribution operations. Entergy owns and operates power plants with approximately 30,000 megawatts of electric generating capacity, and is the second-largest nuclear generator in the United States. The company has 2.7 million utility customers in Arkansas, Louisiana, Mississippi, and Texas.

Entergy Nuclear has applied for a permit to build new reactors at the Grand Gulf site in Port Gibson, Mississippi, 60 miles southwest of Jackson near the Mississippi River in Claiborne County. One reactor currently operates at the site, and Entergy is seeking approval to possibly build two additional reactors. Entergy will file an application for a COL for the two reactors in October 2007.

NuStart Energy Development has announced its intention to seek a permit to actually build and operate new reactors at the site. NuStart has selected Grand Gulf Nuclear Station as one of the sites for which it is applying for COLs for new nuclear plants. Grand Gulf has been designated by NuStart as the location for GE's electric ESBWR design, and plans call for the COL to be submitted to the NRC in late 2007 or early 2008. After an estimated two-year review process, the NRC could issue the COL in 2010; construction of the reactor is expected to take approximately four years, with the reactor commencing operations in 2014.

Florida Power & Light   Florida Power & Light Company is the principal subsidiary of FPL Group, Inc., an organization that has a presence in 26 U.S. states. Florida Power & Light Company serves 4.4 million customer accounts in Florida. FPL Nuclear owns and operates four nuclear power plants at St. Lucie, near Ft. Pierce, Florida; Turkey Point, near Florida City, Florida; Seabrook Station, in Seabrook, New Hampshire; and Duane Arnold Energy Center, near Cedar Rapids, Iowa.

In April 2006, FPL notified the NRC of its intent to submit a license application in 2009 for a new nuclear power plant in Florida. Filing an application will enable FPL an opportunity to evaluate increased usage of nuclear energy. At this time, FPL has not selected a site or specific reactor technology for the proposed unit. A decision to build is not expected for several years and, according to FPL, the process of siting, licensing, and constructing a nuclear unit could take approximately 12 years.

TXU   Dallas-based TXU manages a portfolio of regulated and deregulated energy businesses. TXU's unregulated business, TXU Energy, provides electricity to more than 2.4 million customers. TXU Power has over 18,300 megawatts of generation in Texas, including 2,300 megawatts of nuclear-fired and 5,837 megawatts of lignite/coal-fired generation capacity.

TXU plans to develop applications to file COLs with the NRC for two to six gigawatts of new nuclear-fueled power generation capacity at one to three sites. The utility expects to submit the COL applications in 2008, which could potentially bring the new capacity on line between 2015 and 2020.

Progress toward Centralized Waste Management

The U.S. nuclear industry continues to produce waste, which is for the most part kept locally on site in secured structures. With new reactors expected to come on line in the United States around 2015 to 2017, a resolution regarding the contentious Yucca Mountain waste disposal facility must be found. Under the DOE's latest schedule, the agency projects that Yucca Mountain will begin receiving utility spent fuel as early as March 31, 2017.

The DOE plans to complete the repository license application by the end of November 2007 and will make repository-related documents available for inspection in December 2007. Repository plans are then scheduled to be submitted in a license application to the NRC in June 2008, the same month a final environmental impact statement on railroad access to the site will be completed. The NRC is expected to formally accept the DOE's license application in September 2008.

If this timetable holds true, the Yucca Mountain repository would be complete by April 2016 and the start-up and preoperations testing of the underground disposal facility would be completed by the end of December 2016. Once all approvals and testing are completed, Yucca Mountain would begin receiving spent nuclear fuel in April 2017.

Conclusion

The United States is at a major nuclear power crossroads. One path, the path of inaction or status quo, will result in a slow erosion of this nation's nuclear power electric generation capacity. If no new reactors are built in the years to come, the current U.S. reactor base will slowly be decommissioned once each reactor's 40-year operating license or 20-year license extension expires. As each of the 103 nuclear reactors is decommissioned, this will put additional strain on other U.S. electricity generation assets, namely conventional generation, which is fueled by increasingly hard-to-find quantities of fossil fuels. In the worst-case scenario, conventional fuel generation won't be able to keep pace with demand growth and severe electric power shortages will result.

The other path at this important nuclear crossroad leads to the further expansion of U.S. nuclear power assets. This nuclear expansion is ongoing on a global basis. Nuclear energy's improving clean-power image is prompting greater numbers of nations to consider the technology as part of their twenty-first-century energy solution. These countries include nations such as Tanzania, Portugal, and Mexico. While the developing African nation of Tanzania may not have the financial resources to actually construct such a facility, the western European nation of Portugal, which in October 2004 dismissed the introduction of nuclear power, is now taking a fresh look at the technology due to increased domestic power consumption and rising energy and oil imports. The Portuguese do have some previous experience with nuclear energy: Uranium was mined in the nation for about 50 years, but these mining operations ceased in 2001 for economic reasons.

One possibility being considered is a joint project by Portugal and Spain which calls for the construction of a large LWR. This has great potential since the two nations recently unified their electricity transmission grids, which will assist in the distribution of electricity produced by the jointly owned nuclear unit.

On the North American continent, Mexico is taking a fresh look at building a second nuclear power plant, 10 years after the second of its twin 654-megawatt BWRs at Laguna Verde began commercial operation. In 2005, the Mexican Ministry of Energy charged the Federal Energy Commission, or CFE, to analyze a policy shift that would emphasize "alternative generation portfolios." This makes it possible for the Mexican government to explore nuclear technology options due to its lower lifetime operation costs.

Simply stated, if new reactor technology is good enough for Tanzania, Portugal, and Mexico, it should be good enough for further expansion in the United States. For decades, the U.S. fleet of 103 reactors has generated millions of kilowatt-hours of relatively low-cost electricity from steam produced from the nuclear fission process. The U.S. nuclear industry is under very stringent oversight by the NRC, which has resulted in decades of safe performance. While the U.S. nuclear industry hasn't received a license for a new commercial reactor for decades, and there was little interest for a time in building new reactors, operators have made tremendous strides in the efficient operation of these assets.

After decades in suspension relative to rapid global growth, the U.S. nuclear industry has begun to show the early signs of rebirth. Several factors are responsible for what many are calling a "nuclear renaissance." Steadily increasing demand for electricity, greater global competition and rising prices for limited supplies of fossil fuels, improvements in reactor safety technology, changing public perceptions regarding energy generation requirements, increased emission concerns and global warming fears, and increased government funding have all been catalysts for U.S. nuclear expansion.

With numerous electric utilities considering constructing nuclear reactors in response to growth forecasts for future electricity demand, the prospects are indeed very bright for the U.S. nuclear power industry. While nuclear power won't be the solution to all future U.S. generation demand growth, the industry is favorably positioned and now benefits from both energy security and economic issues. Nuclear power will never replace the United States' extensive coal-fired, natural gas, and alternative fuel electricity-producing assets. It will, however, play an increasingly important role as part of this nation's diverse mixture of power generation assets. This diversity of generation assets will enable the United States to literally power its economic expansion and maintain its citizens' standard of living well into the twenty-first century.

APPENDIX A

U.S. Reactors

Table A.1 U.S. Reactor List

Reactor Name	Type	Capacity MW(E) Net	Operator[A]	Reactor Supplier[B]	Grid Connection	Commercial Operation
Arkansas Nuclear 1	PWR	840	ENTERGY	B&W	8/17/1974	12/19/1974
Arkansas Nuclear 2	PWR	1,000	ENTERGY	CE	12/26/1978	3/26/1980
Beaver Valley 1	PWR	821	FIRSTENERGY	West	6/14/1976	10/1/1976
Beaver Valley 2	PWR	831	FIRSTENERGY	West	8/17/1987	11/17/1987
Braidwood 1	PWR	1,185	EXELONG	West	7/12/1987	7/29/1988
Braidwood 2	PWR	1,177	EXELON	West	5/25/1988	10/17/1988
Browns Ferry 1	BWR	1,065	TVA	GE	10/15/1973	8/1/1974
Browns Ferry 2	BWR	1,118	TVA	GE	8/28/1974	3/1/1975
Browns Ferry 3	BWR	1,114	TVA	GE	9/12/1976	3/1/1977
Brunswick 1	BWR	872	CPL	GE	12/4/1976	3/18/1977
Brunswick 2	BWR	811	CPL	GE	4/29/1975	11/3/1975
Byron 1	PWR	1,194	EXELON	West	3/1/1985	9/16/1985
Byron 2	PWR	1,162	EXELON	West	2/6/1987	8/21/1987
Callaway 1	PWR	1,137	AMERUE	West	10/24/1984	12/19/1984
Calvert Cliffs 1	PWR	845	CONSTELL	CE	1/3/1975	5/8/1975
Calvert Cliffs 2	PWR	858	CONSTELL	CE	12/7/1976	4/1/1977
Catawba 1	PWR	1,129	DUKE	West	1/22/1985	6/29/1985
Catawba 2	PWR	1,129	DUKE	West	3/18/1986	8/19/1986
Clinton 1	BWR	1,026	AMERGEN	GE	4/24/1987	11/24/1987

Columbia 2^C	BWR	1,108	ENERGYNW	GE	5/27/1984	12/13/1984
Comanche Peak 1	PWR	1,084	TXU	West	4/24/1990	8/13/1990
Comanche Peak 2	PWR	1,124	TXU	West	4/9/1993	8/3/1993
Cooper	BWR	757	NPPD	GE	5/10/1974	7/1/1974
Crystal River 3	PWR	838	PROGRESS	B&W	1/30/1977	3/13/1977
Davis Besse 1	PWR	873	FIRSTENERGY	B&W	8/28/1977	7/31/1978
Diablo Canyon 1	PWR	1,087	PGEC	West	11/11/1984	5/7/1985
Diablo Canyon 2	PWR	1,087	PGEC	West	10/20/1985	3/13/1986
Donald Cook 1	PWR	1,016	IMPCO	West	2/10/1975	8/27/1975
Donald Cook 2	PWR	1,077	IMPCO	West	3/22/1978	7/1/1978
Dresden 2	BWR	850	EXELON	GE	4/13/1970	6/9/1970
Dresden 3	BWR	850	EXELON	GE	7/22/1971	11/16/1971
Duane Arnold 1	BWR	562	NUCMAN	GE	5/19/1974	2/1/1975
Enrico Fermi 2	BWR	1,111	DETED	GE	9/21/1986	1/23/1988
Farley 1	PWR	833	SOUTH	West	8/18/1977	12/1/1977
Farley 2	PWR	842	SOUTH	West	5/25/1981	7/30/1981
Fitzpatrick	BWR	825	ENTERGY	GE	2/1/1975	7/28/1975
Fort Calhoun 1	PWR	476	OPPD	CE	8/25/1973	6/20/1974
Grand Gulf 1	BWR	1,263	ENTERGY	GE	10/20/1984	7/1/1985
H.B. Robinson 2	PWR	710	CPL	West	9/26/1970	3/7/1971
Hatch 1	BWR	856	SOUTH	GE	11/11/1974	12/31/1975
Hatch 2	BWR	883	SOUTH	GE	9/22/1978	9/5/1979
Hope Creek 1	BWR	1,049	PSEG	GE	8/1/1986	12/20/1986
Indian Point 2	PWR	965	ENTERGY	West	6/26/1973	8/15/1974

(Continued)

Table A.1 (Continued)

Reactor Name	Type	Capacity MW(E) Net	Operator[A]	Reactor Supplier[B]	Grid Connection	Commercial Operation
Indian Point 3	PWR	985	ENTERGY	West	4/27/1976	8/30/1976
Kewaunee	PWR	539	NUCMAN	West	4/8/1974	6/16/1974
LaSalle 1	BWR	1,146	EXELON	GE	9/4/1982	1/1/1984
LaSalle 2	BWR	1,147	EXELON	GE	4/20/1984	10/19/1984
Limerick 1	BWR	1,134	EXELON	GE	4/13/1985	2/1/1986
Limerick 2	BWR	1,134	EXELON	GE	9/1/1989	1/8/1990
McGuire 1	PWR	1,100	DUKE	West	9/12/1981	12/1/1981
McGuire 2	PWR	1,100	DUKE	West	5/23/1983	3/1/1984
Millstone 2	PWR	866	DOMINION	CE	11/9/1975	12/26/1975
Millstone 3	PWR	1,131	DOMINION	West	2/12/1986	4/23/1986
Monticello	BWR	569	NUCMAN	GE	3/5/1971	6/30/1971
Nine Mile Point 1	BWR	621	CONSTELL	GE	11/9/1969	12/1/1969
Nine Mile Point 2	BWR	1,135	CONSTELL	GE	8/8/1987	3/11/1988
North Anna 1	PWR	925	DOMINION	West	4/17/1978	6/6/1978
North Anna 2	PWR	917	DOMINION	West	8/25/1980	12/14/1980
Oconee 1	PWR	846	DUKE	B&W	5/6/1973	7/15/1973
Oconee 2	PWR	846	DUKE	B&W	12/5/1973	9/9/1974
Oconee 3	PWR	846	DUKE	B&W	9/18/1974	12/16/1974
Oyster Creek	BWR	619	AMERGEN	GE	9/23/1969	12/1/1969
Palisades	PWR	767	NUCMAN	CE	12/31/1971	12/31/1971
Palo Verde 1	PWR	1,243	APS	CE	6/10/1985	1/28/1986

Palo Verde 2	PWR	1,335	APS	CE	5/20/1986	9/19/1986
Palo Verde 3	PWR	1,247	APS	CE	11/28/1987	1/8/1988
Peach Bottom 2	BWR	1,112	EXELON	GE	12/18/1974	7/5/1974
Peach Bottom 3	BWR	1,112	EXELON	GE	9/1/1974	12/23/1974
Perry 1	BWR	1,235	FIRSTENERGY	GE	12/19/1986	11/18/1987
Pilgrim 1	BWR	685	ENTERGY	GE	7/19/1972	12/1/1972
Point Beach 1	PWR	512	NUCMAN	West	11/6/1970	12/21/1970
Point Beach 2	PWR	514	NUCMAN	West	8/2/1972	10/1/1972
Prairie Island 1	PWR	522	NUCMAN	West	12/4/1973	12/16/1973
Prairie Island 2	PWR	522	NUCMAN	West	12/21/1974	12/21/1974
Quad Cities 1	BWR	864	EXELON	GE	4/12/1972	2/18/1973
Quad Cities 2	BWR	864	EXELON	GE	5/23/1972	3/10/1973
R.E. Ginna	PWR	498	CONSTELL	West	12/2/1969	7/1/1970
River Bend 1	BWR	978	ENTERGY	GE	12/3/1985	6/16/1986
Salem 1	PWR	1,121	PSEG	West	12/25/1976	6/30/1977
Salem 2	PWR	1,119	PSEG	West	6/3/1981	10/13/1981
San Onofre 2	PWR	1,070	SCE	CE	9/20/1982	8/8/1983
San Onofre 3	PWR	1,080	SCE	CE	9/25/1983	4/1/1984
Seabrook 1	PWR	1,159	FPL	West	5/29/1990	8/19/1990
Sequoyah 1	PWR	1,150	TVA	West	7/22/1980	7/1/1981
Sequoyah 2	PWR	1,127	TVA	West	12/23/1981	6/1/1982
Shearon Harris 1	PWR	900	CPL	West	1/19/1987	5/2/1987
South Texas 1	PWR	1,280	STP	West	3/30/1988	8/25/1988
South Texas 2	PWR	1,280	STP	West	4/11/1989	6/19/1989

(Continued)

Table A.1 *(Continued)*

Reactor Name	Type	Capacity MW(E) Net	Operator[A]	Reactor Supplier[B]	Grid Connection	Commercial Operation
St. Lucie 1	PWR	839	FPL	CE	5/7/1976	12/21/1976
St. Lucie 2	PWR	839	FPL	CE	6/13/1986	8/8/1983
Surry 1	PWR	810	DOMINION	West	7/4/1972	12/22/1972
Surry 2	PWR	815	DOMINION	West	3/10/1973	5/1/1973
Susquehanna 1	BWR	1,105	PP&L	GE	11/16/1982	6/8/1983
Susquehanna 2	BWR	1,140	PP&L	GE	7/3/1984	12/12/1985
Three Mile Island 1	PWR	786	AMERGEN	B&W	6/19/1974	9/2/1974
Turkey Point 3	PWR	693	FPL	West	11/2/1972	12/14/1972
Turkey Point 4	PWR	693	FPL	West	6/21/1973	9/7/1973
Vermont Yankee	BWR	506	ENTERGY	GE	9/20/1972	11/30/1972
Virgil C. Summer 1	PWR	966	SCEG	West	11/16/1982	1/1/1984
Vogtle 1	PWR	1,152	SOUTH	West	3/27/1987	6/1/1987

Vogtle 2	PWR	1,149	SOUTH	West	4/10/1989	5/20/1989
Waterford 3	PWR	1,089	ENTERGY	CE	3/18/1985	9/24/1985
Watts Bar 1	PWR	1,121	TVA	West	2/6/1996	5/5/1996
Wolf Creek	PWR	1,165	WOLF	West	6/12/1985	9/3/1985
Total		99,209				

[A]Operator Name Codes: AMERUE = Amerenue; AMERGEN = Amergen Energy Co.; APS = Arizona Public Service Company; CONED = Consolidated Edison Co.; CONSTELL = Constellation Nuclear Group; CPL = Carolina Power & Light Co.; DETED = Detroit Edison Co.; DOE/PRWR = Department of Energy and Puerto Rico Water Resources; DOMINION = Dominion Generation; DPC = Dairyland Power Cooperative; DUKE = Duke Power Co.; ENERGYNW = Energy Northwest; ENTERGY = Entergy Nuclear; EXELON = Exelon Nuclear Co.; FIRSTENERGY = First Energy Nuclear Operating Co.; FPC = Florida Power Corp.; FPL = Florida Power & Light co.; IMPCO = Indiana Michigan Power Co.; IPL = Interstate Power and Light Co.; NAES = North Atlantic Energy Service Corp.; NMPC = Niagara Mohawk Power Corp.; NNEC = Northeast Nuclear Energy Co.; NPPD = Nebraska Public Power District; NUCMAN = Nuclear Management Co.; OPPD = Omaha Public Power District; PGEC = Pacific Gas & Electric Co.; PROGRESS = Progress Energy Corp.; PP&L = Pennsylvania Power & Light Co.; PINN = Pinnacle West; PSEG = Public Service Electric & Gas Co.; RCPA = Rural Cooperative Power Assoc.; RGE = Rochester Gas & Electric Corp.; SCE = Southern California Edison; SOUTH = Southern Nuclear Operating Co.; STP = STP Nuclear Operating Co.; TXU = TXU Electric Co.; TVA = Tennessee Valley Authority; VYNPC = Vermont Yankee Nuclear Power Corp.; WOLF = Wolf Creek Nuclear Operation Corp.

[B]Reactor Supplier Names Codes: B&W = Babcock & Wilcox Co.; CE = Combustion Engineering Co.; GE = General Electric Company (U.S.); WEST = Westinghouse Electric Corporation.

[C]Columbia, formerly Washington Nuclear Power, Unit 2 (WNP-2).

SOURCE: Energy Information Administration.

Appendix B

U.S. Reactor Shutdown List

Table B.1 U.S. Reactor Shutdown List

NRC Code	Reactor Name	Type	Capacity MW(E) Net	Gross	Operator[A]	NSSS Supplier[B]	Construction Start	First Criticality	Grid Connection	Commercial Operation	Shutdown or Cancel
US-155	BIG ROCK POINT	BWR	67	71	CPC	GE	1-May-60	27-Sep-62	8-Dec-62	29-Mar-63	29-Aug-97
US-4	BONUS	BWR	17	18	DOE/PRW	GNEPRWR	1-Jan-60	1-Jan-64	14-Aug-64		1-Jun-68
US-144	CVTR	PHWR	17	19	CVPA	WEST	1-Jan-60	1-Mar-63	18-Dec-63		1-Jan-67
US-10	DRESDEN-1	BWR	197	207	COMED	GE	1-May-56	15-Oct-59	15-Apr-60	4-Jul-60	31-Oct-78
US-1	ELK RIVER	BWR	22	24	RCPA	AC	1-Jan-59	1-Nov-62	24-Aug-63	1-Jul-64	1-Feb-68
US-16	ENRICO FERMI-1	FBR	65	61	DETED	UEC	1-Aug-56	23-Aug-63	5-Aug-66		29-Nov-72
US-267	FORT ST.VRAIN	HTGR	330	342	PSCC	GA	1-Sep-68	31-Jan-74	11-Dec-76	1-Jul-79	29-Aug-89
US-213	HADDAM NECK	PWR	560	587	CYAPC	WEST	1-May-64	24-Jul-67	7-Aug-67	1-Jan-68	4-Dec-96
US-133	HUMBOLDT BAY	BWR	63	65	PGEC	GE	1-Nov-60	16-Feb-63	18-Apr-63	1-Aug-63	2-Jul-76
US-3	INDIAN POINT-1	PWR	257	277	CONED	B&W	1-May-56	2-Aug-62	16-Sep-62	1-Oct-62	31-Oct-74
US-409	LACROSSE	BWR	48	55	DPC	AC	1-Mar-63	11-Jul-67	26-Apr-68	7-Nov-69	30-Apr-87
US-309	MAINE YANKEE	PWR	860	900	MYAPC	CE	1-Oct-68	23-Oct-72	8-Nov-72	28-Dec-72	1-Aug-97
US-245	MILLSTONE-1	BWR	641	684	NNEC	GE	1-May-66	26-Oct-70	29-Nov-70	1-Mar-71	1-Jul-98

US-130	PATHFINDER	BWR	59	63	NSP	AC	1-Jan-59	1-Jan-64	25-Jul-66		1-Oct-67
US-171	PEACH BOTTOM-1	HTGR	40	42	PEC	GA	1-Feb-62	3-Mar-66	27-Jan-67	1-Jun-67	1-Nov-74
US-312	RANCHO SECO-1	PWR	873	917	SMUD	B&W	1-Apr-69	16-Sep-74	13-Oct-74	17-Apr-75	7-Jun-89
US-206	SAN ONOFRE-1	PWR	436	456	SCE	WEST	1-May-64	14-Jun-67	16-Jul-67	1-Jan-68	30-Nov-92
US-320	THREE MILE ISLAND-2	PWR	880	959	GPU	B&W	1-Nov-69	27-Mar-78	21-Apr-78	30-Dec-78	28-Mar-79
US-344	TROJAN	PWR	1095	1155	PORTGE	WEST	1-Feb-70	15-Dec-75	23-Dec-75	20-May-76	9-Nov-92
US-29	YANKEE NPS	PWR	167	180	YAEC	WEST	1-Nov-57	19-Aug-60	10-Nov-60	1-Jul-61	1-Oct-91
US-295	ZION-1	PWR	1040	1085	COMED	WEST	1-Dec-68	19-Jun-73	28-Jun-73	31-Dec-73	1-Jan-98
US-304	ZION-2	PWR	1040	1085	COMED	WEST	1-Dec-68	24-Dec-73	26-Dec-73	17-Sep-74	1-Jan-98

[A]Operator Name Codes: COMED = Commonwealth Edison Co.; CONED = Consolidated Edison Co.; CPC = Consumers Power Co.; CYAPC = Connecticut Yankee Atomic Power Co.; DETED = Detroit Edison Co.; DOE/PRWR = Department of Energy and Puerto Rico Water Resources; DPC = Dairyland Power Cooperative; GPU = General Public Utilities; MYAPC = Maine Yankee Atomic Power Co.; NSP = Northern States Power; PEC = Philadelphia Electric Co.; PGEC = Pacific Gas & Electric Co.; PORTGE = Portland General Electric Co.; PSCC = Public Service Co. of Colorado; RCPA = Rural Cooperative Power Assoc.; SCE = Southern California Edison; SMUD = Sacramento Municipal Utility District; YAEC = Yankee Atomic Electric Co.

[B]NSS Supplier Name Codes: ACTUALLY = Allis Chalmers; B&W = Babcock & Wilcox Co.; CE = Combustion Engineering Co.; GA = General Atomic Corp.; GE = General Electric Company (U.S.); GNE/PRWRA = General Nuclear Engineering and Puerto Rico Water Resources; UEC = United Engineers and Contractors; WEST = Westinghouse Electric Corporation.

SOURCE: Energy Information Administration.

Appendix C

Global Reactor Closings

Table C.1 Anticipated Worldwide Reactor Closures before 2010

Reactor	Nation	Design	Capacity (MW)	Projected Closure	Reason
Kozloduy 3	Bulgaria	VVER	408	2006	EU–Bulgaria agreement
Kozloduy 4	Bulgaria	VVER	408	2006	EU–Bulgaria agreement
Phenix	France	FBR	233	2009	Prototype retirement
Biblis A	Germany	PWR	1167	2008	Nuclear closure policy/law
Biblis B	Germany	PWR	1240	2009	Nuclear closure policy/law
Brunsbuettel	Germany	BWR	771	2009	Nuclear closure policy/law
Neckarwestheim 1	Germany	PWR	785	2008	Nuclear closure policy/law
Ignalina 2	Lithuania	RBMK	1185	2009	EU–Lithuania agreement
Bohunice 1	Slovakia	VVER	408	2006	EU–Slovakia agreement
Bohunice 2	Slovakia	VVER	408	2008	EU–Slovakia agreement
Dungeness A1	United Kingdom	GCR	225	2006	Aging
Dungeness A2	United Kingdom	GCR	225	2006	Aging
Oldbury A1	United Kingdom	GCR	230	2008	Aging
Oldbury A2	United Kingdom	GCR	230	2008	Aging
Sizewell A1	United Kingdom	GCR	210	2006	Aging
Sizewell A2	United Kingdom	GCR	210	2006	Aging
Wylfa 1	United Kingdom	GCR	490	2009	Aging
Wylfa 2	United Kingdom	GCR	490	2009	Aging

SOURCE: IAEA, press notices and reports.

Appendix D

NRC Reactor Certification Status

Table D.1 **Certification Process for New Reactors in the United States**

Reactor Design	Lead Vendor(s)	Design Category	Status at NRC
System 80+	Westinghouse BNFL	PWR	Certified
ABWR	GE, Toshiba, Hitachi	BWR	Certified
AP600	Westinghouse BNFL	PWR	Certified
AP1000	Westinghouse BNFL	PWR	Certified
ESBWR	GE	BWR	Pre-certification
SWR-1000	Framatome ANP	BWR	Pre-certification, deferred
ACR700	AECL	PHWR/ PWR hybrid	Pre-certification
PBMR	Eskom	HTGR	Pre-certification, deferred
GT-MHR	General Atomic	HTGR	Pre-certification
IRIS	Westinghouse BNFL	PWR	Pre-certification
EPR	Framatome ANP	PWR	Pre-certification
ACR1000	AECL	PHWR/ PWR hybrid	No application decision
4S	Toshiba	Sodium-cooled	No application decision

Note: Reactor design names are defined in the text. Vendors of ESBWR, ACR700, EPR, and IRIS vendors have indicated intentions to begin certification in the near future.
SOURCE: U.S. Nuclear Regulatory Commission.

Appendix E

Diagram of a Boiling Water Reactor (BWR)

In a typical commercial boiling water reactor (shown in Figure E.1):

- The reactor core creates heat.
- A steam-water mixture is produced when very pure water (reactor coolant) moves upward through the core, absorbing heat.
- The steam-water mixture leaves the top of the core and enters the two stages of moisture separation, where water droplets are removed before the steam is allowed to enter the steam line.
- The steam line directs the steam to the main turbine, causing it to turn the turbine generator, which produces electricity.

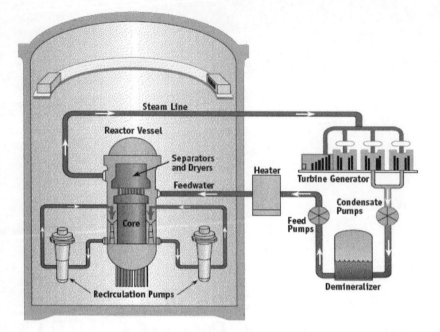

Figure E.1 Boiling Water Reactor
SOURCE: U.S. Nuclear Regulatory Commission.

The unused steam is exhausted to the condenser, where it is condensed into water. The resulting water is pumped out of the condenser with a series of pumps, reheated, and pumped back to the reactor vessel. The reactor's core contains fuel assemblies that are cooled by water, which is force-circulated by electrically powered pumps. Emergency cooling water is supplied by other pumps, which can be powered by on-site diesel generators.

APPENDIX F

Pressurized Water Reactor (PWR)

I n a typical commercial pressurized light–water reactor (shown in Figure F.1):

- The reactor core generates heat.
- Pressurized water in the primary coolant loop carries the heat to the steam generator.
- Inside the steam generator, heat from the primary coolant loop vaporizes the water in a secondary loop, producing steam.
- The steam line directs the steam to the main turbine, causing it to turn the turbine generator, which produces electricity.

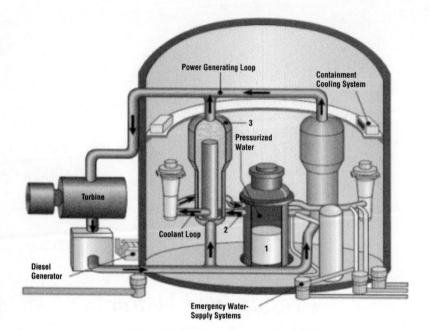

Figure F.1   Pressurized Light-Water Reactor
SOURCE: U.S. Nuclear Regulatory Commission.

The unused steam is exhausted to the condenser, where it is condensed into water. The resulting water is pumped out of the condenser with a series of pumps, reheated, and pumped back to the steam generator.

The reactor's core contains fuel assemblies that are cooled by water, which is force-circulated by electrically powered pumps. Emergency cooling water is supplied by other pumps, which can be powered by on-site diesel generators.

Appendix G

Map of World Nuclear Reactors

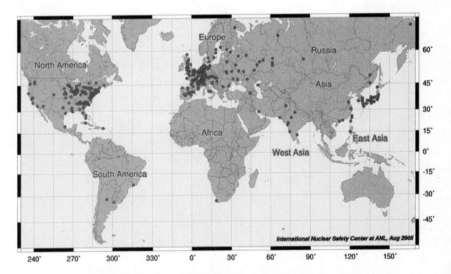

Figure G.1   Map of World Nuclear Reactor Locations
SOURCE: International Nuclear Safety Center.

Appendix H

Global Nuclear Generation

Table H.1 World Net Nuclear Electric Power Generation, 1980–2004 (Billion Kilowatt–Hours)

Region/Country	Fipscd	1980	1981	1982	1983	1984	1985	1986	1987	1988	1989	1990	1991	1992	1993	1994	1995	1996	1997	1998	1999	2000	2001	2002	2003	2004
Bermuda	BD	0	0	0	0	0	0	0	0	0	0	0	0	0	0	0	0	0	0	0	0	0	0	0	0	0
Canada	CA	35.88	37.80	36.17	46.22	49.26	57.10	67.23	72.89	78.18	75.35	69.24	80.68	76.55	90.08	102.44	92.95	88.13	77.86	67.74	69.82	69.16	72.86	71.75	71.15	85.87
Greenland	GL	0	0	0	0	0	0	0	0	0	0	0	0	0	0	0	0	0	0	0	0	0	0	0	0	0
Mexico	MX	0	0	0	0	0	0	0	0	0	0	2.79	4.03	3.72	4.68	4.03	8.02	7.48	9.94	8.80	9.50	7.81	8.29	9.26	9.98	8.73
Saint Pierre and Miquelon	SB	0	0	0	0	0	0	0	0	0	0	0	0	0	0	0	0	0	0	0	0	0	0	0	0	0
United States	US	251.12	272.67	282.77	293.68	327.63	383.69	414.04	455.27	526.97	529.35	576.86	612.57	618.78	610.29	640.44	673.40	674.73	628.64	673.70	728.25	753.89	768.83	780.06	763.73	788.53
North America	r1	287.00	310.47	318.94	339.90	376.89	440.79	481.27	528.16	605.15	604.71	648.89	697.28	699.05	705.06	746.91	774.38	770.34	716.44	750.24	807.57	830.86	849.97	861.07	844.85	883.13
Antarctica	AY	0	0	0	0	0	0	0	0	0	0	0	0	0	0	0	0	0	0	0	0	0	0	0	0	0
Antigua and Barbuda	AC	0	0	0	0	0	0	0	0	0	0	0	0	0	0	0	0	0	0	0	0	0	0	0	0	0
Argentina	AR	2.22	2.68	1.78	3.23	4.29	5.43	5.38	6.14	4.85	4.79	7.03	7.70	6.75	7.32	7.82	7.07	6.92	7.45	7.13	6.75	5.99	6.54	5.39	7.03	7.31
Aruba	AA	NA	NA	NA	NA	NA	NA	0	0	0	0	0	0	0	0	0	0	0	0	0	0	0	0	0	0	0
Bahamas, The	BF	0	0	0	0	0	0	0	0	0	0	0	0	0	0	0	0	0	0	0	0	0	0	0	0	0
Barbados	BB	0	0	0	0	0	0	0	0	0	0	0	0	0	0	0	0	0	0	0	0	0	0	0	0	0
Belize	BH	0	0	0	0	0	0	0	0	0	0	0	0	0	0	0	0	0	0	0	0	0	0	0	0	0
Bolivia	BL	0	0	0	0	0	0	0	0	0	0	0	0	0	0	0	0	0	0	0	0	0	0	0	0	0
Brazil	BR	0	0	0.05	0.17	2.73	2.92	0.12	0.92	0.31	1.51	1.94	1.37	1.66	0.42	0.05	2.39	2.31	3.01	3.14	3.78	4.94	14.27	13.84	13.40	11.60
Cayman Islands	CJ	0	0	0	0	0	0	0	0	0	0	0	0	0	0	0	0	0	0	0	0	0	0	0	0	0
Chile	CI	0	0	0	0	0	0	0	0	0	0	0	0	0	0	0	0	0	0	0	0	0	0	0	0	0
Colombia	CO	0	0	0	0	0	0	0	0	0	0	0	0	0	0	0	0	0	0	0	0	0	0	0	0	0
Costa Rica	CS	0	0	0	0	0	0	0	0	0	0	0	0	0	0	0	0	0	0	0	0	0	0	0	0	0
Cuba	CU	0	0	0	0	0	0	0	0	0	0	0	0	0	0	0	0	0	0	0	0	0	0	0	0	0
Dominica	DO	0	0	0	0	0	0	0	0	0	0	0	0	0	0	0	0	0	0	0	0	0	0	0	0	0
Dominican Republic	DR	0	0	0	0	0	0	0	0	0	0	0	0	0	0	0	0	0	0	0	0	0	0	0	0	0
Ecuador	EC	0	0	0	0	0	0	0	0	0	0	0	0	0	0	0	0	0	0	0	0	0	0	0	0	0
El Salvador	ES	0	0	0	0	0	0	0	0	0	0	0	0	0	0	0	0	0	0	0	0	0	0	0	0	0
Falkland Islands	FK	0	0	0	0	0	0	0	0	0	0	0	0	0	0	0	0	0	0	0	0	0	0	0	0	0
French Guiana	FG	0	0	0	0	0	0	0	0	0	0	0	0	0	0	0	0	0	0	0	0	0	0	0	0	0
Grenada	GJ	0	0	0	0	0	0	0	0	0	0	0	0	0	0	0	0	0	0	0	0	0	0	0	0	0
Guadeloupe	GP	0	0	0	0	0	0	0	0	0	0	0	0	0	0	0	0	0	0	0	0	0	0	0	0	0

Guatemala	GT	0	0	0	0	0	0	0	0	0	0	0	0	0	0	0	0	0	0	0	0	0	0	0	0
Guyana	GY	0	0	0	0	0	0	0	0	0	0	0	0	0	0	0	0	0	0	0	0	0	0	0	0
Haiti	HA	0	0	0	0	0	0	0	0	0	0	0	0	0	0	0	0	0	0	0	0	0	0	0	0
Honduras	HO	0	0	0	0	0	0	0	0	0	0	0	0	0	0	0	0	0	0	0	0	0	0	0	0
Jamaica	JM	0	0	0	0	0	0	0	0	0	0	0	0	0	0	0	0	0	0	0	0	0	0	0	0
Martinique	MB	0	0	0	0	0	0	0	0	0	0	0	0	0	0	0	0	0	0	0	0	0	0	0	0
Montserrat	MH	0	0	0	0	0	0	0	0	0	0	0	0	0	0	0	0	0	0	0	0	0	0	0	0
Netherlands Antilles	NT	0	0	0	0	0	0	0	0	0	0	0	0	0	0	0	0	0	0	0	0	0	0	0	0
Nicaragua	NU	0	0	0	0	0	0	0	0	0	0	0	0	0	0	0	0	0	0	0	0	0	0	0	0
Panama	PM	0	0	0	0	0	0	0	0	0	0	0	0	0	0	0	0	0	0	0	0	0	0	0	0
Paraguay	PA	0	0	0	0	0	0	0	0	0	0	0	0	0	0	0	0	0	0	0	0	0	0	0	0
Peru	PE	0	0	0	0	0	0	0	0	0	0	0	0	0	0	0	0	0	0	0	0	0	0	0	0
Puerto Rico	RQ	0	0	0	0	0	0	0	0	0	0	0	0	0	0	0	0	0	0	0	0	0	0	0	0
Saint Kitts and Nevis	SC	0	0	0	0	0	0	0	0	0	0	0	0	0	0	0	0	0	0	0	0	0	0	0	0
Saint Lucia	ST	0	0	0	0	0	0	0	0	0	0	0	0	0	0	0	0	0	0	0	0	0	0	0	0
Saint Vincent/ Grenadines	VC	0	0	0	0	0	0	0	0	0	0	0	0	0	0	0	0	0	0	0	0	0	0	0	0
Suriname	NS	0	0	0	0	0	0	0	0	0	0	0	0	0	0	0	0	0	0	0	0	0	0	0	0
Trinidad and Tobago	TD	0	0	0	0	0	0	0	0	0	0	0	0	0	0	0	0	0	0	0	0	0	0	0	0
Turks and Caicos Islands	TK	0	0	0	0	0	0	0	0	0	0	0	0	0	0	0	0	0	0	0	0	0	0	0	0
Uruguay	UY	0	0	0	0	0	0	0	0	0	0	0	0	0	0	0	0	0	0	0	0	0	0	0	0
Venezuela	VE	0	0	0	0	0	0	0	0	0	0	0	0	0	0	0	0	0	0	0	0	0	0	0	0
Virgin Islands, U.S.	VQ	0	0	0	0	0	0	0	0	0	0	0	0	0	0	0	0	0	0	0	0	0	0	0	0
Virgin Islands, British	VI	0	0	0	0	0	0	0	0	0	0	0	0	0	0	0	0	0	0	0	0	0	0	0	0
Central & South America	**r2**	**2.22**	**2.68**	**1.83**	**3.40**	**7.03**	**8.36**	**5.50**	**7.06**	**5.16**	**6.30**	**8.97**	**9.07**	**8.41**	**7.73**	**7.88**	**9.46**	**9.23**	**10.46**	**10.26**	**10.52**	**10.93**	**20.81**	**19.23**	**20.43**	**18.91**
Albania	AL	0	0	0	0	0	0	0	0	0	0	0	0	0	0	0	0	0	0	0	0	0	0	0	0
Austria	AU	0	0	0	0	0	0	0	0	0	0	0	0	0	0	0	0	0	0	0	0	0	0	0	0
Belgium	BE	11.91	12.22	14.75	22.83	26.36	32.69	37.30	39.76	40.89	39.10	40.59	40.72	41.28	39.83	38.59	39.29	41.17	45.04	43.86	46.57	45.75	44.03	44.99	45.01	45.80

(Continued)

211

Table H.1   (Continued)

Region/ Country	Fipscd	1980	1981	1982	1983	1984	1985	1986	1987	1988	1989	1990	1991	1992	1993	1994	1995	1996	1997	1998	1999	2000	2001	2002	2003	2004
Bosnia and Herzegovina	BK	NA	NA	NA	NA	NA	NA	NA	NA	NA	NA	NA	NA	NA	0	0	0	0	0	0	0	0	0	0	0	0
Bulgaria	BU	5.81	8.59	10.13	11.61	12.00	12.38	11.38	11.72	15.11	14.60	13.53	12.41	10.99	13.27	14.56	16.40	17.77	16.44	16.05	15.02	17.27	18.24	20.22	16.04	15.60
Croatia	HR	NA	NA	NA	NA	NA	NA	NA	NA	NA	NA	NA	NA	0	0	0	0	0	0	0	0	0	0	0	0	0
Czech Republic	EZ	NA	NA	NA	NA	NA	NA	NA	NA	NA	NA	NA	NA	NA	12.00	12.33	11.62	12.21	12.49	12.52	12.69	12.91	14.01	17.80	24.58	25.01
Denmark	DA	NA	NA	0	0	0	0	0	0	0	0	0	0	0	0	0	0	0	0	0	0	0	0	0	0	0
Faroe Islands	FO	0	0	0	0	0	0	0	0	0	0	0	0	0	0	0	0	0	0	0	0	0	0	0	0	0
Finland	FI	6.63	13.84	15.83	16.72	17.80	17.98	18.00	18.53	18.45	18.01	18.26	18.54	18.30	18.93	18.46	18.26	18.50	19.04	20.76	21.83	21.36	21.63	21.18	21.60	21.55
Former Czechoslovakia	CZ	4.50	5.10	5.80	6.20	7.30	11.90	17.90	20.93	21.95	23.16	23.40	22.52	23.27	NA	NA	NA	NA	NA	NA	NA	NA	NA	NA	NA	NA
Former Yugoslavia	YO	0	0.27	2.39	3.69	4.17	4.04	4.04	4.24	3.90	4.45	4.39	4.17	NA	NA	NA	NA	NA	NA	NA	NA	NA	NA	NA	NA	NA
France	FR	63.42	99.24	102.63	135.99	180.47	211.19	239.56	249.27	260.29	288.72	298.38	314.77	321.52	349.78	341.98	358.37	377.47	375.71	368.59	374.53	394.40	400.02	414.92	419.02	425.83
Germany	GM	NA	NA	NA	NA	NA	NA	NA	NA	NA	NA	NA	140.06	150.86	145.80	143.17	145.44	152.02	161.81	153.56	161.50	161.13	162.74	156.60	156.81	158.97
Germany, East	GC	11.89	11.22	10.22	11.53	11.74	12.74	10.91	10.65	11.06	11.05	5.33	NA	NA	NA	NA	NA	NA	NA	NA	NA	NA	NA	NA	NA	NA
Germany, West	GE	43.70	53.63	63.58	65.83	92.58	125.90	119.58	130.52	145.08	140.44	139.82	NA	NA	NA	NA	NA	NA	NA	NA	NA	NA	NA	NA	NA	NA
Gibraltar	GI	0	0	0	0	0	0	0	0	0	0	0	0	0	0	0	0	0	0	0	0	0	0	0	0	0
Greece	GR	0	0	0	0	0	0	0	0	0	0	0	0	0	0	0	0	0	0	0	0	0	0	0	0	0
Hungary	HU	0	0	0.01	2.33	3.55	6.11	7.00	10.35	12.67	13.09	13.04	13.04	13.27	13.11	13.35	13.32	13.47	13.27	13.25	13.39	13.47	13.42	13.26	10.46	11.32
Iceland	IC	0	0	0	0	0	0	0	0	0	0	0	0	0	0	0	0	0	0	0	0	0	0	0	0	0
Ireland	EI	0	0	0	0	0	0	0	0	0	0	0	0	0	0	0	0	0	0	0	0	0	0	0	0	0
Italy	IT	2.07	2.54	6.59	5.47	6.50	6.60	8.29	0.05	0	0	0	0	0	0	0	0	0	0	0	0	0	0	0	0	0
Luxembourg	LU	0	0	0	0	0	0	0	0	0	0	0	0	0	0	0	0	0	0	0	0	0	0	0	0	0
Macedonia	MK	NA	NA	NA	NA	NA	NA	NA	NA	NA	NA	NA	NA	0	0	0	0	0	0	0	0	0	0	0	0	0
Malta	MT	0	0	0	0	0	0	0	0	0	0	0	0	0	0	0	0	0	0	0	0	0	0	0	0	0
Netherlands	NL	3.95	3.44	3.67	3.37	3.49	3.67	3.96	3.36	3.47	3.79	3.33	3.16	3.61	3.75	3.77	3.82	3.95	2.29	3.62	3.64	3.73	3.78	3.72	3.82	3.63
Norway	NO	0	0	0	0	0	0	0	0	0	0	0	0	0	0	0	0	0	0	0	0	0	0	0	0	0
Poland	PL	0	0	0	0	0	0	0	0	0	0	0	0	0	0	0	0	0	0	0	0	0	0	0	0	0
Portugal	PO	0	0	0	0	0	0	0	0	0	0	0	0	0	0	0	0	0	0	0	0	0	0	0	0	0
Romania	RO	0.00	0.00	0.00	0.00	0.00	0.00	0.00	0.00	0.00	0.00	0.00	0.00	0.00	0.00	0.00	0.00	0.91	5.13	4.90	4.81	5.23	5.04	5.11	4.54	5.27
Serbia and Montenegro	YR	NA	NA	NA	NA	NA	NA	NA	NA	NA	NA	NA	NA	NA	NA	NA	NA	NA	NA	NA	NA	0	0	0	0	0

Slovakia	LO	NA	NA	NA	NA	NA	NA	NA	NA	NA	NA	NA	NA	NA	11.62	11.52	10.87	11.26	10.45	10.82	12.46	15.67	16.25	17.06	16.97	16.18
Slovenia	SI	NA	NA	NA	NA	NA	NA	NA	NA	NA	NA	NA	NA	3.77	3.76	4.29	4.56	4.36	4.79	4.79	4.48	4.55	5.04	5.31	4.96	5.21
Spain	SP	5.19	9.57	8.77	10.66	23.09	28.04	37.46	41.27	48.31	53.75	51.56	52.80	52.99	53.26	52.55	52.68	53.51	52.54	56.04	55.91	59.10	60.52	59.87	58.78	60.43
Sweden	SW	25.33	35.98	37.26	39.06	48.51	55.81	66.88	64.34	65.59	62.81	64.78	72.92	60.37	58.33	69.50	66.44	70.56	66.43	69.90	69.53	54.45	68.50	64.20	64.04	73.43
Switzerland	SZ	12.88	13.63	13.45	13.97	16.39	20.06	20.08	20.45	21.49	21.54	22.42	21.65	22.28	22.18	23.15	23.65	23.89	24.14	24.54	24.54	25.12	25.47	25.87	26.11	25.61
Turkey	TU	0	0	0	0	0	0	0	0	0	0	0	0	0	0	0	0	0	0	0	0	0	0	0	0	0
United Kingdom	UK	32.29	33.19	38.72	43.91	47.26	53.77	51.77	48.21	55.64	63.60	62.46	67.02	72.97	84.89	83.87	84.52	89.94	93.24	94.51	90.38	80.81	85.38	83.64	84.25	73.68
Europe	**r3**	**229.56**	**302.45**	**333.79**	**393.16**	**501.20**	**602.87**	**654.11**	**673.64**	**723.88**	**758.11**	**761.26**	**783.78**	**795.48**	**830.50**	**831.07**	**849.22**	**890.98**	**902.80**	**897.73**	**911.28**	**914.94**	**944.07**	**953.74**	**957.00**	**967.52**
Armenia	AM	NA	NA	NA	NA	NA	NA	NA	NA	NA	NA	NA	NA	0	0	0	0	2.10	1.43	1.42	2.08	1.84	1.99	2.09	1.82	2.21
Azerbaijan	AJ	NA	NA	NA	NA	NA	NA	NA	NA	NA	NA	NA	NA	0	0	0	0	0	0	0	0	0	0	0	0	0
Belarus	BO	NA	NA	NA	NA	NA	NA	NA	NA	NA	NA	NA	NA	0	0	0	0	0	0	0	0	0	0	0	0	0
Estonia	EN	NA	NA	NA	NA	NA	NA	NA	NA	NA	NA	NA	NA	0	0	0	0	0	0	0	0	0	0	0	0	0
Former U.S.S.R. NA	UR NA	72.88	64.05	98.62	109.73	141.94	169.96	151.55	176.25	203.71	212.69	201.31	201.50	NA	NA	NA	NA	NA	NA	NA	NA	NA		NA		NA
Georgia	GG	NA	NA	NA	NA	NA	NA	NA	NA	NA	NA	NA	NA	0	0	0	0	0	0	0	0	0	0	0	0	0
Kazakhstan	KZ	NA	NA	NA	NA	NA	NA	NA	NA	NA	NA	NA	NA	0.48	0.38	0.37	0.10	0.09	0.29	0.10	0.001	0	0	0	0	0
Kyrgyzstan	KG	NA	NA	NA	NA	NA	NA	NA	NA	NA	NA	NA	NA	0	0	0	0	0	0	0	0	0	0	0	0	0
Latvia	LG	NA	NA	NA	NA	NA	NA	NA	NA	NA	NA	NA	NA	0	0	0	0	0	0	0	0	0	0	0	0	0
Lithuania	LH	NA	NA	NA	NA	NA	NA	NA	NA	NA	NA	NA	NA	13.87	12.26	7.32	10.64	12.67	10.85	12.88	9.37	8.00	10.79	13.44	14.71	14.35
Moldova	MD	NA	NA	NA	NA	NA	NA	NA	NA	NA	NA	NA	NA	0	0	0	0	0	0	0	0	0	0	0	0	0
Russia	RS	NA	NA	NA	NA	NA	NA	NA	NA	NA	NA	NA	NA	113.62	113.24	92.91	94.34	103.32	104.50	98.33	110.91	122.46	125.36	134.14	141.17	137.47
Tajikistan	TI	NA	NA	NA	NA	NA	NA	NA	NA	NA	NA	NA	NA	0	0	0	0	0	0	0	0	0	0	0	0	0
Turkmenistan	TX	NA	NA	NA	NA	NA	NA	NA	NA	NA	NA	NA	NA	0	0	0	0	0	0	0	0	0	0	0	0	0
Ukraine	UP	NA	NA	NA	NA	NA	NA	NA	NA	NA	NA	NA	NA	70.11	71.44	65.36	66.98	76.00	75.43	70.64	67.35	71.06	71.67	73.38	76.70	82.69
Uzbekistan	UZ	NA	NA	NA	NA	NA	NA	NA	NA	NA	NA	NA	NA	0	0	0	0	0	0	0	0	0	0	0	0	0
Eurasia	**r4**	**72.88**	**64.05**	**98.62**	**109.73**	**141.94**	**169.96**	**151.55**	**176.25**	**203.71**	**212.69**	**201.31**	**201.50**	**198.08**	**197.32**	**165.96**	**172.05**	**194.18**	**192.50**	**183.37**	**189.71**	**203.35**	**209.81**	**223.05**	**234.40**	**236.71**
Bahrain	BA	0	0	0	0	0	0	0	0	0	0	0	0	0	0	0	0	0	0	0	0	0	0	0	0	0
Cyprus	CY	0	0	0	0	0	0	0	0	0	0	0	0	0	0	0	0	0	0	0	0	0	0	0	0	0
Iran	IR	0	0	0	0	0	0	0	0	0	0	0	0	0	0	0	0	0	0	0	0	0	0	0	0	0
Iraq	IZ	0	0	0	0	0	0	0	0	0	0	0	0	0	0	0	0	0	0	0	0	0	0	0	0	0
Israel	IS	0	0	0	0	0	0	0	0	0	0	0	0	0	0	0	0	0	0	0	0	0	0	0	0	0
Jordan	JO	0	0	0	0	0	0	0	0	0	0	0	0	0	0	0	0	0	0	0	0	0	0	0	0	0
Kuwait	KU	0	0	0	0	0	0	0	0	0	0	0	0	0	0	0	0	0	0	0	0	0	0	0	0	0

(Continued)

Table H.1 (Continued)

Region/Country	Fipscd	1980	1981	1982	1983	1984	1985	1986	1987	1988	1989	1990	1991	1992	1993	1994	1995	1996	1997	1998	1999	2000	2001	2002	2003	2004
Oman	MU	0	0	0	0	0	0	0	0	0	0	0	0	0	0	0	0	0	0	0	0	0	0	0	0	0
Qatar	QA	0	0	0	0	0	0	0	0	0	0	0	0	0	0	0	0	0	0	0	0	0	0	0	0	0
Saudi Arabia	SA	0	0	0	0	0	0	0	0	0	0	0	0	0	0	0	0	0	0	0	0	0	0	0	0	0
Syria	SY	0	0	0	0	0	0	0	0	0	0	0	0	0	0	0	0	0	0	0	0	0	0	0	0	0
United Arab	TC	0	0	0	0	0	0	0	0	0	0	0	0	0	0	0	0	0	0	0	0	0	0	0	0	0
Yemen	YM	0	0	0	0	0	0	0	0	0	0	0	0	0	0	0	0	0	0	0	0	0	0	0	0	0
Middle East		0	0	0	0	0	0	0	0	0	0	0	0	0	0	0	0	0	0	0	0	0	0	0	0	0
Algeria	AG	0	0	0	0	0	0	0	0	0	0	0	0	0	0	0	0	0	0	0	0	0	0	0	0	0
Angola	AO	0	0	0	0	0	0	0	0	0	0	0	0	0	0	0	0	0	0	0	0	0	0	0	0	0
Benin	BN	0	0	0	0	0	0	0	0	0	0	0	0	0	0	0	0	0	0	0	0	0	0	0	0	0
Botswana	BC	0	0	0	0	0	0	0	0	0	0	0	0	0	0	0	0	0	0	0	0	0	0	0	0	0
Burkina Faso	UV	0	0	0	0	0	0	0	0	0	0	0	0	0	0	0	0	0	0	0	0	0	0	0	0	0
Burundi	BY	0	0	0	0	0	0	0	0	0	0	0	0	0	0	0	0	0	0	0	0	0	0	0	0	0
Cameroon	CM	0	0	0	0	0	0	0	0	0	0	0	0	0	0	0	0	0	0	0	0	0	0	0	0	0
Cape Verde	CV	0	0	0	0	0	0	0	0	0	0	0	0	0	0	0	0	0	0	0	0	0	0	0	0	0
Central African Republic	CT	0	0	0	0	0	0	0	0	0	0	0	0	0	0	0	0	0	0	0	0	0	0	0	0	0
Chad	CD	0	0	0	0	0	0	0	0	0	0	0	0	0	0	0	0	0	0	0	0	0	0	0	0	0
Comoros	CN	0	0	0	0	0	0	0	0	0	0	0	0	0	0	0	0	0	0	0	0	0	0	0	0	0
Congo (Brazzaville)	CF	0	0	0	0	0	0	0	0	0	0	0	0	0	0	0	0	0	0	0	0	0	0	0	0	0
Congo (Kinshasa)	CG	0	0	0	0	0	0	0	0	0	0	0	0	0	0	0	0	0	0	0	0	0	0	0	0	0
Cote d'Ivoire (Ivory Coast)	IV	0	0	0	0	0	0	0	0	0	0	0	0	0	0	0	0	0	0	0	0	0	0	0	0	0
Lebanon	LE	0	0	0	0	0	0	0	0	0	0	0	0	0	0	0	0	0	0	0	0	0	0	0	0	0
Djibouti	DJ	0	0	0	0	0	0	0	0	0	0	0	0	0	0	0	0	0	0	0	0	0	0	0	0	0
Egypt	EG	0	0	0	0	0	0	0	0	0	0	0	0	0	0	0	0	0	0	0	0	0	0	0	0	0
Equatorial Guinea	EK	0	0	0	0	0	0	0	0	0	0	0	0	0	0	0	0	0	0	0	0	0	0	0	0	0

Country	Code																					
Eritrea	ER	NA	NA	NA	NA	NA	NA	NA	NA	NA	NA	NA	NA	0	0	0	0	0	0	0	0	0
Ethiopia	ET	NA	NA	NA	NA	NA	NA	NA	NA	NA	NA	NA	NA	0	0	0	0	0	0	0	0	0
Gabon	GB	NA	NA	NA	NA	NA	NA	NA	NA	NA	NA	NA	NA	0	0	0	0	0	0	0	0	0
Gambia, The	GA	NA	NA	NA	NA	NA	NA	NA	NA	NA	NA	NA	NA	0	0	0	0	0	0	0	0	0
Ghana	GH	NA	NA	NA	NA	NA	NA	NA	NA	NA	NA	NA	NA	0	0	0	0	0	0	0	0	0
Guinea	GV	NA	NA	NA	NA	NA	NA	NA	NA	NA	NA	NA	NA	0	0	0	0	0	0	0	0	0
Guinea-Bissau	PU	NA	NA	NA	NA	NA	NA	NA	NA	NA	NA	NA	NA	0	0	0	0	0	0	0	0	0
Kenya	KE	NA	NA	NA	NA	NA	NA	NA	NA	NA	NA	NA	NA	0	0	0	0	0	0	0	0	0
Lesotho	LT	NA	NA	NA	NA	NA	NA	NA	NA	NA	NA	NA	NA	0	0	0	0	0	0	0	0	0
Liberia	LI	NA	NA	NA	NA	NA	NA	NA	NA	NA	NA	NA	NA	0	0	0	0	0	0	0	0	0
Libya	LY	NA	NA	NA	NA	NA	NA	NA	NA	NA	NA	NA	NA	0	0	0	0	0	0	0	0	0
Madagascar	MA	NA	NA	NA	NA	NA	NA	NA	NA	NA	NA	NA	NA	0	0	0	0	0	0	0	0	0
Malawi	MI	NA	NA	NA	NA	NA	NA	NA	NA	NA	NA	NA	NA	0	0	0	0	0	0	0	0	0
Mali	ML	NA	NA	NA	NA	NA	NA	NA	NA	NA	NA	NA	NA	0	0	0	0	0	0	0	0	0
Mauritania	MR	NA	NA	NA	NA	NA	NA	NA	NA	NA	NA	NA	NA	0	0	0	0	0	0	0	0	0
Mauritius	MP	NA	NA	NA	NA	NA	NA	NA	NA	NA	NA	NA	NA	0	0	0	0	0	0	0	0	0
Morocco	MO	NA	NA	NA	NA	NA	NA	NA	NA	NA	NA	NA	NA	0	0	0	0	0	0	0	0	0
Mozambique	MZ	NA	NA	NA	NA	NA	NA	NA	NA	NA	NA	NA	NA	0	0	0	0	0	0	0	0	0
Namibia	WA	NA	NA	NA	NA	NA	NA	NA	NA	NA	NA	NA	NA	0	0	0	0	0	0	0	0	0
Niger	NG	NA	NA	NA	NA	NA	NA	NA	NA	NA	NA	NA	NA	0	0	0	0	0	0	0	0	0
Nigeria	NI	NA	NA	NA	NA	NA	NA	NA	NA	NA	NA	NA	NA	0	0	0	0	0	0	0	0	0
Reunion	RE	NA	NA	NA	NA	NA	NA	NA	NA	NA	NA	NA	NA	0	0	0	0	0	0	0	0	0
Rwanda	RW	NA	NA	NA	NA	NA	NA	NA	NA	NA	NA	NA	NA	0	0	0	0	0	0	0	0	0
Saint Helena	SH	NA	NA	NA	NA	NA	NA	NA	NA	NA	NA	NA	NA	0	0	0	0	0	0	0	0	0
Sao Tome and Principe	TP	NA	NA	NA	NA	NA	NA	NA	NA	NA	NA	NA	NA	0	0	0	0	0	0	0	0	0
Senegal	SG	0	0	0	0	0	0	0	0	0	0	0	0	0	0	0	0	0	0	0	0	0
Seychelles	SE	0	0	0	0	0	0	0	0	0	0	0	0	0	0	0	0	0	0	0	0	0
Sierra Leone	SL	0	0	0	0	0	0	0	0	0	0	0	0	0	0	0	0	0	0	0	0	0
Somalia	SO	0	0	0	0	0	0	0	0	0	0	0	0	0	0	0	0	0	0	0	0	0
South Africa	SF	3.93	5.32	8.80	6.17	10.49	11.10	8.45	9.14	9.29	7.26	9.70	11.30	11.78	12.65	13.60	12.84	13.01	10.72	11.99	12.66	14.28
Sudan	SU	0	0	0	0	0	0	0	0	0	0	0	0	0	0	0	0	0	0	0	0	0
Swaziland	WZ	0	0	0	0	0	0	0	0	0	0	0	0	0	0	0	0	0	0	0	0	0
Tanzania	TZ	0	0	0	0	0	0	0	0	0	0	0	0	0	0	0	0	0	0	0	0	0

(Continued)

Table H.1 (Continued)

Region/Country	Fipscd	1980	1981	1982	1983	1984	1985	1986	1987	1988	1989	1990	1991	1992	1993	1994	1995	1996	1997	1998	1999	2000	2001	2002	2003	2004
Togo	TO	0	0	0	0	0	0	0	0	0	0	0	0	0	0	0	0	0	0	0	0	0	0	0	0	0
Tunisia	TS	0	0	0	0	0	0	0	0	0	0	0	0	0	0	0	0	0	0	0	0	0	0	0	0	0
Uganda	UG	0	0	0	0	0	0	0	0	0	0	0	0	0	0	0	0	0	0	0	0	0	0	0	0	0
Western Sahara	WI	0	0	0	0	0	0	0	0	0	0	0	0	0	0	0	0	0	0	0	0	0	0	0	0	0
Zambia	ZA	0	0	0	0	0	0	0	0	0	0	0	0	0	0	0	0	0	0	0	0	0	0	0	0	0
Zimbabwe	ZI	0	0	0	0	0	0	0	0	0	0	0	0	0	0	0	0	0	0	0	0	0	0	0	0	0
Africa	**r6**	**0**	**0**	**0**	**0**	**3.93**	**5.32**	**8.80**	**6.17**	**10.49**	**11.10**	**8.45**	**9.14**	**9.29**	**7.26**	**9.70**	**11.30**	**11.78**	**12.65**	**13.60**	**12.84**	**13.01**	**10.72**	**11.99**	**12.66**	**14.28**
Afghanistan	AF	0	0	0	0	0	0	0	0	0	0	0	0	0	0	0	0	0	0	0	0	0	0	0	0	0
American Samoa	AQ	0	0	0	0	0	0	0	0	0	0	0	0	0	0	0	0	0	0	0	0	0	0	0	0	0
Australia	AS	0	0	0	0	0	0	0	0	0	0	0	0	0	0	0	0	0	0	0	0	0	0	0	0	0
Bangladesh	BG	0	0	0	0	0	0	0	0	0	0	0	0	0	0	0	0	0	0	0	0	0	0	0	0	0
Bhutan	BT	0	0	0	0	0	0	0	0	0	0	0	0	0	0	0	0	0	0	0	0	0	0	0	0	0
Brunei	BX	0	0	0	0	0	0	0	0	0	0	0	0	0	0	0	0	0	0	0	0	0	0	0	0	0
Burma	BM	0	0	0	0	0	0	0	0	0	0	0	0	0	0	0	0	0	0	0	0	0	0	0	0	0
Cambodia	CB	0	0	0	0	0	0	0	0	0	0	0	0	0	0	0	0	0	0	0	0	0	0	0	0	0
China	CH	0	0	0	0	0	0	0	0	0	0	0	0	0.50	2.47	13.50	12.38	13.62	11.35	13.46	14.09	15.90	16.60	25.17	41.66	47.95
Cook Islands	CW	0	0	0	0	0	0	0	0	0	0	0	0	0	0	0	0	0	0	0	0	0	0	0	0	0
East Timor	TT	NA	NA	NA	NA	NA	NA	NA	NA	NA	NA	NA	NA	NA	NA	NA	NA	NA	NA	NA	NA	NA	NA	NA	0	0
Fiji	FJ	0	0	0	0	0	0	0	0	0	0	0	0	0	0	0	0	0	0	0	0	0	0	0	0	0
French Polynesia	FP	0	0	0	0	0	0	0	0	0	0	0	0	0	0	0	0	0	0	0	0	0	0	0	0	0
Guam	GQ	0	0	0	0	0	0	0	0	0	0	0	0	0	0	0	0	0	0	0	0	0	0	0	0	0
Hawaiian Trade Zone	HQ	NA	NA	NA	NA	NA	NA	NA	NA	NA	NA	NA	NA	NA	NA	NA	NA	NA	NA	NA	NA	NA	NA	NA	NA	NA
Hong Kong	HK	0	0	0	0	0	0	0	0	0	0	0	0	0	0	0	0	0	0	0	0	0	0	0	0	0
India	IN	3.00	3.02	2.02	3.49	3.84	4.70	4.73	4.75	5.19	3.80	5.61	5.17	6.01	5.90	4.72	6.46	7.42	10.45	10.64	11.45	14.06	18.23	17.76	16.37	15.04
Indonesia	ID	0	0	0	0	0	0	0	0	0	0	0	0	0	0	0	0	0	0	0	0	0	0	0	0	0
Japan	JA	78.64	82.92	94.97	105.24	127.00	149.66	158.78	188.60	173.90	174.52	192.16	202.79	212.10	236.79	255.67	276.69	287.09	306.22	315.73	300.79	305.95	03.87	280.34	228.01	271.58
Kiribati	KR	0	0	0	0	0	0	0	0	0	0	0	0	0	0	0	0	0	0	0	0	0	0	0	0	0
Korea, North	KN	0	0	0	0	0	0	0	0	0	0	0	0	0	0	0	0	0	0	0	0	0	0	0	0	0
Korea, South	KS	3.28	2.73	3.56	8.45	11.11	15.78	26.68	37.05	37.79	45.00	50.24	53.50	53.70	55.23	55.72	63.68	70.23	73.23	85.21	97.91	103.52	106.53	113.15	123.19	124.18

Laos	LA	0	0	0	0	0	0	0	0	0	0	0	0	0	0	0	0	0	0	0	0	0	0	0	0	0
Macau	MC	0	0	0	0	0	0	0	0	0	0	0	0	0	0	0	0	0	0	0	0	0	0	0	0	0
Malaysia	MY	0	0	0	0	0	0	0	0	0	0	0	0	0	0	0	0	0	0	0	0	0	0	0	0	0
Maldives	MV	0	0	0	0	0	0	0	0	0	0	0	0	0	0	0	0	0	0	0	0	0	0	0	0	0
Mongolia	MG	0	0	0	0	0	0	0	0	0	0	0	0	0	0	0	0	0	0	0	0	0	0	0	0	0
Nauru	NR	0	0	0	0	0	0	0	0	0	0	0	0	0	0	0	0	0	0	0	0	0	0	0	0	0
Nepal	NP	0	0	0	0	0	0	0	0	0	0	0	0	0	0	0	0	0	0	0	0	0	0	0	0	0
New Caledonia	NC	0	0	0	0	0	0	0	0	0	0	0	0	0	0	0	0	0	0	0	0	0	0	0	0	0
New Zealand	NZ	0	0	0	0	0	0	0	0	0	0	0	0	0	0	0	0	0	0	0	0	0	0	0	0	0
Niue	NE	0	0	0	0	0	0	0	0	0	0	0	0	0	0	0	0	0	0	0	0	0	0	0	0	0
Pakistan	PK	0.002	0.15	0.17	0.23	0.32	0.33	0.41	0.50	0.19	0.07	0.40	0.36	0.52	0.39	0.56	0.50	0.34	0.37	0.38	0.07	0.38	1.98	1.80	1.81	1.93
Papua New Guinea	PP	0	0	0	0	0	0	0	0	0	0	0	0	0	0	0	0	0	0	0	0	0	0	0	0	0
Philippines	RP	0	0	0	0	0	0	0	0	0	0	0	0	0	0	0	0	0	0	0	0	0	0	0	0	0
Samoa	WS	0	0	0	0	0	0	0	0	0	0	0	0	0	0	0	0	0	0	0	0	0	0	0	0	0
Singapore	SN	0	0	0	0	0	0	0	0	0	0	0	0	0	0	0	0	0	0	0	0	0	0	0	0	0
Solomon Islands	BP	0	0	0	0	0	0	0	0	0	0	0	0	0	0	0	0	0	0	0	0	0	0	0	0	0
Sri Lanka	CE	0	0	0	0	0	0	0	0	0	0	0	0	0	0	0	0	0	0	0	0	0	0	0	0	0
Taiwan	TW	7.81	10.17	12.52	18.14	23.60	27.79	25.84	31.80	29.40	27.10	31.55	33.53	32.47	32.99	33.48	33.93	36.33	34.85	35.41	36.91	37.00	34.09	38.01	37.37	37.94
Thailand	TH	0	0	0	0	0	0	0	0	0	0	0	0	0	0	0	0	0	0	0	0	0	0	0	0	0
Tonga	TN	0	0	0	0	0	0	0	0	0	0	0	0	0	0	0	0	0	0	0	0	0	0	0	0	0
US Pacific Islands	IQ	0	0	0	0	0	0	0	0	0	0	0	0	0	0	0	0	0	0	0	0	0	0	0	0	0
Vanatu	NH	0	0	0	0	0	0	0	0	0	0	0	0	0	0	0	0	0	0	0	0	0	0	0	0	0
Vietnam	VM	0	0	0	0	0	0	0	0	0	0	0	0	0	0	0	0	0	0	0	0	0	0	0	0	0
Wake Island	WQ	0	0	0	0	0	0	0	0	0	0	0	0	0	0	0	0	0	0	0	0	0	0	0	0	0
Asia & Oceania	**r7**	**92.73**	**99.00**	**113.24**	**135.54**	**165.87**	**198.25**	**216.43**	**262.70**	**246.46**	**250.48**	**279.93**	**295.38**	**305.31**	**333.76**	**363.64**	**393.64**	**415.03**	**436.47**	**460.82**	**461.21**	**476.80**	**481.30**	**476.22**	**448.41**	**498.62**
World Total	**ww**	**684.38**	**778.64**	**866.42**	**981.72**	**1,196.85**	**1,425.54**	**1,517.66**	**1,653.98**	**1,794.85**	**1,843.39**	**1,908.81**	**1,996.14**	**2,015.60**	**2,081.63**	**2,125.16**	**2,210.04**	**2,291.53**	**2,271.31**	**2,316.01**	**2,393.13**	**2,449.89**	**2,516.67**	**2,545.30**	**2,517.76**	**2,619.18**

SOURCE: Energy Information Administration.

References

Bell, J. 2006. With a big nuclear push, France transforms its energy equation. *Wall Street Journal* (March 28): A1, A18.

Bisconti, A. 2006. Nuclear power opinion polls. Bisconti Research, Washington, D.C. (May), www.bisconti.com.

Dowling, C. 2006. Oil's decline. *Bloomberg Markets* (October): 65–68, www.bloomberg.com.

Echávarri, L., and Y. Sokolov. 2006. Uranium 2005: Resources, production and demand. OECD Nuclear Energy Agency and the International Atomic Energy Agency, Paris (June), www.oecd.org.

Energy Information Admininstration (EIA) web site: www.eia.doe.gov.

Gertner, J. 2006. The nuclear option. *New York Times Magazine* (July 16): 36–47, 56, 62, 64.

Gunter, P. 2005. Best of the nuclear power boondoggles: Yesterday and today. Nuclear Information and Resource Service, Washington, D.C. (May), www.nirs.org.

Hannum, W., G. March, and G. Stanford. 2006. Recycling nuclear waste. *Energybiz* (March/April): 28, www.energycentral.com.

Hinds, D., and C. Maslak. 2006. Next-generation nuclear energy: The ESBWR. *Nuclear News* (January): 35–40.

How Stuff Works Web site: www.howstuffworks.com.

Jones, D., and G. Tolley. The economic future of nuclear power. University of Chicago (August).

Martin, R. 2002. The history of nuclear plant safety. The About Nuclear Website (Fall), www.users.owt.com.

Moore, P. 2006. Going nuclear: A Green makes the case. *Washington Post* (April 16): p. B01, www.washingtonpost.com.

National Academy of Sciences. 2003. *A century of innovation: Twenty engineering achievements that transformed our lives.* Washington, D.C.: National Academies Press: 226–227, www.nap.edu.

Nuclear Regulatory Commission. 2003. A short history of nuclear regulation, 1946–1999 (June), www.nrc.gov/who-we-are/short-history.html.

Nuclear Regulatory Commission (NRC) Web site: www.nrc.gov.

Platts. 2006. Platts OPEC guide (September), www.platts.com.

World Nuclear Association Web site: www.world-nuclear.org.

Index